John Cuthbert Hedley

The Light of Life

In Sermons

John Cuthbert Hedley

The Light of Life
In Sermons

ISBN/EAN: 9783744660464

Printed in Europe, USA, Canada, Australia, Japan

Cover: Foto ©Lupo / pixelio.de

More available books at **www.hansebooks.com**

SET FORTH IN SERMONS

BY THE
Right Rev. JOHN CUTHBERT HEDLEY, O.S.B.,
BISHOP OF NEWPORT.

LONDON: BURNS & OATES, LIMITED.
NEW YORK, CINCINNATI, CHICAGO : BENZIGER BROTHERS.
—
1899.

BURNS AND OATES, LTD., PRINTERS, LONDON, W.

CONTENTS.

THE LIGHT OF THE WORLD.

*Preached in the Church of the English Martyrs,
Preston, on Sunday, October 8th, 1898.*

"The Lord is my light, and my salvation" (Ps. xxvi. 1).

AT the present time, even those who read little and
reflect little can hardly help noticing that there is a
tendency to make the thought of God more obscure
than the thought even of that most High Name ought
to be. I will not say that men are forgetting God or
neglecting Him. There have always been in the world
such forgetfulness and such neglect. But now our
best thinkers—our most cultivated intelligences—are
occupying themselves with the attempt to make God
more and more remote; to thicken the veil that hides
the effulgence of His heavenly throne; to increase
the darkness which necessarily hangs over the great
gulf separating the Creator from the creature; to
deaden the echoes of the Voice which must always
be distant, but which we believe is intended to be
heard and recognised over all the universe. In other
words, there is an active and determined endeavour
to persuade the men and women whom God has
made that they cannot know Him; that beyond
the vague idea of His existence, there is nothing
in His sacred Name for the intelligence to grasp;
that the consecrated and treasured words to which

2

we are accustomed are mere empty air, and not rational conceptions ; that to call Him Maker, Father, Friend, Judge, Last End, is even to contradict that deepest, that most fundamental view of the mind which regards Him as the Infinite and the Absolute.

This false and disastrous teaching it is not my intention on the present occasion to attempt to meet. I will only say this—that the names which human speech applies to the Infinite, must necessarily be inadequate, but that they need not therefore be false. I can form no full or complete conception of what is meant by God's goodness, His truth, His justice, or His holiness. But I know, first, that these attributes in Him cannot be in contradiction with what human reason recognises as goodness, truth, justice, or holiness ; next, that such qualities in the Godhead are entirely unmixed with any defects ; and, thirdly, that no human contemplation or investigation through endless ages can ever exhaust the riches or the glories of them. "When a man hath done, then he shall begin ; and when he leaveth off, he shall be at a loss."[1]

But, speaking to-day of God as light, I will ask any intelligent man if the mere fact of Creation does not seem to involve illumination. Could God have made man and left him in the dark ? As to his body, it is evident that God has furnished him with every sense which is needed in order to find his way about in the material world, and to use that world.

[1] Ecclus. xviii. 6.

Could God have created a world such as this, and placed man therein, and yet not have given him faculties to know it? What kind of a Creator would that have been? He would have been either feeble and impotent, or sinister and malignant. But the Infinite could be none of these things. Now the principal part, the essential part, of a man is his spiritual soul with its spiritual powers. Those powers can, no doubt, exercise themselves upon the material world. But they can do much more than that. They are capable of views, of flights, of reachings out, of apprehensions, which easily pass the horizon of the visible and the material. They undoubtedly point to a wider world — to a nobler activity — just as a great ship, lying in one of our ports, with sails all furled, or engines cold, will speak to the visitor of limitless heaving oceans, where all that canvas will be set, and all that strong machinery will play in hot and ceaseless energy. So the spirit of man indicates a great universe of the spiritual. And from other sources we know well that such a universe exists. For God is the spiritual universe. God, with His immensity, His holy will, His heavens, His ministers, His eternity, a measureless universe, an unexplored universe, the only universe which the soul can travel in, and not find limits and disappointments! Is it possible that there can be no communication between that world of spiritual things and the spirit of man? Can God have created the soul, and yet left her blind, deaf, and insensible to the august voices, forces, events, of a world in comparison with which all the planets and the systems are as a little dust? Is His arm so short? Is His will so weak? Is His wisdom so much at fault? Is His love so cold? "For we are His people, and the sheep of His pasture."[1] "Know ye that He is God; He made us, and not we ourselves."[2]

What, therefore, should we expect from a God and Father, infinitely loving and infinitely powerful? We should expect illumination. We should expect a light, enabling every man to know God, to recognise an immortal destiny, and to see his path through this tangled world.

But this religious light would not be an overpowering, an overwhelming light. You must remember we are speaking of intellectual light, not physical. Now, the eye of sense, as long as it is healthy, cannot mistake light when there is light; light acts upon it like a stimulant. But the intellectual eye is different. Floods of light may be round about, and yet the eye of the mind may be unaffected; it may not heed; it may be turned in a wrong direction; it may obey the will and refuse to see; it may be so distracted or taken up with a multitude of occupying, flattering, pleasing, degrading ideas, that it may be practically blind to religious light. For a man does not consist of reason or intelligence alone. He has passions, pride, desires. There are fogs and darknesses. Truth may

shine, but man may either never see it, or may disregard it, or pervert it, or basely prefer to take up
with something else.   Our God and Father has made
us so—or, at least, since the Fall we find ourselves
so.   It were always in His power, doubtless, to overwhelm our mind with light, and to compel our assent.
But if He did that, and if that were our natural
condition, there would be no responsibility, no
merit; no fight and no crown; no room for Our
Saviour's grace.   In a word, we should not be
what we are, and the whole scheme of Creation
would be different.

It is most important to insist on this view of
human nature, because it prepares us for two
things: first, the recognition that God has always
given His creatures sufficient religious light; and,
next, that this light has been exposed, and will
always be exposed, to obscuring conditions, arising
from what human nature is, and what the world
is.   It is not easy to find a single word which
will express what it is that, in all ages, has striven
to obscure religious light.   But if we must
have one, I would prefer the word Worldliness,
or Secularism.   It is a good Scripture word.   The
world, in Holy Scripture, means the body of influences which tend to make a man look to this
earth, and not to life everlasting.   A swimmer leaps
into the sea and starts to swim to some pleasant
point where rest awaits him.   All is smooth, calm, and
smiling.   But ere he has made a score of strokes some
strong-running current below the surface seizes him.

Will he master it, or will it carry him out to sea and strangle him ? It is the question of our human life. In all the world's history it has been the question with religious truth. God has given light to His children. Will the world kill it ? "And the serpent cast out of his mouth after the woman water, as it were a river ; that he might cause her to be carried away."[1]

It has become almost an axiom among modern men of science that the idea of God is not an early, a primitive, a universal notion among men, but has slowly developed or grown, more or less perfectly according to circumstances. They will tell you that several savage tribes have been found to have no idea of God at all. Where there are any gods, we are told, they are not the remnant of primitive revelation, but have grown out of the terror felt for dead ancestors ; ghosts have passed into deities, lower deities into higher ones. In spite of the great names arrayed in support of this view, such as Spencer, Huxley, Lubbock, and Tylor, I am happy to say that the most recent investigations in authropology are certainly demonstrating it to be false. It is true that to the superficial observer, traveller, or reader, the description of the greater number of savage religions seems to consist of gross fetish-worship, the honour of sacred animals *(totems)*, sanguinary rites, and absence of morality. But it has now been shown that, anterior in date to this savage mythology, un-

[1] Apoc. xii. 15.

derlying it, as the limestone underlies the coal measures, there is the primitive belief in a supreme Being.
This is a matter that can only be brought out by
long and careful detail—by the weighing of first-hand
evidence. But I am speaking of books published
during the last six months, and it will be as interesting to you as it was to me, to learn that com-
petent investigators now believe that the superstitions,
the idol-worship, the fantastic rites, and the degrading
customs of even the lowest savages (that is, their
mythology) overlie a deep and most ancient belief in
one God. It is not asserted that they possess such
a clear-cut or consistent idea of the only and infinite
God as you find in Catholic theology ; but there is
demonstrably in their traditions the belief in a Being
who is a Creator, mighty, kindly, the rewarder and
the punisher—who sanctions truth, unselfishness,
loyalty, chastity, and other virtues.

Thus the Australian natives, low as they are in
civilisation, have the clear tradition of a creating, all-
seeing, undecaying Being, quite different from the
spirits to whom some of their rites are directed. The
Fijians, a very remarkable race, have a supreme Being,
eternal, Creator of men. The Zulus, a race of practical warriors, still remember, although his worship is
almost non-existent, a Lord in Heaven, maker of
men. The Melanesians have a primitive immortal
Being. The Bushmen, houseless and wandering, pray
to a Divine Father, who existed before the sun, a
maker of all things. The Andamanese, who for a
long time, as we know, have been pointed out by our

superior thinkers as utterly godless, now are shown to have the tradition of a God resembling "fire," but invisible; a God not born, never to die, a Creator, a reader of the heart, merciful, and judge of men. The Indians of British Guiana prove to hold a Maker, a Father, an ancient of days. The Negro tribes of East Central Africa, in spite of so much that has been said, have in their traditions an eternal, immortal Being, who was before all men. The dwellers on the Gold Coast, and in the trackless forests and swamps of West Africa—such as the Ashanti and Fanti peoples—though hostile and separated, have the universally diffused notion of a supreme deity. Even the Dinkas of the Upper Nile tell you of an all-powerful Being, dwelling in Heaven, seeing all things, and a Creator. It is needless to speak of the Indians of the North American continent, who so easily recognised their own Great Spirit in the God of the Christians; or of the South American, the Peruvian religion, whose complex and repulsive ritual could not conceal an immemorial belief in a supreme Being, whom many interests had combined to thrust almost out of sight. Let this enumeration be pardoned. But I have gone round the globe, and the tale is everywhere the same. The Monotheistic belief is primitive; the multiplication of gods, fetishes, and spirits, with the ritual ensuing, is later. It would seem that God had given a religion, and that some malignant hand had striven to choke religion by mythology.[1]

[1] For details see *The Making of Religion*, by Andrew Lang (Longmans, 1898).

And is not this precisely what St. Paul states? He tells us that the invisible things of God, His power and His divinity, were clearly seen in the beginning; but that afterwards men became "vain in their thoughts, and their foolish heart was darkened"—and they "changed the glory of the incorruptible God into the likeness of the image of a corruptible man."[1] Here we have described the process which has been at work through all the ages of the world's existence, and has brought about the "degeneration" or the obscuration of the primitive idea of God. It was not merely that half-civilised primitive tribes dropped their civilisation, fell into a savage state, and so lost the knowledge of God. It was rather that they lost it as they *advanced* in civilisation, or in comparative civilisation. What has happened? I take the account from the books of which I am speaking—and it is this. In every tribe or community, from the beginning, there would be four influences constantly operating. First, they would cease to wander and would grow settled; this would incline them to seek to make God a local God, favouring them, and hostile to their enemies. Next, the idea of a state would grow up; and the chiefs or rulers would look out for means to strengthen that idea by fear and authority; hence the worship of dead ancestors, who must be propitiated by rites, offerings, and even blood. But, thirdly, there would be, especially on the part of the more powerful, the more cunning, and the more rich of the community,

---

[1] Rom. i. 21, *seqq.*

the continual pressure of self-indulgence, and this would urge them to find gods who would approve of their pleasures.   And, lastly, there would be progress in the arts, which of itself, as history shows, tends to the expression of the Divine idea in material form, and thus (unless there is some check and counterpoise) to corrupt and degrade it.   Now this fourfold influence— localisation, statecraft, self-indulgence, and the artistic impulse, makes up what we just now called "world- liness, or secularism."   This is the direction in which human nature, stimulated by the evil spirits, will work.   And the writers to whom I refer show, by a long and detailed comparison of facts, how, in peoples of various stages of civilisation, from that of the Australian black to the cultured Greek of antiquity, all over the world, and in all ages, this fourfold spirit has wrought upon the primitive idea of God—setting up side by side with it all kinds of fantastic legends and gross rites, draw- ing to itself all the attention of the various communi- ties, and thus crowding out and almost obliterating the pure and ancient religious light.   Yet the light was there—and there was knowledge of God.   Were these heathen peoples within the reach of salva- tion ?   Nay—for barbarism and paganism still cover the larger part of the earth's surface—what are we to say at this moment of the multitudes who sit in darkness and in the shadow of death ?   First, we must say this—that it is of Catholic faith that Al- mighty God gives to all men sufficient grace to be saved ; next, that no man is condemned, or can be condemned, merely for inculpable ignorance ; thirdly, we must remember that responsibility is proportioned to capacity. This is so with children, with persons of feeble intellect, and with savages. The difference between the intelligence of these classes and the highest trained minds of advanced civilisation is very difficult to realise. The ideas of the savage about God and on morality may be vague, limited, and even inconsistent. But it is certain that the ideas are there, at least in rudiment. This being so, is it not quite certain that in all savage and heathen peoples there are multitudes of humble, obedient hearts, not by any means without occasional liftings up to a father and a judge, who seldom transgress essential morality ? I believe these are the people of the " two talents," and I, for one, should not like to think that they did not enter into the joy of their Lord. For if there is one thing more certain than another it is that it is not the simple that are cast out, but the wilfully perverse. And if we can be sure, as it seems to me we can, both from Holy Scripture and from the science of anthropology, that the idea of God as a Maker and a rewarder is found in the traditions of every people in the universe, it follows as a necessary consequence—it is hardly an assumption to conclude —that the poor, the suffering, the simple, the patient multitudes in every age must have turned to Him, dimly and intermittently perhaps, but with sufficient apprehension to bring them within the reach of His infinite mercy and compassion.

But there is, as you are aware, one race among

the peoples of antiquity in whose annals we can study the conflict between secularism and light under very different conditions. The race of Abraham, had it been left to the light of nature, might have never risen higher than the Bedouin of the desert, or the plundering and fighting Arabs of Western Asia. In their history, as in that of so many other tribes and nationalities, the investigator might have found nothing better than half worn-out traces of a primitive revelation, darkened by superstition and evil. Instead of that, we have the revelation of Jehovah, enforced by a strenuous schooling of two thousand years. We hear the voice of God, speaking to Abraham, to Jacob, to Moses, to the Prophets—instructing, exhorting, reproving, until the name and attributes of the God of Heaven are not only written large upon the consciousness of the Hebrew nation, but are enshrined in a history, a ritual, a literature, and a poetry which are now the precious inheritance of the world at large. And yet, do we not see, in the history of the Old Testament, the same worldliness at work against the light of God ? Is there anything more striking than the story of that conflict, in which God, as it would seem, has to put forth all His strength—to raise up judges, kings, and prophets ; to control battles, to interfere with the laws of nature, to rule, as it were, with His own hand, in order to keep safe above the turbid flood the sacred lamp of light ? First, this people would localise the God of gods ; would look upon Him as only the God of their own tribe. How often was it thundered over Israel that He was "the Only One, and there was no other"[1]; that the "Lord Jehovah is the One God"[2]; that "all the families of the nations shall adore Him"[3]; and that the gods of the Gentiles are demons?"[4] Then, over and over again, as Israel grew in stability, in power, and in riches, the spirit of earthly state-craft sets itself against the religion of Jehovah—at times recurring to the idolatry of Egypt or of Phœ-nicia, at other times attempting in some other way to throw in its lot with what seemed to be the success of the nations of the world. But by Moses and the Prophets God said, "You shall have no strange gods before Me"[5]; and the abominations, the dark rites, the magic, the devil-worship, which worldly wisdom and the lust of power have elsewhere inva-riably called in to help them to their ends, were banished from Israel by God's visible interference. Again, among the chosen people, as everywhere that human nature is found, the light had to contend against the lusts of the flesh and of the eyes, and against the arts of advancing civilisation. You read how they sat down, in the very shadow of Sinai, to eat and drink, and rose up to play—to indulge in sinful orgies. You read how they disobeyed God, and kept things which were "anathema"[6]; how they rushed into the licentious worship of Baal and Astaroth; how they fell into schism among them-selves; how Isaias accuses them of substituting

---

[1] Deut. xxxii. 39.   [2] *Ib.* vi. 4.   [3] Ps. xxi. 28.
[4] *Ib.* xcv. 5; I Par. xvi. 26.   [5] Exodus xx. 3.   [6] Josue vii.

ritual for real religion;[1] how God complains by Jeremias[2] that even "they that held the law knew Me not, and the pastors transgressed against Me"; and how in Ezechiel he calls them a "provoking people."[3] In any other race this spirit of license would have led to the atheism, materialism, and debauchery of Greece and Rome, of the ruling classes of the East, or of China; the Jewish people would have been absorbed in the great sea of Roman heathenism or Oriental stagnation. But the Holy Spirit of God never ceased to speak to them by the Prophets. The truth was never long obscured; from Moses to David, from David to Isaias, from Isaias to Malachy, from Malachy to the Machabees, the Divine revelation was protected, and shone out more and more brightly in each generation, until that same Holy Spirit, in the fulness of time, was ready to speak through Jesus Himself.

Thus, both in the heathen world and under the law, we see how the Divine light was kept alive. Heathenism is justly called darkness, and the Gentiles are said to sit "in the shadow of death." Even Judaism is only a shadow of something better. But these expressions are comparative. Absolutely speaking, God's light has always been in the world. Still, with the coming of the Redeemer there was to be a reinforcement of revelation which can justly be described as the rising of the sun after the darkness of the night. You read of that coming light in the far

---

[1] Isaias i.   [2] *Ib.* ii. 8.   [3] Ezechiel ii. 6.

off prophecies of David and of Isaias. You hear it saluted at its dawning by the sage and Saint who holds Jesus in his arms, and greets Him as the " light of revelation to the nations of the earth and of salvation for His people Israel." That light, stronger and brighter, with new safeguards and a new ministry, was now to illuminate the whole world, driving the darkness back and never overcome or clouded over by any of the forces of this world, or of the rulers of this world, the evil spirits. True, those forces were still to be in existence. They were to fight to the very end. The history of the conflict of Christianity — the light of Pentecost—with worldliness — the history of false teaching and of its origin, displays the same causes at work as those which menaced the Mosaic revelation and well-nigh extinguished the revelation of the primitive age.

Christianity is, first and foremost, light. It is conduct also, no doubt ; but conduct cannot be first, for the very simple reason that a man must find the way before he can walk in it. And if it be insisted that to find out what conduct is right, is, after all, a very different thing from accepting certain dogmas about God and the Incarnation, I would at once reply that if there is a God, the most essential laws of man's conduct must be those which concern his behaviour to God, and his obedience to the scheme or dispensation by which God has signified His purpose of saving him. In speaking of Christianity, then, I do not mean the Christianity of those who profess that a very arbitrary and narrow morality is all the Christianity we can be certain of. I mean the Christianity of St. Paul, of St. Peter, and of St. John. I mean God in His unity and Trinity ; Jesus Christ, in His Divine and human nature ; the work of the Holy Spirit in the soul of man ; the Divine voice of the Church, and that sacramental system which is the living touch of the living Jesus, and which culminates in the real Eucharistic Presence.

That this is the Christianity of the New Testament cannot be disputed by any one who takes even the broadest view of what we find there. There we have God as Creator, ruler, judge, rewarder, and avenger. There we have the Son of God, the Redeemer, Who is to be loved and worshipped in God. There we have the Holy Spirit, proceeding from the Father and the Son. There we have the clear outline of the pastorate, or teaching Church, instituted by Christ, endowed with Christ's promised never-failing assistance to the end of time, defining and ruling by its bishops in matters of faith and practice, and taking means to perpetuate itself by ordination. There we have the sacramental system—certain external acts, such as baptism and the eating of the Eucharist, the anointing with oil, and the laying on of hands, producing spiritual and interior effects.

Here, then, we have a revelation as grand and as far-reaching as if God had once again come down in clouds and fire on Sinai. It was a revelation which not only confirmed all the natural law, as already God had done in the Ten Commandments, and brought out clearly those beliefs

which had been gradually developing under the
Jewish dispensation, but enriched the world with
Jesus Christ for ever; Jesus Christ in His life
and His Cross, Jesus Christ in His perpetual
voice as heard in the Church, Jesus Christ in the
continued touch of His hand, through the Sacraments. Here was light; light on what I may call
the character of God, revealing His love, His mercy,
His justice, His retribution; light on the soul of
man, its end, its sin, and its forgiveness, its state on
earth and in the world to come; light on worship;
light on right and wrong; light on man's interior
life and perfection; light on innumerable questions,
social and political.

It does not require any deep philosophical insight
or profound reflection to understand that when intellectual or spiritual light is given to the human race,
and is given by human instruments and handed on,
like the torches were handed on, from one human
hand to another, either God must specially interfere to
protect it, or it will be exposed to such danger of
obscuration, of diminution and of alteration, as human
brains and human hands are likely to occasion. First
of all, the records of such spiritual illumination might
be lost or falsified, by not being written; or, if written,
copied erroneously; or, if manuscripts and books,
might be destroyed. Next, we must remember that
there are very few human statements whose precise
meaning may not be the subject of dispute. In
ancient history, even the plain matters of fact are by
no means clearly understood in later times. How

much more true is this of spiritual truths, of religious systems, of moral maxims! Let me take, for example, one or two well-known specimens of the kind of sentences one meets in the New Testament. There is first the great formula of the Incarnation, "the Word was made Flesh." There is, secondly, the great sacramental injunction, "This is My Body: take and eat: Do this in commemoration of Me." There is, thirdly, the great justification phrase, that "unless we believe, we shall be condemned." What did Christ mean?—what did St. John or St. Paul mean—by enunciations like these? What is the Word? What was the Flesh? What is the Eucharist? What is justifying faith? These expressions cover vast controversies. Were they understood in the generation in which they were uttered? Were they understood in the fourth century?—in the sixteenth? Are they understood in the nineteenth? It is certain that men have never left them alone. All through the Christian ages they have been discussed, analysed, developed. Hundreds, nay thousands, of keen intelligences have pulled them to pieces, compared them, tried to put them together again. Every century, with its new ideas, its changed standpoints, its freshly opening horizons, has made its guess, written its gloss upon them. Is it possible that they have not been altered and transfigured in such a way that their very authors would hardly recognise them? The bare and formal words may still be found in our Bibles; but are they not fossils?—like the forms of dead and gone monsters which we find in the hard rock, covered deep with the deposits of ages, and stony as the rock itself? I say that if it is not so —and Catholics maintain that it is not so—it must be because God has interfered, by what we may justly call a miraculous intervention.

For the Catholic view, as you do not need to be told is that the Faith delivered to the Saints can neither be altered nor petrified. It can neither be corrupted into error, nor deadened into lifeless formularies. These great utterances of which I spoke just now can neither lose the meaning which they had in the mouth of Christ or of His Apostles, nor can they become mere silent print without a message for each generation as it passes. In other words, there must be both preservation from error and development of truth. What would be the use of a revelation unless these things went with it?

The present age is tolerant of what it is pleased to call speculative error. Our great thinkers will tell you that religious truth is impossible of attainment; and, on the whole, that it is better so, because to investigate is much more healthy than to know. But if so, Christianity is certainly impossible. For Christianity, even to those who are least in love with dogma, does rest upon certain facts and pronouncements. But even Christians in this country are infected with this propensity to accept doubt as a creditable state of mind, and to put up with what may, in all probability, be quite wrong. As to this, we can only say that if there is no reasonable certainty to be had as to the meaning of the religious truths and facts proclaimed in the four Gospels and in the Epistles, then God's Word and revelation may be asserted to be in vain ; then, we have the Incarnation, the Resurrection, the Pentecostal descent, the formation of the Church, and the writings of St. Paul, all given us, virtually, to no purpose ; for what is the difference to me between a revelation which is mainly doubtful in its meaning and a revelation which does not exist ? And if you tell me—what, however, our great thinkers would not admit—that I have got my reason and my intelligence, and that other men have also reason and intelligence ; and that by study and investigation, without any supernatural help, no little meaning can be made out of the New Testament, I would first of all point to the thousands and the millions who have neither the time nor the ability to make such studies ; and I would remind the objectors that revelation was meant for them also ; and I would say, in the second place, without denying that intelligent study can do much, that, when there is question of a revelation—of the light given by the Heavenly Father in order that His creature may know Him and be led to Him—unless I can be practically certain of every point in it, I do not understand why He should have given it at all. This does not mean that every human being should, or could, be acquainted with every detail of the Divine message to the world ; but that there must be no portion of it as to which, given the occasion, given the questioning of a soul, given the need of a human spirit, a satisfying and secure certainly could not be arrived at. But the general Protestant mind tolerates doubt ; and we can see the consequences. They shirk the creeds of Christianity ; they do not know whether they should pray to Christ ; they are in the dark as to the Sacraments ; they are very vague as to forgiveness and justification ; and they have most unsettled ideas as to the world to come. To me, it would appear that unless we could be certain on these and similiar vital subjects, God's revelation is to no effect. When the sailor, taking his ship through the straits and rocks, spreads out his chart and finds neither channels marked nor soundings given, would he not be justified in saying that the hand that gave that chart meant not to help him, but rather to leave him to his fate ?

On the other hand, there could not be a revelation without some kind of progressive development. The Catholic Church has always taught that religious truths, as expressed from the beginning, contain much more than the ordinary mind takes in at once. These implicit truths are brought out and made explicit as time goes on. The reason is, that the mind of man, as I said just now, cannot let a truth alone. Every mind has questions to put ; and every question, if it be a reasonable question, demands, and should have, an answer. And when the right answer is given, that very answer lends itself to further questioning ; and thus the Divine edifice of Catholic teaching is built up. You are all familiar, at this time of day, with this aspect of revelation—its growth. I will give two very simple examples. It is part of the

Christian revelation that God the Son became man. Not long after St. John died some one began to question whether God the Son, or the Word, was God in the same sense as God the Father. Any one ever so little acquainted with the speculations of the heathen philosophers about the Word of God, and with those Divine utterances which are contained in the Book of Wisdom, can understand how the question would suggest itself. The Church was shocked when the question was raised, because a very short reflection showed that it was a vital one; to say "No" was to deny the Trinity and to do away with the Incarnation. Therefore the Church spoke (at the Council of Nicæa) and defined that when the Word was called God it meant God in its full and adequate sense, as "consubstantial" with the Father. That is development. Here is another instance. Christ said to His Apostles, "Whose sins you shall forgive they are forgiven." Two questions arose at different times on this. First, was this power conferred on the Apostles only, or on the Christian ministry in general? And, again, could that power be exercised on a sinner who did not confess his sins? You know how those questions were answered. And I say that unless they could be answered, one way or the other, God's revealed mind on that particular point must have remained dead, inert, inoperative. For, in order to be effective in saving souls, God's revelation must be always a living revelation, meeting the questions of every generation and the requirements of every century. No possible Bible could have contained the answers to all possible questions ; and if such a Bible had been possible the questions themselves would not have existed when it was written ; for every period of the world has fresh questions to ask and fresh circumstances to meet. When I ask, "What must I do to be saved?" you cannot send me to dead print—to ancient formulas covered with the commentaries of nineteen centuries. You must send me to a living authority, which can interpret those formularies, rescue them from the rubbish that has been shot upon them, and place their Divine truth in living contact with the fibres of my spiritual being.

Looking back into Christian history we can see that, on the whole, the protection of God over his revelation is evident and undeniable. The Catholic Church, which holds as its fundamental principle the perpetual authority and inerrancy of the teaching body commissioned by Christ, is not only the most conspicuous fact in Christian history, but is a fact which dwarfs all heresies into insignificance. Arianism was widespread at one time ; but it showed from the beginning that tendency to alteration which foretells approaching decay, and it speedily died and was shovelled into the earth. Protestantism—the principle of the Bible as read by private judgment—has been very active in some places and at certain times ; but its unreasonable worship of the Bible has always tended to discredit Christianity itself, by making men either refuse to accept the mysteries of the Bible, or, as now, driving them to question as they please the inspiration of anything whatever that the Bible contains. Hence, now, together with the Socinianism and the Unitarianism which have always formed the fringe of Protestantism, there is the widespread cancer of rationalistic criticism. So that the good old sound Protestantism, which never was strong in logic or argument, only survives in those classes whose inherited prejudice is undisturbed by such a thing as reflection, and it is chiefly kept alive by onslaughts on Popery. For anything like reflection is fatal to Protestantism ; because, although its great watchword, " The Bible alone," sounds wonderfully satisfying, the moment you attempt to apply it to any book, chapter, or verse of the Bible, then the confusion begins.

Still, the " heresies," as Catholics call them, after St. Paul, have been sufficiently conspicuous and long-lived to form a feature of Christian history ; and it is therefore worth while to see how they have been brought about by causes virtually the same as those which obscured and almost obliterated the primitive revelation of God. I enumerated four of these causes— localisation, statecraft, self-indulgence, and the progress of the arts. These make up what we call worldliness, or the pressure of the world against God and the holy light. It is evident that we must expect these influences to assert themselves in Christian times as in the days before His coming. Human nature remains what it is.

Taking these headings in a somewhat different order, I would ask you to observe, first, how often human nature's hankering after license and indulgence

has given rise to heresies. I do not want to prove to
you that Arius, or Nestorius, or Berengarius, or
Luther, was an evil-living man, who started dogmatic
errors in order to justify himself in giving reins to his
passions. There is a very large amount of truth in
this view. But I will take broader ground. There
are three chief heretical periods—first, the heresies
principally on the subject of Our Lord, in the
early centuries; next, the mediæval heresies, and
lastly, the Protestant heresies. In the first period,
the history of which fills our text-books with statement and counter-statement, with terms and proposi-
tions, with councils and edicts and persecution—what
was the worldly influence which chiefly made itself
felt as the foe of God's Divine illumination? It was
the absolutism of the Roman Empire. The rulers of
that Empire were Christians, it is true. But they
could not, in a generation, or even in a century, shake
off that lust of Cæsarism—that frenzy of irresponsible
power—which marked the great pagan world-empire.
They now had, in their midst, the world-wide Church,
no longer in the catacombs, but visible in her youth
and strength. Was the Church to rule the spiritual
world, or was the Empire? The conflict was sure to
come. The Arian heresy was as good an opportunity
as any other. That heresy never really spread among
the people, or the parish priests, or the monks. It
was men of the Church's hierarchy who took it up—but
it was the ingrained heathenism of the Cæsars that
gave it life and power. At least as late as the days
of St. Gregory the Great, heresy and schism meant

the effort of the Empire to enslave the Church and to corrupt the Divine light. Here was the spirit of license in its most portentous manifestation. But it was beaten in the conflict.

There would be no difficulty, if any one disputed it, in showing how that same spirit of license and self-indulgence gave rise to the heresies of the Middle Ages, with their immoral doctrines and their hideous practices. And when we come to Luther, Calvin, and Cranmer, it is simply notorious that their so-called "Reformation" not only sprung from moral laxity, but established moral laxity as a principle—I mean the principle of justification by faith only; a principle which logically leads to the conclusion that sin is of no consequence and repentance impossible. It is a principle which one-half of Protestantism have always been too honest to act upon—but, all the same, it has encouraged, and it does encourage, millions in moral laxity.

Another element of the worldly influence was statecraft — with which I may join the wish to localise the light of revelation. My brethren, think of England, of Prussia, of Holland, of Russia—and it will be clear to you at once how strong has been the effort, at certain periods of Christian history, to form local and national religions. The astute politicians who carried out what we now behold in this country, for example, acted on a twofold principle; they wanted independence, and they wanted stability for their institutions. Hence, they carefully cut and trimmed the revelation of God to fit their local and national views. They maintained their Church—but, as Cardinal Newman once said, they "tied it up, pared its claws, and kept it low." First, they made it impossible for the Church to make a definition or give a decision. Next, they practically abolished the sacramental system, and so reduced the Divine order of the priesthood to a mere name. Further, by abolishing the Holy Sacrifice, and substituting for that world-wide act of worship a cold, if decent, ritual of their own, they made public worship itself a kind of national function, like their Parliament or their courts of justice. And it is not unusual, in our own day, to hear people speak of the "English religion." In the English religion there is supposed to be manliness, honesty, truth, and independence. The Gospel virtues of obedience, humility, and purity are not emphasised in this religion. It is considered to be antagonistic to priestcraft, to ceremonies, and to sentiment of every kind. And if you wish to brand any doctrine or practice with the reddest brand, you have only to say it is un-English. Such a spirit as this was sure, one day or other, to rise up in conflict with the light· Let any one consider the effect of the Reformation in England on the Christian creeds—and how few educated Englishmen will recite any creed—and he will be able to measure the deadliness of localising and nationalising the revelation of God.

The only remaining worldly element that we need notice is that which I have called the advance of the arts. In the savage this advance led to idolatry—

and we can observe a similar impulse constantly showing itself among the Hebrews. But in modern times, advancing civilisation and the progress of science has not resulted in idolatry, but in what may be called naturalism. This is the heresy which refuses to admit the spiritual world—grace, eternal life, the Incarnation, or God Himself. I call it a heresy, although it looks more like sheer paganism. But it is not paganism. It is really a perversion of the Christian revelation. It clings to a kind of supreme Being—a God shadowy, far off, indescribable, Who must be decorously recognised and saluted, but need not be prayed to, and indeed has no office now that the world has been set going, except to round off expressions of sentiment, and perhaps to provide for all sorts of people after death. This is the God of the scientist, the "superior" novelist, and the newspaper man. They all claim the name of Christian—because there are parts of the New Testament which they really approve and commend ; such, they will tell you, as the sermon on the Mount. This kind of spirit, like the others, was certain to lift itself up against the light. Just as the primitive savage was tempted to make an idol, so the modern student of nature is led to nature. Had the heathen kept the light of God bright, there would have been no harm in multiplying images ; although, as a matter of fact, it must always in those early times have been dangerous. That the civilised and scientific mind should see God in every natural law and every natural fact is not only excusable, but praiseworthy. It is only when the modern mind stops short at the natural phenomenon, just as the savage stopped short at the image of wood or stone— it is only then that the light of God is obscured and lost.

We have thus, my brethren, two great facts in Christian history—the light of the Christian revelation, and the war made on that revelation by human passion, national temper, and the spirit of naturalism. We have, in Christian times, the same conflict which had been going on in the ancient world ever since the primitive revelation was given. We have a conflict which was to be expected. However clear was, or might be, the illumination from on high, the mists and fogs of earth were sure to affect it. But in Christian history we have it proved to demonstration that there is a Divine protection cast over God's light which has never allowed the light to fail. Heresies have risen and died down. Absolutism and Cæsarism have done their worst. Nationalism has tried to narrow the boundaries of the Christian light, and science has too uniformly turned its back upon it. But it shines on still, and an inquirer is reduced to the choice between two alternatives—either he must admit that, out of all that Christ and His Apostles have left us, he can grasp with certainty only a few shreds and scraps, or he must accept the Catholic principle and submit to the Catholic Church. The Catholic principle is Divine protection for the Divine light. To reject that principle is to make that light as if it had never been given.

As to Catholics—ourselves—the least that can be
said is that all who rejoice, as we do, in the grand
system of religious truth which is guarded and
kept in all its lustre by the divinely constituted
Church, should strive to raise themselves to the
level of that great position. It is not merely by
praying for grace to be worthy of their faith, nor by
striving to live according to its precepts, nor by
practising it and using the means of grace which it
offers, that they discharge their duty as children of
the light. There is yet another obligation, an obligation most intimately connected with those just
mentioned, but yet an obligation distinct in itself.
It is the obligation to learn and know their faith.
No one can "comprehend, with all the Saints, what
is the breadth and length, and sublimity and depth"
of Christ, nor can be "filled unto all the fulness of
God,"[1] without an effort to hear, to read, to meditate.
It is among the ignorant that the forces of worldliness most easily destroy and corrupt the light
of Christ ; the ignorant—not the uneducated, but
those who, living more or less in a sphere of
culture and intellectual thought, omit from their
readings and their studies the noblest subject of all—
the great science of the Christian inheritance. How
comes it to pass, in an age when all men read, and
every matter of interest on the earth's face is written
up for our instruction and our pleasure, that Christ
and His Holy Spirit, the Church and the sacramental

[1] Eph. iii. 18, 19.

kingdom, Our Lady and the Saints, are so little known, so badly neglected ? Is not this holy science, this light of salvation, the very illumination that our spirits need ? The natural light of this world—the sunlight—is the world's life. It awakens energy, disperses evil influences, and stimulates the germs of being ; and every living thing lifts itself towards the light, turning the tendril and the leaf to its benignant potency, and expecting the vigour of health, the colours of beauty, and the ripeness of perfection. So it might be—so it should be—with the immortal spirits on whom the sun of revelation shines. Let them believe it. If Catholicism is to be living, luxuriant, and strong, Catholics must love the light— the light of Christ's holy life, the long roll and charter of the Church's treasure. Let the priest instruct and the people learn. Let Catholic books be multiplied, and let every household love to use them well. Then will each child of the Church be able to say with truthful confidence, " The Lord is my light and my salvation."

THE DIVINE GIFT OF FAITH.

Preached at the re-opening of St. Anne's Church, Liverpool, on Rosary Sunday, October 7th, 1888.

"And the ruler believed and his whole house" (John iv. 53).

THE word "*belief*" is mentioned three times in the Gospel of this Sunday ;[1] and there are two kinds of faith alluded to. First, the ruler, being rebuked for not believing that Jesus can work at a distance as easily as by His presence, humbly and reverently accepts the reproof, and with touching simplicity acquiesces in Our Lord's declaration, and goes home. Next, when he sees that a great miracle has been wrought on his child, he believes in Jesus in the full and adequate sense of faith. This is the faith which has saved the world. This is the faith which in every age has had to struggle with unbelief, with worldliness, and with pride. This is the faith which, with that abundant grace of which it is the forerunner, has covered the earth "like the covering waters of the sea." Does it seem at this moment to be ebbing—to be losing its hold on the race which it is meant to save? Men say so. A great poet and writer, lately passed away, has written in mournful verse—as if he had this very passage of Isaias in his thought—how the waters of belief which once flowed

---

[1] The Twentieth after Pentecost.

over so wide a tract have now receded and left the
land bare :

> The sea of faith !
> It once was at the full, and round earth's shore
> Lay like the folds of a bright girdle furled.
> But now I only hear
> Its melancholy, long, withdrawing roar.

Is this so ? Men " hear " what they listen for. The
unbeliever, the cynical doubter, is too ready to pronounce that unbelief and doubt are winning the battle.
Whatever the truth may be, one thing is certain.
Faith, to you, and to me, and to all who open their
eyes on this earthly light in the generation which is
ours, is as vital and as powerful and as much within
our reach as ever it has been in the past : vital, for
without it the spirit is paralysed—crawls, and does
not fly ; powerful, for it still flows like a heavenly
spring from Our Saviour's fountains ; and within our
reach, in spite of culture, of self-consciousness, of
criticism, of physical science, and every other feature
of that " progress " which is said to make this age so
different from the ages which have gone before.

I wish this morning, by God's help, briefly to set
forth one side of the relation between God's gift,
which is faith, and that reason of man which must
always operate when truth, whether revealed or
otherwise, has to be received into the soul. To be a
Christian believer means to hold certain truths about
God and immortality and our Blessed Saviour. I do
not propose to prove the existence of God, or the
immortality of the soul, or the divinity of Jesus
Christ. I am taking these things for granted. And

4

I say at once that the Christian theory is that the Christian possesses, or may possess if he wishes, a certain mental or spiritual gift quite beyond his natural endowments, which I do not say proves his religion to him, but gives his religion that character of stability, of mental security and of devotedness, without which it would only be a speculation or a philosophy, and not a religion.

There are two questions which modern doubt is constantly insisting upon. The first is, " What right have children and ignorant people to believe at all, not having examined ? " And the second, " How is it possible for a learned investigator, in the face of the innumerable difficulties which his investigations must bring to light, ever to have a firm faith ? " As the world may be really divided into these two classes —the unlearned, who cannot or do not discuss ; and the critical or the scientific, who are always ready to discuss—it is evident that, if we cannot answer these questions satisfactorily, very few can have faith at all. And it is to this, as a result of strict argument, that so many grave and serious writers of the present day wish to drive their generation. Faith, they will tell you, is acceptance ; but you cannot accept what has so much reason against it ; neither can you accept, in any manly sense of the word, what you have not argued out to yourself. And if one replies that faith is acceptance on authority and not through argument, they will rejoin that this only moves the difficulty a step further back. No authority can be Divine or valid which proposes for our acceptance what reason rejects or doubts. In short, the view of the keenest minds of the day is that faith depends on what a man can make out by his faculties. If a man has not used his faculties he may have superstitions and prejudices—faith, if you will have it so—but no rational persuasion. If he has used his faculties and can make nothing out, he may not have faith, but that is no fault of his, because it is simply that he cannot accept. And therefore modern books of the highest culture are filled with a melancholy pessimism. You find these cultivated minds envying those who can believe; admiring the ancient days of faith; entering into the simple views of the simple multitudes; speaking with a kind of regretful enthusiasm of the times of unity and heroism; and dwelling with lingering love on the innocent faith of little children. But with all this admiration there is mingled a self-satisfied, condescending pity. These enthusiasts knew no better! A child believes and is happy, but that is only possible because he is a child. The world in its childhood believed and was happy in its faith. Now humanity has grown up to man's estate; faith has vanished like the illusions of childhood; and if the happiness has departed too, yet still man is more manly, the race is more reasonable than it was. So the intellect of to-day argues. But the argument, after all, is not wholly made up with pride or with pitying superiority. The best minds cannot conceal a kind of regret—a sense of something wanting. They admit aspirations of human nature which seem to have no answer except from faith. They cannot sit down quietly and leave the unknown future to itself. They find it difficult to take their ease or their pleasure with the haunting feeling upon them of an invisible world just out of reach of their sense. There is a moral universe all around them, as importunate to be penetrated as the earthly one—with heights as dizzy and oceans as deep, and a firmament as beautiful and infinite, as the world which it is their delight and their pride to investigate. Can it be—this is the thought that comes back and comes back—can it be that my spirit truly has the power and faculty to pierce all this populous darkness, to reach indefinitely into this universe of spiritual relations, and that I, like the hooded falcon, have taken the blinding pressure of some master's hand for the quenching of the essential light of day?

My proposition is, that there is within our reach a gift by which the child and the unlearned can reasonably hold fast to religious truth, and by which the most active-minded questioner may reasonably remain steady and fervent in spite of all the difficulties which his intellect may raise. Let no one exclaim that this is mere enthusiasm ; that either you hold truth on reasonable evidence or not ; if you do, any further gift is unnecessary ; if you do not, any influence that impels you is either childish simplicity or fanatical enthusiasm.

In reply to this, let us for one moment observe how the mind acts in holding or rejecting anything. No one will dispute the principle that when a thing is sufficiently proved, and nothing urged against it has absolutely disproved it, it may be reasonably held. It is *sufficiently* proved ; not with evidence which is so overwhelming as to compel the assent of the mind in spite of itself, but still so as to remove reasonable doubt. The motive may be tradition, authority, custom, universal agreement, fitness, design, or some other of those on which men in ordinary affairs reasonably believe. Thus, the reader of the newspaper believes many items of intelligence ; the scholar believes his master, the child his parent ; men believe their friends, or make inferences from what they see, using rough and ready reasoning. Thus, a man acts on the conviction that his food is wholesome, that the land will grow his crop, that his doctor is a capable man. Thus one hands money to one's banker, accepts what the shopkeeper sells, drives over a bridge, even buries one's departed friends, without any scientific or exhaustive inquiry. These things, I say, may be, and often are, quite sufficiently proved for reasonable acceptance. Difficulties raised against their acceptance, as long as they are merely difficulties, and do not *disprove* the facts, need not cause the most reasonable mind to reject them. Such difficulties will no doubt affect the mind's attitude ; they will cause hesitation, lead to inquiry, lessen the feeling of conviction. But unless, as I have said, they really do upset the evidence, they are always compatible with acceptance. A truth in this condition may be reasonably believed. And if such a truth, or proposition, were only a natural or scientific or social matter, it might there

be left to take care of itself.   But *religious* truths are
exposed to an attack, the danger of which they
partly share with all other truths except absolute
demonstrations, and partly owe to their own nature.
Three things may happen.   My mind may, for a
time, lose sight of the evidence; it may, even with
the evidence before it, be keenly impressed with
certain importunate difficulties; or it may have to
struggle with a moral repugnance, arising from
passion, or egotism, or temperament, making it
extremely averse from the acceptance of this or that
particular truth.   Now, God's gift, in one word, is
intended to meet these three dangers.   It is intended,
first, to keep clearly and calmly before the mind the
sufficient evidence of Christian truth.   It is intended,
next, to turn the mind away from the contemplation
of difficulties ;   and, lastly, it is intended to endow
our spirits with those moral dispositions, such as
humility, simplicity, and trust in God, which make
belief easy.   There is in this nothing unreasonable.
The most firmly-rooted truths may be exposed to
attacks of the kind described.   The danger springs
from the mind's constitution.   However satisfied the
physical philosopher may be of a law like gravita-
tion, for instance, there are difficulties he cannot
answer.   However satisfied I may be that God really
exists, there are moments when the clouds rise and
the firmament is hidden ;   there are times when
difficulties are troublesome.   However satisfactory
are the proofs of Christ's Divine mission the young
child can only take them in so far as he sees he may

trust the teacher who tells him of them. But he reasonably does so. Then comes the gift. The little foothold of reason—which is never wanting— is genuine and firm ground, but it is not very secure against the rushing tempest. But the angel stoops from Heaven and holds the child of God. He brings a supernatural motive ; he brings attention and concentration ; he gives the mind the impulse to sweep away, as it can do, what it must not dwell upon ; he lifts the mind's gaze to the face of that God Who may be trusted as never friend was trusted ; and he pours through the whole being that transformation which turns the will to prayer and the heart to love.

Now since such truths as God's existence, and Christ's divinity and a teaching Church, are really vital truths for man's heart to hold firmly, it is reasonable to hold—as the Christian theory holds— that there is a special gift of God which is meant to enable the heart to adhere to them. And when we turn to the New Testament we find, accordingly, that the gift of faith plays a most prominent part in what I may call the philosophy of the kingdom of God. Faith is a kind of postulate, without which you cannot advance a step. Faith is required not only for the due acceptance of those matters which are delivered on authority, such as the revelation of Jesus Christ and the constitution of His Church, but also for the things which our reason can in some way discover for herself—God's existence, immortality, and the law of reward and punishment. Faith is described by St.

Paul[1] as an essential part of the equipment of the children of God. He classes it with hope and charity as one of the Christian gifts or virtues by excellence, with which the redemption of Christ furnishes man to carry on his warfare. He calls it armour, he calls it a shield. It is the root of justification, the kindling of prayer, the spring of love. When the inspired writer would describe the soul of Stephen, he calls him full of the Spirit of God and of faith[2]; when he would set Barnabas before us, he says that he is full of the Holy Ghost and of faith[3] ; as if faith were the very presence of the Spirit in the spirit of man. And the power of this endowment of the soul of man could not be more impressively described than when the great Apostle says it is the very substance of the far off things we hope for ; not the shadow, as one might think, but the reality ; the very demonstration of the things which appear not, and which, therefore, cannot be demonstrated.[4] This grand hyperbole makes faith a faculty of spiritual sight ; and as sight brings to us things far away, by that wondrous vital immutation which makes us master of a circle of the universe so much beyond our own beings, so faith takes in the things above and the things around, the things of the future and of the mysterious present, and makes us master of a spiritual world in the presence of which the world of sense withers and decays.

Thus faith is a seeing power, provided by God

---

[1] I Cor. xiii. 13.   [2] Acts vi. 5.
[3] *Ib.* xi. 24.   [4] Heb. xi. 1.

through Christ's Blood. But the strangest thing yet remains. It is not altogether a seeing-power — by which I mean a power working in and through our intellectual nature ; it has to do with that other faculty of our complex humanity which is as poorly off, since the Fall, as our intellect—I mean, the will. In the Acts the converts are said to "obey the faith."[1] In the Epistle to the Romans St. Paul calls faith "an obedience,"[2] and he repeats the phrase in the Epistle to the Galatians[3] ; and these two Epistles are by excellence the Epistles of Faith. St. Paul's view was that "every understanding" was to be "brought into captivity unto the obedience of Christ."[4] But this means that this intellect of man—so independent, so self-sufficing, so proud—must be willing to accept a master ; that belief is one of those acts which must be pressed—unbelief repressed, like pride or sensuality or anger ; it means that free speculation is incompatible with Christianity ; it means that a certain force, the pressure of something external, must be brought to bear on that faculty by which we take in the truth, or else the truth will not be taken in. It means that belief is a duty, and not to believe is to sin. There is no escaping this consequence. However freely we may grant that no man can be judged who has not had the chance of coming in presence of the truth—that birth, bringing up, and surroundings may be such as to lessen guilt or to remove it altogether—yet the fact must remain that, in

[1] Acts vi. 7. [2] Rom. i. 5. [3] *Ib.* iii. 25. [4] 2 Cor. x. 5.

the abstract, unbelief is sin. For unbelief is disobedience, pride, indifference to God. The truth of
God is sufficiently in the world ; the gift is at hand ;
it rests with man (to whom God never refuses necessary grace) to accept or reject it. O men ! who refuse
the daylight, and keep fast to the caves of earthly
wisdom—to the brooding darkness of carnal prudence—can you acknowledge even the shadow of a
God and not suspect that He has a message for your
immortal spirit ? Is not this very darkness full of
stir and motion ? Is not the very solitude unnatural
and strained ? Being what you are, you must be
more than you now are, or perish. You have sus-
picions and suggestions of a wider world, but they
will never grow clear—you have longings and ideals,
but they will never be possessed—unless you turn
your spirit to the God Who made it, and seek for
that Divine illumination which nothing can shut out
from you except the wilfulness or the indifference of
your own hearts !

The Christian view, then, is that the heart of a
believer is so supernaturally assisted that, with fair
play, it ought to rest in the calm and tranquil enjoyment of the reasonable assurance of religious truth.
With fair play! That word raises the vision of a
state which has been too seldom realised on earth—
the state of faith at peace. We must suppose a time
when the Faith is gently taught to babes almost
before the use of their reason ; when the young grow
up in faith's atmosphere ; when Christ's religion is a
part of men's speech and thought, in the Church and

in the family, in the State and in the household. A
time when there is no heresy, no questioning speech,
no wrangling of controversy. A time when the great
features of Christ's revelation—His person, His word,
His Church, His Eucharistic presence, His sacramental work—are clear and luminous before every
mind, like stately vessels at anchor on a peaceful sea.
Then would faith grow like the light grows from
dawn to noon on a summer's day. Then would
Divine charity increase and deepen as the colours
deepen on the earth and sea when the sun is up.
Then would God seem to be very near to man, and
the unseen world to be almost palpable, so that if
God's hand were felt there would be little surprise, or
if angels visited the earth, or Saints were said to
have wrought wonders, men would be inclined to
think it true. Then would the civil State be a Christian state, and kings would receive their crowns in
the sanctuary, and statesmen kneel before the altar,
and soldiers honour the God of battles, and parliaments bow to revealed truth. Then would men care
for the poor and seek out misery, and take measures
that all might have food and raiment, and so be fitted
to hear the tidings of salvation. Then the family
would be as the holy home of Nazareth. Then
would great churches cover the land for the pomp
and glory of the Eucharistic King. Then would the
lamp of the sanctuary be lighted wherever men were,
that none might be without that Presence. Then
would physical science and all good arts make progress in proportion to the purity of men's hearts.

There would still be sin—and deadly sin, alas!—but not the deadliest sins of all. There would be no intellectual pride and indifference to God, or rebellion against the Holy Spirit; and the sins of passion black as they were, would generally result in driving the sinner more closely into the arms of that Saviour whose invisible kingdom was so vividly realised. Then would death be of inexpressible interest, yet peaceful and full of loving hope, for the light of the resurrection of Jesus would illuminate the open grave; and then would the world beyond the grave be known and familiar, and the suffering souls would be helped unceasingly, whilst the Saints in their be-atitude would be as helping brothers, honoured and loved, and Most Holy Mary would be the Queen whose power was boundless, and whose compassion embraced all the world. Then would Christ reign, and Christ be Master, in all the realms which He hath redeemed by His Precious Blood. Such a picture is not wholly ideal. There have been periods and communities where it has been realised, and in the present, as in the past—in the future, too—until the great Judgment is held, there will always be men and women and families, and even gatherings of families, who live by faith, and possess their religion in peace unbroken.

But in these days, and in most days, it is rather faith in conflict that we see than faith at peace. The prime movers of the war against faith are put down, especially in the Apocalypse, as the powers of dark-ness, the spirits which are permitted to rule in this lower world. There are many good and honest men who would be shocked and angry to hear that they were the devil's agents ; but whether by their fault or without it, such they too often are. Any one who tries to prevent the full teaching of faith, or to poison the well of faith by making belief impossible, or to obtrude the difficulties of faith, is doing the work of God's enemy. And the conflict begins when the little child is prevented from learning the revelation of God. To teach a child, that is to teach men, is a gradual and a laborious process. One must first of all have been clearly taught one's self. No doubter can teach Christianity. Then one must have the command of many years of the child's life ; one must have the command of the child's day : and one must so put religion into even profane teaching that he may understand that religion governs everything else. Therefore, those who forbid the plain teaching of religion, or shut the mouths of teachers, or banish religious teaching to the Sundays, or leave the child to ignorant parents—all these are in battle against faith. When the child has grown up and can take his own part, the conflict is none the less hot. Books suggest doubt, newspapers criticise everything, a man's company laugh at his faith or argue with it, and the pressure of business fills his mind and thought. There is little sign of God in the surround-ings of a Christian in the days in which we live. The world seems to take one road, leaving Christ to carry His Cross along another. There are few out-ward reminders of the invisible. God's kingdom is

too straitly confined to the Church, and even good
men and believing men expose their faith to danger
by their communications with unbelief, their lack of
teaching, and their indifference.   We lose heavily
in this conflict.   Some of us live all our lives
on unfamiliar terms with God.   Some are afraid
of the supernatural.   Some are ashamed of their
religion.   Few become truly interior men, valuing
prayer and union with God.   There are some
whom marriage or friendship leads to apostasy.
There are some who make shipwreck on the
rocks of Biblical criticism or intellectual difficulties.   Of all these it may be truly said that they
know not " the gift of God."[1]   It is true that even one
who knows it may reject it.   But how many there
are who, if they knew better what a power they had
in faith, would never go astray.   The man of science
and of thought, for example, who encounters difficulties in believing, would remember that he acts
reasonably if he throws himself on his supernatural
faith.   He can easily satisfy himself that there is
proof enough for prudent acceptance.   That being
so, he has to pray, he has to reject, he has to turn
to God with humble trust, he has to concentrate
himself on the holy doctrine taught by God.   Then
he may hope that his doubts will cease.   This is the
power and purpose of the gift of faith.   That of
which our reason gives us reasonable certitude, faith
teaches us to clasp to our hearts.   The doubts which

[1] John iv. 10.

thought and learning urge, faith helps us to avert our eyes from, nay, to detest. It is better to believe too much than too little, even in matters which are not important, because it is most essential to cherish the spirit of faith. On the other hand, to miss any vital mystery or part of God's holy revelation through want of faith is to kill by starvation the immortal spirit which God meant by these means to feed and to save. A time of conflict has its advantages as it has its drawbacks. But if there is a loving and Almighty God, if there is a Saviour, if there is a gift of acceptance such as Peter and Paul and John describe, then the victory must be in the end with the believer, whatever be the tides and vicissitudes of the conflict. Therefore we are forbidden to despair of faith. I, for one, believe that faith is at this moment as actual and as powerful as ever it was. Kings have gone, and establishments have been starved; but the millions hold the faith. Heresy and doubt may speak aloud, and they get on the house-tops to speak; but for every word of contradiction there is a deepening of the fervour of the believers; they hold their faith more consciously, with more intention, and with greater tenacity of love. If the press is against us, we can use the press ourselves. If Governments are hard upon us, we can appeal to the people, who now make the governments. If there is no other way, there is still the way of martyrdom; and nothing spreads the faith like the martyr's blood Therefore let us have confidence. " This is the victory which overcometh the world—your faith." Have confidence that in spite of appearances God will somehow win. We shall win in the Education battle ; whatever happens, if we act and move on the lines of faith we shall win. We shall win in the struggle to bring back the misguided millions of our fellow-countrymen. The efforts of priests and of people may not succeed at this moment ; but as surely as a man gives his money to the bank and receives it with usury, so surely does every step taken in faith produce its effect in God's time. We shall win in the battle over the Bible. Without fanaticism, without denying the explanations of science, we shall hold—the millions will continue to hold—the Bible to be the very Word of God. And we shall win in the fight over the Vicar of Christ. We shall win back his independence. No Catholic should be half-hearted in this. Nothing but the temporal independence of the Pope, under the guarantee of Europe, can satisfy either the Holy Father himself or the wishes and intention of Catholics. As soon as the Catholics of Europe take the matter up it will be done. There will be no fighting, no blood-shed, no disturbance. It will be done by the votes of the millions as soon as the millions learn a little more explicitly the lesson of their faith. And on this Rosary Sunday, above all, who can doubt or waver in his confidence ?—this Sunday which commemorates so many triumphs of the cause of Christ —this day which, even in this generation, has received a new lustre and a fresh renown from events which can only be referred to the interposition of the same Heavenly Father Who scattered the pride of the infidel in days gone by. Thank God for your faith. Thank Him under the roof of this noble and beautiful church—at once the result of faith and the stimulus of faith. These stones have been placed by those who believe. This temple is to mark the faith —to express the faith – to draw men together in the faith—to erect a throne for Jesus, the author and finisher of faith—to bring the world a little more into harmony with faith. Let us sing the *Te Deum*—but only to use the occasion as an incentive to better efforts to live the life of faith. May these walls last —aye, as long as faith lasts ; for the day will come when they and the faith they symbolise will have to perish and depart. On that day earthly tabernacles will pass away, and Faith, after her pilgrimage and her conflict during the long centuries, will lay her head down on the bosom of the earth which she has sanctified, and as the banners of the Judge begin to flame in the Eastern sky, will breathe her last breath —to rise again transformed into that something immortal and unspeakable which we call Vision of the Face of God.

THE PIETY OF CHRISTIAN FAITH.

Preached at St. Osburg's, Coventry, September 1st,
1895.

"Thy faith hath made thee whole" (Luke xvii. 19).

FAITH, in this passage, evidently means what we should call piety. For, if you observe, all the ten lepers had already professed their belief in Our Lord's pardon and power. They had cried out, "Jesus, master, have pity on us"; they had obeyed His commands; and even as they were on their way to show themselves to the priests, their leprosy had left them. It is clear that Our Lord had further designs of beneficence in their behalf. He intended to infuse regenerating grace, or at least strengthening and illuminating grace, into their souls. But, as a condition of the bestowal of His spiritual mercy, they were to return to Him in the spirit of those who realised what He was and what He had done for them. They were to return in affectionate gratitude and loyalty. "It is Jesus!" they were expected to say, "it is the Blessed Son of God! See what He has done for us! Let us go back to Him, let us thank Him, adore Him, praise Him, cling to Him." But only one returned, and he was rewarded with that second and greater visitation of the Redeemer's power which is signified by these words : " Thy faith hath made thee whole."

Here we have a universal lesson for all time. It is the spirit of piety which sets in motion the grace of the Redeemer. Mere faith is not enough. We may believe—we do believe—in the Incarnation, in the Church, in the Real Presence, in the Sacraments. Through this faith, not without love, we are cleansed from sin, and admitted into the kingdom of God— into the Christian inheritance—into the Church and fellowship of the Saints. All this happens, as it were, without any great warmth or energy on our own part. Even in the Sacrament of Penance our recon- ciliation is, one may say, a single effort, a single step, which lands us inside the Holy Spirit's kingdom. We are like men who have swum across a swift and dangerous river, and who stand panting and exhausted on the bank, safe and sound, with a grand country before them. But they have to exert themselves and to labour before they can reap its harvest, or reach its golden cities.

Piety is that manifestation of faith which loves and honours Jesus Christ and all persons and things who or which are connected with Him. It is one of the seven gifts which the Holy Spirit, as prophesied by Isaias, poured upon the most perfect human soul of Jesus—from Whose fulness it overflows upon all who are not in mortal sin. In Him it was the love and honour of His Heavenly Father. In us it is that also ; but as Jesus is Himself our Heavenly Father, in us it comes to be coloured and affected by the whole of the circumstances of the Incarnation.

Piety, therefore, is the Christian use of the
Christian inheritance.   Now, the Christian inheritance is the effect and continuance of the Incarnation.   By our Christian inheritance we differ both
from Gentile and from Jew ; we have advantages
not only over those who have lived, or do live, in the
mere belief of God as known by nature, but over the
chosen people to whom He had made Himself known
in a hundred marvellous revelations.   Our Christian
inheritance is not merely our redemption.   It is that
merciful and continuous dispensation of Christ which
makes, or might make, redemption secure to every
individual soul.   It is the existence, in the midst of
us, of the adequate knowledge of God, of God's
attributes, and of God's will ; a knowledge which
can be made available by every creature, however
inexpert, or ignorant, or destitute of worldly resource.   It is the continuance of the sacramental
touch of Christ's hand ; whereby a visible ministry,
with a whole system of rites and observances, not
only admonishes and edifies men, but effects spiritual
and supernatural results in the state and condition of
our souls.   It is the possession of a Eucharistic Sacrifice, in which the Blood of Calvary is not only commemorated but applied, and of a system of Sacraments
which give life and strength.   Our Christian inheritance is the infallible Church, regeneration, the
Blessed Sacrament, the sacramental forgiveness of
sins, the anointing with oil in the name of the
Lord, the priesthood, the altar, the visible temple
of God, and the whole expression of Catholic tra-

dition and practice as it builds itself visibly up in the world generation by generation. Those who do not claim or who reject these things, or any of them, may call themselves Christians—and it is not for us to refuse that name to any one who in good faith even defectively holds to Christ; but Christians in any complete and adequate sense they cannot be—or else there is little difference between a Christian and a contemporary of holy Job, or between a Christian and a Jew who, under the kings, went up to Jerusalem to keep the feasts of the law.

This great Catholic or Christian dispensation of these latter days is not a code of laws, or a philosophical system, or a school of thought. It is the presence and the action of a Person. That Person is God—God the Son, made man. By that ineffable plan or counsel of love and wisdom, the Incarnation, God has made it possible for Himself to influence and seize on man with much greater efficacy than if He had remained as it were secluded in the heavens. Now that the Divine Redeemer has gone up into Heaven, He is still present on earth by His infallible word, His sacramental touch, His Eucharistic reality, and His ministers; in all which ways His spirit--which is Himself—works not only morally, or symbolically, or mystically, but physically and literally; for the soul is just as real and substantial as the body. Therefore the Christian dispensation is the presence of Christ. And the first duty or tendency of a man who thoroughly believes in it, is to seek Christ and adore Him and thank Him every day of His life. Now this is Piety. Piety therefore is, as we have said, the Christian way of using the great Christian inheritance.

For it must be said, with sorrow, that of the multitudes who use the great treasure which a man having found in a field went and sold all he had and bought that field, there are very many who use it to little purpose. There are those who praise Christianity, but fail to see, or to admit, its unique position and superlative claim. Men talk of it as a stage of culture, between a more or less barbarous past and a more advanced and perfect future. These men believe not the Godhead of Christ, or the supernatural element in Christianity itself. They set it down as a human effort, subject to the drawbacks and imperfections of everything human. Then there are those who make much of what we may call the ethical side of Christianity, but little of the personal. They will praise the sermon on the Mount ; they will preach or otherwise enforce the loving-kindness and the meekness of Jesus ; they will enlarge on Christian humility, truthfulness, and patience ; but to adore Jesus in His annihilation or in His Passion, to petition Him, to thank Him or ask His forgiveness—these things are hardly a part of their religion. And there are Catholics—for it is to Catholics I principally address myself—who are to a greater or less degree affected or tainted with the unbelief, or the half belief, which finds its expression in views like these. They have little zeal for those elements of their holy religion which are by excellence its

Christian elements. They have a decorous way of acknowledging God ; they lead a decent life ; they are seen at church ; they are kind to the poor. But the Sacred Name, the Sacred Heart, Our Lady, the Blessed Sacrament, the Sacrament of Penance, the liturgy of the Church—these are to them almost a yoke, almost a burthen ; they are somewhat super-fluous ; they interfere in too marked a manner with this world's peremptory course ; they savour of ex-tremes and of fanaticism.

I would not now trouble you with these ideas except for one thing. In the service of God and the progress of sanctity there is often a small but im-portant step or turn which is overlooked. Suppose that God has given me faith and fellowship in His Church, it is true that my advance in grace, in near-ness to Himself, must be the work of no one but Himself. I cannot become a saint, or a confessor, or a martyr, or a missionary without His making me so. But it is also true that, unless I step in the right path, He will never do it ; unless I grasp His hand He will never lead me. Let us admit that even this step, this taking hold, is the work of grace ; it suffices to know that such grace is at our disposal, and that we can do what is here referred to if we please. I say, then, that no marked or powerful outpouring of the graces of the Redeemer is possible, either on the individual or on races, peoples, and nations, with-out sincere and childlike Christian piety. Jesus, Who has given us our faith and the forgiveness of our sins, will neither make us saints, nor will He give the grace of conversion to those in darkness, unless we approach Him in gratitude and affection. The inexhaustible riches of the Precious Blood will lie inactive, in a great measure, unless our hearts find their way to Calvary; unless we return glorifying God and giving thanks, and throw ourselves at His feet, He will never say those words of power and might, "Thy faith hath made thee whole."

Piety, therefore, is the measure of the growth and the well-being of God's kingdom upon earth. Let us look at it more closely.

Piety, as we have said, rests on faith. In the wide sense, it *is* faith—faith flaming out into affection. For piety is mainly the growth and creation of the Incarnation. I do not say that, even in the older times, there was not possible a filial and affectionate love of our Heavenly Father. You see its expression in the Psalms. Look, for example, at that most fervent lyrical outburst of trust and affection, the 17th Psalm, in which David seems to be under the influence of gratitude for some signal interference of God against his enemies. It begins, "I will love Thee, O Lord, my strength! The Lord is my firmament, my refuge, my deliverer! My God is my helper, and in Him will I put my trust. . . . Praising, I will call upon the Lord, and I shall be saved. . . . In my affliction I called upon the Lord, and I cried to my God." This is the tenor of the Psalm—interrupted in the middle by a sublime description of God's interference by storm and destruction. Such Psalms, in the mouth of the Jewish people,

were the expression of their appreciation of the
special protection of God, as shown in their deliverance from Egypt, and the conquest and settlement
of the Holy Land.   In David himself, the singer,
there were, first, the feelings of his race ; next his own
sense of God's particular providence over him ; and,
thirdly, the more or less clear revelation of the
promised Redeemer.   Moreover, in a large number
of the Psalms, the Psalmist sooner or later begins to
speak in the very person of the Messias Himself, as in
this one (verse 44), where suddenly the king of a small
nation, fighting his way to safety, cries out, " Thou
shalt make me head of the Gentiles ; a people which
I knew not hath served me   . . .   therefore will I
give glory to Thee, O Lord, among the nations."
But piety of a more marked kind was to characterise
the " latter times."   The Jew loved his God.   But
that God was as yet not known to the multitude as
the God of Bethlehem and Calvary—the God of the
Blessed Sacrament and of the Holy Catholic Church.
Here, in Christian belief, firm and clear, full and
adequate, with all its circumstances and its whole
extension, here is the ocean from which piety springs
up, as beautiful as the goddess who, in the ancient
story, rose from the sea to do reverence to the gods
and to fill the earth with joy.

So that piety is not a mere sentiment.   There are
human feelings which may be easily mistaken for
piety, feelings shallow and evanescent, the shadows
of surrounding things, rather than the manifestations
of internal force and pressure.   We see the peaks of

the distant mountains shine and glitter in the sun ; but the sun goes down, and the mountain tops are only granite and hard snow. So a man is joyous or sad, according to the countenance of his friends, or the state of his path in life, or even the promise of the skies ; and if he has no deeper motives to cling to, he is as mutable as the skies themselves. But piety rests, solidly and fast, on the faith of the In- carnation. Nothing can alter the great work of the Son of God. The sun may shine, or the rain may pour—there may be summer or winter—there may be prosperity or adversity, or even death ; but a believer in Christ and His work holds fast to the unshaken rock. He holds fast, not with his feeling or his fancy, or his senses, but with his reason and intelligence, with the strong grip of that spiritual faculty which makes him man ; with the inex- tinguishable energy of that soul and spirit which can push through darkness and through blinding storm, to the realisation of that which is out of sight except to its own God-given endowment. The other, the lower faculties, may hesitate or rebel. There comes sloth ; there comes pain ; there comes repugnance. Temper varies ; moods change ; the disturbance of passion clouds the atmosphere or sickens the heart. Christ sometimes seems a long way off; the Chris- tian altar seems unreal ; all religious feeling seems to have ebbed away, and left only slippery rocks or arid sand ; bitterness and resentment tempt to des- peration ; or worldly attraction exercises its fascina- tion upon all the springs of being. But none of these

things can destroy piety. Its leaves may be burnt as
by a frost, and its springing stems cut down ; but it
lives on, in the good soil where its roots lie. Sometimes we see the Saint kneeling before his crucifix,
with all his interior powers in darkness or distraction,
and yet with the heart of his spiritual soul steadily
burning before his Saviour, as the lamp burns immovable in the sanctuary, though the winds bluster
on the windows. Sometimes it is the faithful ordinary Christian, who is suffering, or disturbed, or
heavy-hearted, but who resolutely seeks the Blessed
Sacrament, or keeps the resolution of his regular
confession, or takes his reading, or goes through his
prayer. This is piety ; true, solid, essential piety,
fast-rooted in Christian faith.

Yet piety implies more than this. It would not
be going too far to say that it is in the ordinary
providence of God that redeemed men and women
should *feel* the interest and the sweetness of their
Saviour's presence and work. It is the way we are
made. We love father, mother, brother, sister, wife,
child. We are proud of our country or our race.
We have a fount of pity in our breasts. We cheer
up when days are bright, or we admire when nights are
glorious. Our passions, or emotions, are bad masters,
no doubt ; but they are also intended to be good
servants. It is their office to make effort easier, to
carry us on in the right direction by their impetus, to
intensify our intellectual acts, to make the resolutions
of reason and of faith hold the faster and last the
longer. Shall not Jesus also shed the benignant

power of His Name over the sensitive surface of this our human life? It was so intended. One of His prophesied attributes was His power to "draw us"; to draw by the sweetness of His earthly apparition. In the well-known phrase of St. Bernard, "Jesus is honey in the mouth, music to the ear, joy to the heart." His taking human nature, His birth, all His history and sayings, form one of the most powerfully attractive recitals that the human breast could take in. His story is like a strain of music carried to the ear, once and again, then wandering through this key and that, with recurrent imitations and developments, till it comes round always to one great solemn close. And we are so made that it sets vibrating in our composite nature many a thread of impulse and emotion, gratitude, joyfulness, remorse, sympathy, compassion, emulation. This is the reason why piety is the key to advancement in sanctity. To seek Jesus, to set apart times and moments in which to commune with Him, to make of Him a true, real, and constant friend, to give Him our hearts and a large part of our time and attention, this is what a Christian should not fail to do and practise. Such piety as this will lead to prayer, to the Blessed Sacrament, and to the Holy Sacrifice. Such piety will be drawn to the Holy Childhood and to the Cross; to Nazareth and to Olivet. It will love the Holy Gospels. It will cherish the crucifix. It will understand the Sacred Heart. It will be found where, on the walls of churches, you see the Stations of the Passion. Such piety will be the most precious disposition that parent, or priest, or teacher can instil into the child who is learning its religion ; a disposition that will do more to preserve its soul from world and devil than any safeguards or any abundance of argument. Such piety will run through a Christian life like a silver winding stream through a fertile vale, imparting character and beauty, taking up the space, but bringing a thousand gifts and advantages ; stealing a corner here and carrying off a sheaf of the harvest there ; at times full and impetuous, disturbing worldly occupation ; at others, seeming to hallow every green bank and happy home as it glides calmly past ; always delightful, generous, satisfying, and living. Such piety, at life's close, will effect what nothing else can ; it will make a truly Christian death-bed. For neither friends, nor peacefulness, nor freedom from pain, nor honour and respect, can by themselves lift the dying man to the land of redeeming grace ; but only the Body of Christ, and the sacramental touch of His hand, and the murmured invocation of that Sacred Name at which all things bow the knee.

Christian piety, thus understood, beginning as it does with the Person and Sacraments of Christ, finds also its nourishment and growth in all things connected with Our Lord and Saviour. And chiefly in two : on the one hand, in Our Lady and the Saints ; on the other, in the visible ministry of the Catholic Church.

The Blessed Mother of God is, naturally, most dear to Christ ; and to love Him is to love her. But she is also a part of the environment of the Incarna-

tion. That God should have had a Mother, according
to the flesh, is one of the most striking and astounding circumstances of His coming. It is also a circumstance which gives rise to far the greater number
of those touching details which make the Incarnation
so peculiarly well fitted to captivate human attention
and affection. Therefore, the message of the angel,
the visitation, the birth, the finding in the Temple,
and the whole history of Bethlehem and of Nazareth,
although they primarily and nominally introduce Our
Lady, are really filled with Jesus. Now Jesus sanctified all whom He touched. Mary, then, being near
to Him in a way peculiar to herself, was, as reason
would urge and our faith teaches, uniquely sanctified.
This holy creature, this Mother of the Redeemer, this
perfect work of redeeming grace, real Christian piety
turns to, reveres, loves, and invokes. And what is
said of her, is said with due proportion of all the
Saints. We love and reverence them because they
are part of Christ's presence, uttering Him, surrounding Him, explaining Him, and magnifying Him.

The ministry of the Christian Church possesses so
many of the special prerogatives of Our Redeemer
Himself that it may with truth be said that it continues Him on the earth. For it possesses, as a body
and in its earthly Head, Christ's prerogative of un-
erring teaching ; it possesses Christ's sacramental
touch, the power of the Eucharistic consecration, and
a gift, scarcely less wonderful and Divine, of ruling
and persuading the flock of the redeemed. Piety,
therefore, draws men to honour, reverence, and obey

the Christian priesthood. In spite of all drawbacks, all human disguises, and all weaknesses and deficiences, piety recognises in the priesthood the reality of those powers and gifts which the Spirit of Jesus has conferred upon a chosen body of men, in order to make the Incarnation a living influence in the world to the very end of time. Thus piety is not a merely private and secret communing with Jesus Christ and with God. It comes out into the highways and streets. It shows itself in words and acts. It observes times and seasons. It honours persons and places. It builds churches and sets up altars. It lights the lamp of the sanctuary and sacrifices itself for the honour of the Blessed Sacrament. It multiplies the images of Most Holy Mary and the Saints. It rejoices in the festivals of the Christian year, and finds its expansion in a great liturgical function when there seems to be some approach to the fulfilment of that utterance of the Psalmist, that " the earth is the Lord's, and the fulness thereof."

This, it seems to me, is the deep Christian faith, to which the promise is given that he who practises it shall be saved, or made whole, sound, strong, and perfect. Let us take a Christian community which, for one or two generations, has lived near a church like this, and used it to the full. The Church, with its ministers, represents and embodies the Word made Flesh. Here, more than anywhere, is His presence, His word, His power, and His sweet attraction. Hither, therefore, have the faithful people come, Sunday after Sunday, morning after morning, ·

evening after evening. Here has the Mass renewed
each day the sacrifice and the mercy of Calvary.
Here have the Sacraments been given. Here has the
incense of prayer—of adoration, of petition, and of
contrition—gone up perpetually. The flock has remembered Jesus Christ. It has lived up to its Christian privilege. It has returned magnifying God, to
throw itself at the feet of its Saviour. Therefore, I
would prophesy and pronounce of that flock that it
had been made holy and been drawn nearer to God,
and that the fruits of justice and of peace were to be
seen therein. First of all, there would be visible
among its members that spirit which beyond all
other tests seems to mark the follower of Jesus
Christ—I mean the spirit of unworldliness. Worldliness is the tendency to sin for this world's sake ;
not so much for the sake of the flesh, or of the
devil ; but for money, comfort, and what people
will say. The world is the rival of Christ. It
is always present and always attractive. Hermits
have to reckon with their own temptations and with
the demon. The rest of us come under the fascination of our surroundings—that is, of the people and
the things of this world. It was in order to meet
the world, if the phrase may be used, on its own
chosen battlefield, that God Our Father willed the
Incarnation, and created a world in a world—the
world of humility, obedience, and sacrifice of Jesus
Christ, which, like the spreading odour of some
balsamic Oriental essence, was to penetrate through
and through this universe, and everywhere foil and
neutralise its characteristic spirit.

In a flock like this, piety will have killed and cast
out that religious indifference, that secular air, that
tendency to put religion in the background, and to
guide one's self by the rules of vanity, which are the
marks of worldliness. In such a flock, the children
will be imbued as they grow up with the true spirit of
Christianity—the spirit of reverence, obedience, devotion, and regular observance. Parents will learn of
Jesus Himself, how the knowledge of Him must be
instilled little by little, every day, with every task and
in every recreation. The power of Jesus will be felt
in every home, and in every act, public or private,
social or political. A radiation of beneficent grace
will pass from the Blessed Sacrament into the very
air, rewarding the true Christian piety of His people
by making them holy. And not least will that power
be felt in the conversions of those who are not yet of
the flock. It was said of Him, when He visited His
own country about Nazareth, that He could not do
any wonders there because of their unbelief. We
must remember that the power of Jesus is subject, in
a certain sense, to the behaviour of the flock. As
when on earth, during so much of His visible life, he
was in the hands of men, so now, in His word, His
sacramental presence, and His whole sacramental
energy, He is in the hands of priest and people. If
they make much of Him and love and serve Him,
His power works; if not, it is more or less fettered.
What is the reason why for generations Jesus resides
in a neighbourhood, and does no sign? Chiefly
because His people neglect Him. But in a flock

where there is true and devout Christian piety, Christ
draws hearts, and conversions follow, as if some missionary were in the land.   For there is no missionary
like the Sacred Heart itself, when Christian faith and
love unbind its fetters and set it free.

Looking back over fifty years, may we not say that
this church, whose jubilee we celebrate, has been the
focus and the hearth of Christian piety ?   It was built
and opened by a man[1] who had within his soul a
wide, deep, and strong sense of what our Lord Jesus
Christ is to this redeemed world.   Within these walls
he meditated how best a priest could belong to Christ,
in order that he might make a harvest of souls.   Here
he offered sacrifice, here he prayed, here he taught
and exhorted.   And I believe—I am persuaded—
that from him, and from the priests and holy persons
who have followed in his steps, this flock has learnt
the lesson of Christian piety.   They have made much
of the presence and work of their Divine Redeemer.
They have reverenced these walls, on which the
sacred unction has been now for half a century ; they
have loved their sanctuary ; they have sought here
the society of Jesus ; they have returned again and
again, in acknowledgment of their Christian inheritance, praising and magnifying God.   And their
reward has been the quickening of heavenly influences ; there have been pious families, saintly
individuals, well-brought up children, not a few conversions, and a general nearness to God.   This

---

[1] Archbishop Ullathorne.

church set an example to English Catholicism—
an example of the enthroning of Our Lord and
Saviour, in His dispensations of redemption, in the
nobleness of a consecrated church. And in this city,
where there are such grand results of the faith of our
fathers, this church, which we could wish were even
more worthy, has done, we may be sure, what those
old churches were meant to do—enlarged Christian
inspiration and intensified Christian practice. Therefore we may thank God—for Christ Our Lord and for
the Blessed Sacrament ; for this roof and altar ; for
all the Masses, Sacraments, and prayers of fifty years ;
for the harvest of redeemed souls now in Heaven or
on its threshold ; and, lastly, for the manifold graces
it has brought to the souls of each of us, and the joy
and peace of Christ which God's mercy allows us to
experience on this day of festival, when our spiritual
fathers that are gone seem to speak to us, and when
God's loving and fatherly providence becomes almost
visible and sensible; and when we seem to see behind
these earthly stones the very outlines of that city of
God, of which the Lamb is the light, and its life the
Sacred Heart of Jesus.

THE SACRAMENT OF PIETY.

*Preached at the Oratory, Edgbaston, Birming-
ham, on St. Philip's Day, May 26th, 1897.*

" I will pour out waters upon the thirsty ground, and streams
upon the dry land : I will pour out My spirit upon thy seed,
and My blessing upon thy stock " (Isaias xliv. 3).

THESE words were prophetic of the glorious Christian
inheritance. This promised " outpouring " meant our
faith and our piety ; it meant revelation and devotion
—supernatural illumination and the fervent life and
operation of Christian hearts in all the Christian ages.
To-day, when we joyously celebrate the festival of a
miracle of faith, of an Apostle of Divine love, of a
burning and shining light of piety, it will not be out
of place to recall to our memory one aspect of that
dear and glorious kingdom of which, by the merits
of Jesus Christ, we are made partakers even upon
this poor earth which must pass away.

Let me remind you that this day is the festival,
not only of St. Philip, who is so justly called the
Apostle of Rome, but also of St. Augustine, who
claims the title of the Apostle of England. In this
church, whose community is bound by so close a tie
to St. Philip, St. Philip's feast is naturally kept ; but
we may bear in mind that outside, throughout the
country, they are celebrating that of St. Augustine.

How full of devout suggestion is this thought! Both
these heroic hearts were formed and nourished in the
city of Rome. One brought the Faith to England,
thirteen centuries ago ; the other, a thousand years
later, stood in the narrow Roman street where then,
as now, the English College was, and watched and
blessed the English students who were to die for that
very faith on English soil. St. Augustine represents
that Catholic and Roman teaching which is the unshaken rock on which Christianity rests ; St. Philip is
the type, by excellence, of that deep, rich, full, and
fertile Catholic life which should be, and may be, and
in such myriad instances is, the outcome and the fruit
of that faith ; and I will use the two entwined names
to introduce to you the subject on which I ask you
to hear a few reflections—that is to say, the relation
between Christian faith and Christian piety.

It is not necessary to make out any formal definition of piety. To Catholics who read the lives of
the Saints there can be no difficulty in seeing what it
means. When I read of St. Philip in his early youth,
at Florence, bright, charming, and modest, learning
in the cloisters of San Marco, from Fra Angelico's
inspired work, to love Jesus, and Mary, and the holy
angels—I feel what piety is. When I realise the
picture of St. Philip saying Mass—of the look of his
countenance, his tears, his visible trembling, his ever
throbbing heart—I know what piety can be. When
I think of him in his old age, in his poor room in the
Vallicella, a beautiful old man, white as an ermine,
with white transparent hands—trembling all over

when he utters one of his favourite ejaculations—his eyes filling with tears at the sight of a holy picture, or the relics of the Saints—or alone with no light but what falls on his crucifix, praying through the night —then no words are wanted to define piety. And if I did want words, it would only be those words of his own—" A man who is truly enamoured of God comes at length into such a state that he is constrained to say, 'Lord, let me sleep!'"

We generally mean by piety, the practice of religion considered as the expression of an affectionate spirit towards God. It is something more than " religion "—for religion is not worth very much without it. Yet there can be no true and real piety without true and solid religion. In the New Testament, the Greek word which in our translation is translated piety, always signifies this reverent and loving service of God.

You will see from this very description, that when we speak of piety we begin to approach that side of the human heart which is called " emotion." For religion by itself is not emotion, and should never be confused with emotion. Religion is rational conviction, rational resolution, and rational spiritual energy. It rests on belief in God, and it acts by that human aspiration and volition which is proper to a human being, and which is of a different world altogether from feeling, fancy, instinct, or excitation of the nerves. Indeed, it may often happen that all our feelings and impulses are in the hostile camp, and that religion has to fight a grim fight for the citadel in their very teeth. And I do not say that piety herself may not at times be cold, dry, and painful, and yet be genuine piety still. But, taking human nature as we usually find it, to speak of piety is to speak of emotion. Now, in a human heart the region of emotion is a dangerous and a treacherous region. It is by no means all healthy or holy. We may find ourselves at times very near the devil and the flesh ; if we are ignorant or reckless, we may die on a barren mountain top, or be suffocated in a darksome morass. Yet emotion will not be kept out of our lives ; and, moreover, it is a most powerful help in our drawing nearer to God. Therefore, whenever emotion is concerned, we want a guide ; we want clear direction, resolute leading, and a strong arm to support us. And since emotion does generally enter into piety, and generally, indeed, gives piety its glow and penetration, we must find out what it is that best regulates piety, distinguishes true piety from false, and sustains its light and heat.

We find two brief phrases in St. Paul which suggest the answer that I am going to give. In 1 Tim. vi. 3 he speaks of a " doctrine which is according to godliness." The words might be more pointedly translated, " doctrine on which rests or stands piety." Again, in Titus i. 1 he mentions the " truth which is according to godliness." But here, again, the expression means that truth on which piety rests. There is, therefore, according to St. Paul, a truth, or doctrine, which is the base and rock that supports piety. This is what we want. But what is it ?

It need not be denied that the whole Christian revelation, taken in its widest sense, is the ground and support of that loving service of God which is fittingly called piety. But to any one who reads the Epistles of St. Paul it is quite clear that when he speaks of the "faith," the "truth," the "good tidings," "sound doctrine," the "promises of God," the "faithful word," and the like, he is referring, not to Divine revelation in general, or that which the Jew held equally with the Christian, but to the distinctive tenets of Christianity. He preaches Christ, and Him crucified. He preaches the "wisdom of God in a mystery,"[1] that mystery being the Incarnation— a mystery which is "hidden"—which God "ordained before the world." He preaches the "illumination of our Saviour Jesus Christ."[2] In a word, his preaching is chiefly concerned with what he so beautifully calls, in the Epistle to Timothy, the "mystery of piety"—which was manifested in the flesh, which was justified in the spirit—that is, proved to be what it was by supernatural power—which appeared to the angels, hath been preached unto the Gentiles, is believed in the world, and is taken up into Heaven.

The Incarnation, then, is the Sacrament of Piety. The word "sacrament" is here used, not in the more restricted and technical sense in which we apply it to the seven Christian Sacraments, but in its original and wider acceptation, as a solemn doctrine, initiation, promise, and pledge—all in one. A very short

---

[1] 1 Cor. ii. 7.   [2] 2 Tim. i. 10.

consideration will suffice to show us how the great and characteristically Christian dispensation of "God made man" is the ground and support of true and genuine Christian piety.

The first and chief effect of piety, as we all feel, is an attachment—what I may venture to call a "personal" attachment—to God. To seek God, to offer ourselves to God, to entreat God, to praise God, to live for God—in a word, to love God with our whole hearts—this is what we exist for. But an attachment of this kind to the Almighty and Infinite God, on the part of a creature like man—perhaps we have never realised how difficult it is, first to initiate, and still more to keep up. It is not so hard to believe in God —or to bow down before Him—as to admire the wisdom and power of the great Creator and preserver of all things. It is not hard even to be resigned to the order of God's providence, as seen in the course of this world, more especially if we ourselves are fairly comfortable and happy. It is not too much to say that religion, in these days, especially among non-Catholics, seldom gets further than a calm and cold reverence for the Almighty, combined with a greater or less strictness in avoiding what is forbidden by the Ten Commandments. Christian men know that God is a Person—not a mere law or force. But the insistence of the non-Christian and agnostic schools has had its effect even here, and in the eyes of this generation the living Infinite ever tends to grow vague, and the fulness of Being to become thin and unsubstantial—just as the distant mountains which

men have never visited, are distinguished with difficulty from the clouds of the changing sky. God is
so silent! Can He be a living Person? Can He
love me, in any intelligent sense of the word " love "?
Can He care for men—for the units of the human
race—for each heart and each heart's struggle and
story? Can He care for me?

The answer to these questions, which are natural
to all human beings who reflect, has been given once
for all—in the Incarnation. The Lord Jesus Christ
is not two persons, but one Person. He is the
Almighty—and He is a man. Now, you may reason
and argue as you like about the impossibility of the
Divine Essence being able to feel love for mortal
men—or indeed to feel love at all ; but that God *does*
love mortal men, whether He feels it or not—(of
course, He does not)—is absolutely proved by the fact
of His coming to the earth in the way He has done.
That this truth was in imminent danger of being
obscured in the world is evident from the reiteration
with which St. John and St. Paul allude to the life
and death of Christ as demonstrating the love of God.
" God hath so loved the world as to give His only-
begotten Son."[1] " He hath loved me, and hath
delivered Himself for me."[2] " God, Who is rich in
mercy, for His exceeding charity wherewith He loved
us,"[3] hath saved us through Jesus Christ. " God
loved us first "—before we loved Him—" and hath
sent His Son."[4] I need not multiply texts.

[1] John iii. 16.   [2] Gal. ii. 20.   [3] Eph. ii. 4.   [4] 1 John iv. 10.

But observe, that this proof of God's love—this stupendous act of redemption—was not a mere event or transaction, in the nature of a payment, a deliverance, a condescension, a humiliation, a decree, or anything transient and impersonal, as when a sovereign may send a messenger, a rescript, or a sum of money. The Incarnation unites in itself whatever is excellent in all these ways of help and proofs of love. But it is much more.

The Prophet Baruch, the friend and disciple of the great Jeremias, after describing the majesty, the wisdom, and the mercy of God, cries out : " This is our God, and there shall no other be accounted of in comparison with Him. . . . And afterwards He was seen upon earth, and conversed with men."[1] These words were chiefly and adequately fulfilled when there walked and conversed upon the earth a Man, of Whom it was possible to say, That is the Everlasting God. As St. Bernard says, the great Invisible was seen by mortal eyes ;[2] the Word in the flesh, the sun in a cloud, honey in the comb, the light shining through the lamp of clay ! As St. Cyprian said, man has always belonged to God ; but now we can say, God belongs to man.[3] God belongs to man ! He has come down to man. He is accessible to man. No longer must He be sought in the unfathomable abysses, in the unscalable heights. No longer does He shroud Himself where eyes cannot pierce, where sense cannot exercise its function. No

---

[1] Baruch iii. 36-38.   [2] *Serm. 2 de Cœnâ Domini.*
[3] *Serm. de Ascensione.*

longer is He silent, motionless, and awful. He is human, visible, familiar. The eye can take Him in, the memory can retain His form and feature, the imagination can embody Him at will. His human birth, life, words, acts, and passion, furnish a thousand points and places to which the hearts of humanity can attach themselves, in order to lift themselves to God ; as the little birds, when men build, make their nests in the coigns and sheltered places. How easy it is to bring Jesus before the mind—to adore Jesus, to offer one's self to Jesus, to entreat Jesus, to understand Jesus, to compassionate Jesus, to give to Jesus our whole heart ! And Jesus is God Most High. Is not this most truly the Sacrament of Piety !

. It is not any exaggeration, then, but only the unadorned truth, to say that piety rests on the Incarnation ; and that any error, any shortcoming in the belief of the Incarnation, is always detrimental to piety, and may be fatal to piety.

Let me illustrate this—and, at the same time, show what we ourselves should be carefully on our guard against—by mentioning the errors, or the aspects of error, on the subject of the Incarnation, which you may come across every day in books, newspapers, and conversation. I do not go back to the early ages of the Church. In those times heresy succeeded heresy. Some denied that Christ was the Word of God ; others, that the Word was God ; others, that Christ's humanity was real ; others, that He had a human soul or will ; others, again, denied the reality of the hypostatic union, and said that in Christ there were two persons ; others maintained that He was neither God nor man, but a new and strange nature—as the Eutychians. These old-world heresies have passed away, and the stormy discussions which shook the Church have long been laid by the power of the Church's definition. But errors quite as pestilential, quite as deadly, are alive and strong at the present ; or perhaps, indeed, the root of the ancient evils has never been, and never can be, utterly destroyed, and is ever ready to spring and sprout again when the season comes.

The greatest error is the fatal one, of those who refuse to believe that Jesus Christ is God. Such men can never kneel by the crib of Bethlehem, nor prostrate themselves before the Cross of Calvary. They. cannot feel that it is their God Who has said, " Take My yoke upon you," or "Learn of Me." They do not find that Jesus makes worship easier, or intercourse with God more real. To them His sufferings are wasted ; they are strange, pitiful, excessive, almost incredible ; but they have not that Divine power with which, for believing souls, they are endowed, of melting the hardness of human hearts to the detestation of sin and the love of God above all things. To them, Jesus is but one portrait in a gallery of wise and good men ; or of men, very likely, not all wise and not all good, but men whom the world admires or talks about. To them, for all that Jesus has done or can do, God is almost as far away as ever, as incomprehensible, as aloof, as mysterious in His relations with men. And, as there is no opening of the heavens, they turn to the world and make the best of it.

Why should I dwell on this? You know how common is the state of mind which does not recognise the divinity of Christ. It is not merely infidels, or that denomination of Protestants who are called Unitarians, who thus cut themselves off from the benefits of the Sacrament of Piety. It is to be feared that the Unitarian spirit is widely diffused. You see it in the difficulty felt by Protestants in praying directly to Christ; in their avoidance of any invocation of the Sacred Name ; in their shrinking from the details of His human life, and from alluding, in their devotional exercises, to His infancy, His childhood, His hidden life, or His solitary prayer. This reticence is the more marked because Protestant writers and preachers are fond of bringing in, even excessively, such New Testament ideas as the white throne in Heaven, the jasper, the rainbow, the crystal sea, and similar descriptions of God's dwelling-place, on the one hand, whilst on the other they love to go back to the Old Testament, and to find devotion in those majestic and significant revelations of God vouchsafed in the ancient law. But of any loving insistence on Bethlehem or Nazareth, or on Our Lady, there is hardly a trace. And this is still more true of the Sacred Passion. Among the fluent divines of Anglicanism, as among the perfervid exponents of Nonconformity, there prevails what may be called a positive dread of the story of the bloody sweat, the scourging, the crowning with thorns, and the crucifixion. They feel no need for this aspect of Our Lord's life. His sufferings, and especially the length and severity of them, are a stumbling-block to them—they have to be explained away. The Sermon on the Mount they understand, or think they understand. The three hours on the Cross—it seems like a mistake, a failure—to be passed over in silence. The explanation is not difficult. They are not clearly convinced that the Person Who lies in the manger, Who obeys Mary and Joseph, and Who is nailed to the Cross, is the true and living God Himself—Who in His all-wisdom chose this way to draw our hearts, and Who, as the Lord and Master of our hearts, has the prerogative of demanding that all the circumstances of His human career—the great acts and the trivial acts, the dignified acts and the acts of humiliation, His words, one by one, His mysterious suffering, stroke upon stroke—every recorded feature of that wondrous revelation, shall be searched out and pondered and pondered again, in order to read aright His Sacred Heart, in order to come to know Him, in order to receive light from the source of light, and in order to lift and set swelling and flowing in these hearts of ours that blessed tide—the tide of supernatural prayer—without which all men's souls are as the Dead Sea.

Akin to this fatal error—an error which, like most errors, deepens in some directions and runs shallow in others—is that which dares to see in the actions and words of Jesus Christ ignorance and weakness; which pretends to mark a progress in what the modern

phrase calls His views ; which notes and criticises
"mistakes"; and which professes to "idealise" Christ—
to pass over, or even reject, the facts of the Gospels,
whilst pretending to construct the mental ideals to
which humanity should conform itself.   From this,
the step is not a long one to the utter denial of the
historical Christ.   And it is precisely this denial
which is found everywhere around us, even among
those who by the consent of their fellow-countrymen are good, just, and religious men.   There has
lately been published the life of a great Oxford head
of a College.   To him his biographers apply Plato's
eulogy of Socrates, " that of all the men of his time
whom they have known, he was the wisest, and justest,
and best."   This is what this good and wise man says
of Jesus Christ : " Is it possible to feel a personal attachment to Christ, such as is prescribed by Thomas
à Kempis ?   I think that it is impossible, and contrary
to human nature, that we should be able to concentrate our thoughts on a person who lived eighteen hundred years ago.   But there might be such a passionate
longing and yearning for goodness and truth.   The
personal Christ might become the ideal Christ.
. . .   Would it be possible to combine in a
manual of piety religious fervour with perfect good
sense and knowledge of the world ? " [1]

That is a passage on which comment would be
wasted—so admirably does it combine the decent reverence and the thorough worldliness of a very large

[1] " Life of Jowett," Vol. II., p. 151.

non-Catholic school of Christians. But let us turn to
the book he refers to—to the *Following of Christ.*
We there read these words : " O Lord Jesus ! Thou
art all my riches, and all that I have, I have it of Thee.
But what am I, O Lord, that I dare thus speak to
Thee? . . . Remember Thy mercies, and fill my
heart with Thy manifold graces. . . . Turn not
Thy face from me ; defer not Thy visitings of me ;
withdraw not Thy consolations from me. Teach me,
O Lord, to fulfil Thy will."[1] And again : " Of all that
are to thee beloved and dear, let the Lord Jesus be
best beloved to thee and dearest."[2]

These two men lived in different worlds. One
believed in the Incarnation ; the other was without
the primary conception of that which gives to Christianity its essential character.

I cannot help thinking that even Catholics, in this
country, require plain warning that, from the prevalence of ignorance and mistake on the subject of the
Incarnation, their own piety is in danger. We are
told that when the ice of the Polar regions breaks up
and floats in masses and mountains into our own seas,
then the temperature of our own coasts cools and
falls. There are books—books of " devotion " and
" lives " of Christ, written by non-Catholics—as to
which I will say no more than this, that they are
spotted with misbelief. These books are not unfre-
quently to be found in Catholic households. Is it
any wonder that the temperature of our piety should

[1] Book III., chap. iii.   [2] *Ib.* II., chap. viii.

7

fall? My brethren, let no man be over confident.
Piety has much to do, as I have said, with emotion
and feeling.   God in the flesh was intended to arouse
our warmth, our devotion, our ardour, our fancy, our
imagination, and all the powerful faculties of perception and energy of that fertile border-land which lies
in man between pure intelligence and mere animality.
Any man who thinks differently of Christ from what
the Catholic Church believes and teaches, so far in-
flicts a wound on Christian piety.

I do not say that, amongst Catholics, piety may
not sometimes be mistaken, untrue, and exaggerated.
Foolish piety arises from ignorance ; and it is pro-
ductive of two evils ; it fetters and blinds its own
victim so that he cannot as he ought approach to
God ; and it turns away those who witness it from
real piety, by the aversion which it inspires.

The remedy for false piety is the same as the
remedy for the want of piety—namely, the accurate
and full teaching of the Church on the Incarnation.
See how the great central mystery has taken possession of the Catholic heart, as the ages have succeeded
each other ! " Wisdom hath built herself a house ;
she hath hewn out seven pillars ; she hath slain
her victims, mingled her wine and set forth her
table ; she hath sent forth her handmaids to in-
vite to the tower, and to the walls of the city."[1]
This is the description of the devotional system
of the Catholic Church—a great temple, built by

---

[1] Prov. ix 1.

wisdom, and opening its portals to all the needy and
hungry souls of the human race. From the Incarnation come the Sacraments—continuing in the world
the sovereign power of Him Who laid His hands on
the afflicted and healed their bodies and their souls.
From the Incarnation comes, chief of all, the sacred
mystery of the Eucharist — Jesus Himself, under
necessary veils, but none the less the august Object
of adoration and ever-varying love ; for Whom
churches are built, altars raised, and sanctuaries
adorned. From the Incarnation comes that beloved
devotion to the Sacred Heart which sweeps the sins
from so many hearts and strengthens so many to
give their hearts to God ; a devotion as to which
there has been opposition and difficulty even in the
Church, but which well illustrates what has here
been said—that faith is the guide to the aspirations of piety, and that we are safe in following
the instructions of the Church, whether she approves
or whether she forbids. From the Incarnation comes
the prerogative and the office of Mary most holy ; of
Mary, whose true motherhood is the truth which
guards the Incarnation, as the walls and outworks
protect the citadel ; of Mary, who so re-echoes, translates, and enforces Jesus, that she is to every Catholic
heart as a second book of the four Gospels. Finally,
from the Incarnation flows our devotion to the angels
and the Saints, trophies and ministers of the God
made man, and to and for the holy souls in Purgatory, who await the perfect fulfilment of His work.
Thus, and in other ways innumerable, subsidiary to

these great main rivers of Paradise, has Christian
piety spread out over all the land that Christ's redemption was to make to blossom as the rose. And
Christian belief and the living voice of teaching have
always ruled its glad and fertilising waters.

Yet I would not send you to the Canons of Councils
or the tomes of learned divines to learn what Christian piety is. There is a shorter and an easier way.
Go to the lives of the Saints, and as we began with
St. Philip, so we can do no less than end with him.
There is no life among the lives of the Saints which
so fully impresses the looker-on with the conviction
that he sees a man who exists in the living presence
of Jesus Christ. The Holy Gospels, the churches, the
Sacrifice of the Mass, the priesthood, Mary most holy,
the Saints, the catacombs, the sight of sinners, with
the thought of their immortal souls, the beauty of
holiness, the calm passage through a long and un-
wearied Christian course—look at him where you
will, find him where you may, it is always and in all
things as if he saw with his eyes the Lord and
Saviour of his heart. I recall the ten years of his
meditations in the catacombs, and that visitation at
Pentecost which enlarged his heart and forced his
very ribs apart. Whom did he find there? Who
visited him thus miraculously? You know, my
brethren. I recall those words, "I cannot bear so
much, O Lord, I cannot bear so much!" Who was
urging him? There is no room for doubt. I read
how he cried out to his penitents, "Do not fear, do
not hesitate; you can never be too many." Whose

place did he then feel himself to be filling? I see him in his trouble, fixing his eyes upon the crucifix: " O good Jesus, why is it Thou dost not hear me?" And the wave of consolation which inundates his soul shows Who it is that hears, and Who it is that answers. I contemplate that cheerful, bright, and charming spirit so characteristic of him, and hear him say: " He who seeks recreation apart from the Creator, or consolation out of Christ, will never find it." I see him lying upon what was thought to be his death-bed—it was in reality only a fortnight before this 26th of May. He lies motionless, his eyes closed, scarcely breathing. Cardinal Borromeo enters his room, bearing the Most Holy Sacrament. All at once his eyes are open, his tears are flowing, and he cries out aloud, with all the fervour that was his own: " Behold my love! Behold my love! Behold my only good! Give me my love quickly, quickly!" No wonder that all present, the Cardinal, the Fathers, and the assistants, were so overcome that the ceremony could hardly go on. The Holy Communion was given, and he was heard to say: " Now I have received the true Physician of my soul. He who seeks aught but Christ knows not what he seeks. Vanity of vanities, and all is vanity." And then he was lost in God.

May St. Philip intercede for us, and obtain for us the spirit of true, deep, and Catholic piety; that we may hold fast to the teachings of our holy Faith; that we may truly believe in Jesus Christ, and live in His loving Presence; and that every thought, every word, and all the actions of our lives may by His word, His touch, and His blessing be made worthy of God, holy and Divine!

THE HOUSE OF PRAYER.

Preached at the opening of the Church of the Blessed Sacrament, Boscombe, Bournemouth, September 8th, 1896.

"My house is the house of prayer" (Matt. xxi. 13).

THE first time of using a new church is an occasion of solemnity and of spiritual emotion. On this spot, but a few months ago, the pines grew and the creatures of God lived their lives. Now, human minds and hearts have written upon it their ideas and their aspirations. They have written in stone, as men have written since the dawn of time; as Egypt set up her pyramids, and Greece her temples, Jacob his Bethel, and the Hebrews their great sanctuary; and the Christian ages in their long course, generation after generation, those grandest and most distinctive of all Christian buildings, the churches of the Catholic faith. Strong ideas, deep aspirations, pregnant lessons have been written in these hewn and carved and high-towering monuments of human energy. I would fain think that not a heathen, not a Greek or Roman of them all, but intended, dimly and ignorantly perhaps, to honour the one only God by the buildings they called Divine. For our Christian churches—the churches of our forefathers, the churches of our brethren in other lands, the churches

of the day in which we live—they have always meant
one thing. They have been, and they are, illustrations
of one of the most strenuous of human efforts—
perhaps the most strenuous of them—to bridge over
the distance between the human spirit and its Creator
and Last End. In one sense, there exists no distance between man and God, " for in Him we live, and
move, and are."[1] But to spiritual beings distance is
ignorance, distance is aversion. Not to know God,
nor to have Him in the heart, not to stretch out
desires to Him—this is to be distant from Him.
What is all religion but the effort to worship, to
love, to serve—to bring God within the grasp of
human faculty, and to stimulate human faculty to
action? To help us to do this, God has wrought
the Incarnation ; and Jesus Christ is the great revelation of God and the great force that draws us to
Him. To keep fast and close to Christ, man, among
other faithful and loyal works, builds churches. For
a church is the scene of the presence of Christ.
When He Himself was on this earth He required
neither roof nor walls. He spoke and wrought,
sometimes in the synagogues or in the great cloister
of the Temple, but as often under the heavens, standing by the lake, or seated on the slope of the mountain. But it is different now that He has gone up
to the right hand of God. The infallible word, the
holy Sacraments, the Eucharistic presence and sacrifice—these things which He has left us to supply for

[1] Acts xvii. 28.

His bodily and sensible absence, cannot be administered except in a church. I speak, as it will be well understood, of the general rule. All Catholics know that the precious things of our holy religion may be distributed, if need be, in any place and at any time. But the earthly kingdom of God is an orderly and a stately kingdom, and until time's consummation it will carry out its manifold mission to a numberless flock in the strongest light of publicity. Therefore, it builds churches to proclaim its powers, to feed and guide its people, and to draw them to the God for Whom they are created.

Among all the words invented to describe the intercommunion of frail and mortal beings with their God, there is not one that is so expressive as that of Prayer. It is certain, therefore, that a Church must be by excellence a "house of prayer." Even had not Jesus Christ used and consecrated that phrase, it would have forced itself into human consciousness and taken its place in human language. For whatever a church may enclose within its walls and cover with its roof, if it does not lift hearts to God it cannot be a church. Among those who think wrongly in matters of religion, there is often found a disposition to speak contemptuously of churches— and to say that a church symbolises that which is the very opposite of what they term spiritual religion. For religion, they say, is of the heart towards God ; a church means ministrations, ceremonies, and forms. And even those of our countrymen who know something more of what a church is—for they possess and use some of the noblest and most beautiful churches in the world—are accustomed, most of them, to ignore the principal purposes for which those churches were originally built, and to contrast their own cool and decorous methods of worship with what they describe as the enthusiasm and the superstition of ours. I wish we could persuade them all that in no spot of the whole earth is true spiritual prayer made more surely, more easily, and more habitually than in a church where the whole Christian faith is adequately believed and practised. It is easy to show what we mean.

I use prayer in no narrow sense. The word is sometimes confined to express that impulse of the rational being which leads him to ask and supplicate. Ask we must, and supplicate we must. But the play of human faculty in the direction of God is more than mere asking. Prayer covers adoration, love, praise, thanksgiving, and sorrow for sin. In all these and other ways man's heart lifts itself to the heavens.

Prayer, taken thus in its widest sense, is in one respect natural to man ; in another, it is difficult to man ; and, in a third, it is impossible without the supernatural grace of Christ.

How can it not be natural to pray? We have before our eyes the living God. A lesser thought than this would bow the creature's head and draw out the creature's heart. The thought of lesser gods than the living God—of gods falsely so called, yet invested by tradition or fancy with attributes that seemed Divine—has sufficed to kindle the fires of sac-

rifice, to inspire invocation and supplication, over the
wide world, through ages of time. And now, when
the clearer atmosphere of Christian teaching has
made it easier for the mind of man to see what his
own strivings have always had the power to make
him see—I mean, the existence of the true and living
God—weak, helpless, short-lived men turn, not naturally merely, but strongly and constantly, to the Being
Whom they recognise as their Father and their Friend.
If there is any stability in this quickly-passing world,
it must be in Him. If there is any security against
the chances of elemental strife and brute violence, it
must come from Him. If there is any light in the
heart to illuminate matter and its blind laws with the
rays of truth, justice, and goodness, that light must
come direct from Him. The greater and more sublime features of the universe reveal Him. The soul
needs Him and cries for him. The inward struggle
between inevitable death and the consciousness of inextinguishable life can have no outcome, rationally,
except in the certainty that a Redeemer liveth—a
strong Master in Whose hands are the keys of death
and of all the nether world. The cry of suffering
must be, without Him, no better than the wailing or
the howling of the beast. The impulses of affection,
the joys of sacrifice, the holy and pure delight of
resisting and subduing what is base and contemptible
in this nature of ours—unless a heart can take God
into its confidence, what are they but ploughing the
sands, beating the air ? The living God gives human
life its meaning, human endurance its purpose, human

fears their relief, human aspirations their satisfaction; therefore the heart of man naturally lifts itself up to Him. There are many dark spots in our modern civilisation. There are tens of thousands, living huddled together in our cities and large towns, on whom poverty, misery, and vice have brought such a blight that they seem to have no longer any respect or reverence for prince or priest, for law or religion, for God or man. Yet it is a most striking fact that among the very worst the idea of God is not strange at all; for when sorrow, or deserved punishment, or the terrors of life and death, really touch their callous hearts, it is of God they speak, and very often it is to God they turn. It is not the poor or the ignorant who are militant against God; but the half-instructed and those puffed up with the conceit of differing from their fellows. Like the harvests which the storm has beaten down, the faculties of men are always trying, when the wind and the rain have ceased and the sun of faith shines for a time, to rise up again and stand erect, in the light and the air of God.

For all this, it cannot be denied that prayer is difficult. To human nature, prayer as it ought to be —adequate, warm, sustained—is far from easy. It is not that it is against the grain, or painful, to turn to God. It is not that one has to master a science, or learn a foreign language, before one can come face to face with Him. It is rather that man finds so many other things to do. This world is so vast, so various, and so attractive; the powers and faculties which can grasp it and enjoy it are so keen and so manifold;

and this human nature, infinite as it may be in its
possibilities, is yet so shallow a vessel for the wine of
strong volition or emotion, so incapable of entertain-
ing more than one occupying interest at a time—
that God is pushed into the dimness of distance, and
an effort is required not to forget Him in the hurry
and pressure of the things He has made. It is as if
our religious aspirations were like the stars, which
disappear before the on-coming of the hot and garish
sun. They are there all the time, in their watches
in the eternal firmament ; but their light is ineffectual,
because a fiercer and a more violent influence fills the
spaces of the air ; and even the moon at the full is
sometimes seen hanging pale and feeble in the morning sky when the overbearing sun as yet is still below
the Eastern hills. For alas ! God is not our sun here
below. It is not yet the day of the new Jerusalem.
Our mortal frame is so made that things earthly warm
it more than God does ; our mortal eyes are so
tempered that the baser and more lurid light which
is shed by things perishable is brighter to them than
the distant shining of the Everlasting. So we are
made. And thus prayer is difficult. It is difficult,
not so much to the simple, the suffering, the old,
and the forlorn. For these, the fascination of things
around them has largely died away. It is not so
hard for these to pray, in the night and in the
day ; unless the world has hardened them in selfishness and degradation ; unless the flood of human
interests even in its subsidence has left wreckage and
malaria behind. It is the young, with hope dancing

in their heart, who find it hard to be constant to prayer; it is the easy and the comfortable—those who are dreadfully content with their earthly lot, those who have "peace in their possessions,"[1] who turn with difficulty to Him to Whom their heart is cold; it is the busy, the prosperous, the reckless, the fighters, who find no time to worship and to praise; it is the frivolous, the thoughtless, and the small, easily occupied minds, who cannot bring themselves to face the ideas of judgment and eternity which are needed to keep the unstable heart steady in its communion with its Father in Heaven.

Thus, it is not strange that prayer is impossible without Divine grace. I speak of more continuous and intense prayer. It is true that even the shortest and poorest act of Christian prayer is the work of grace. But this is what I may call a common and universal grace, which is invariably given to all; for since God wishes all to be saved, the grace to pray must be, and is, at hand to every one. Here, however, I am rather speaking of prayer as a predominant occupation of one's life and one's powers; of prayer which is kept up day by day; of loving adoration, of fervent oblation of one's self, of grateful giving of thanks, of habitual invocation against temptation and peril, of continuous sorrow for sin—in a word, of that all-pervading intercommunion with our Divine Master, Father, and Friend, which is the only ideal worthy of the efforts of an immortal soul. For this,

---

[1] Ecclus. xli. 1.

great and special graces are required. But I speak of this, not to make such prayer seem the more difficult, or such grace too remote a gift for you or me to hope for. Grace is the manifestation of the love of our Heavenly Father, through Jesus Christ our Lord. It is certain that He is so anxious to pour it into our hearts, that He requires very little of us, His children, whom He loves so truly. There can be no real difficulty, therefore, on the side of grace. But I mention the need of grace in order that we may feel and fully understand how great, how august, how Divine a thing is Christian prayer, in its adequate sense. There are found on the Western continent great trees that fill us with wonder. What earth is it that nourishes them—what sun and rains, by which they flourish and grow so mighty! But what are all the trees of all the forests—all the flowers of every clime—all the life, movement, vicissitudes, and beauty of the earth's surface, to the act or production, the growth or flower, of the immortal spirit, which it puts forth by grace to its Creator, and which is called prayer! Divine in origin, mounting to the highest heavens, penetrating the unapproachable light of God's supreme majesty, unchangeable, eternal! It does not need that the angels should gather it in golden vials and offer it like precious perfume to the Highest. But the angels do gather it thus—because their charge is to minister, and there is nothing so precious that the universe has ever sent up to the heavens as Christian prayer For even the sacrifice of the Incarnate was gathered

up in a prayer—an act of the Sacred Heart—and
all Christian prayer in that prayer received its
consecration.

It is not in vain that to this noblest exercise of the
spirit of man there is assigned a "house"—a home.
It is not in vain that three Evangelists report those
striking words, far more significant than at first sight
they appear, with which Our Lord, four days before
His passion, rebuked the profaners of the Jewish
Temple. It will be observed that He speaks as one
quoting the ancient Scriptures: "It is written, My
house shall be called a house of prayer to all nations."
The words are found in the prophecy of Isaias[1]
It is a passage which clearly foretells the in-
gathering of the Gentiles, and the establishment of
an earthly kingdom far more august than that of
Israel. For thus saith the Lord, "The children of
the stranger that adhere to the Lord, to worship
Him, to love His Name, to be his servants . . . I
will bring them into My holy mount, and will make
them joyful in My house of prayer, and their victims
shall please Me upon My altar ; for My house shall
be called the house of prayer for all nations." These
words, like the great prophecy of Malachias[2] is
either unfulfilled to this day, or it finds its fulfilment
in the Christian church, the Christian altar, and the
Christian sacrifice. And when Our Lord and Saviour
uttered that reproof to the buyers and sellers, He saw
in the future something greater than the Temple ;

[1] lvi. 7.   [2] i. 2.

He saw His own great Church—not a mere building of stone and cedar wood, set on a hill amid the hills of Juda, but churches great and small over all the world, churches built and churches falling into decay, churches multiplying and succeeding one another wherever the apostolic inheritance spread— but every one of them an embodied manifestation of the one, only, universal Church, living and working its inexhaustible wonders by His own commission and power.

There is little need to explain to any believing Catholic why a church, and this church amongst others, is truly the house of prayer. These walls are new, this roof is newly raised. There is no con- secration on these stones, of story, or tradition, or romance, such as brings the pilgrim to other spots to muse and meditate on the past. To merely human fancy, the sea, which through the centuries has heaved and beat upon this coast, the cliffs which are so full of history, the pine woods so gracious and so solemn, are more impressive than this new building standing among new buildings. And yet not a believer, not a thoughtful heart, that has entered these doors on this the first day of its use, but feels, with the patriarch of ancient times, that this place is full of awe, and is even the gate or vestibule of a kingdom, barely out of sight, which can only be called heaven upon earth.

It would be enough if God had merely willed that we should worship Him together and in one place. Had He only so decreed, we should not need His revelation to know that where we were gathered together there was He in the midst of us. For it is true that He is everywhere, and that the cry of the human soul can reach Him wherever it is uttered; yet He has often chosen this place and that—and He has called holy the place of His choice, and has promised that His eyes and His heart should be there. And it is for human nature's sake that He has thus hallowed such a favoured spot—in order to draw us more surely ; for He knoweth our frame.

A church would be impressive, too, were it only for the spectacle of prayer in common. There is the public recognition of the living God ; there is the protestation that those who gather here put God and religion before all else in this world they live in. There is the loyalty of professing that God's service is not to be hidden behind doors and walls, but celebrated openly with every faculty we have. Here each shows his faith to every other, and each calls upon each to show his faith in turn. And such is the nature of our being, that this example, this unison, this fervour, this multitudinous confession of our Heavenly Father's sovereignty, kindles sevenfold the flame of our own devotion, and so lifts us nearer to His love.

This would all be true if our churches were only meeting-houses, provided we met in the obedience and the love of God. Our churches are much more. They are the scenes of a peculiar presence of the Redeemer of the world. They are the precincts where His word is uttered and His touch is felt.

The prerogative of infallible teaching denotes that He Who speaks is Christ and no one else. It is not that the priest who stands up in this place to preach is infallible. But he has infallibility behind him. If he teaches what is wrong in a grave matter concerning faith or morality, he is sure to be corrected by the great teaching Church, which cannot err, and which in some fashion or other will undoubtedly bring her voice to bear upon him. And the ministry of the holy Sacraments is just as truly the touch of Christ. Frail man as he is, the priest, given certain conditions, can communicate, not bodily healing, but supernatural sanctifying or strengthening grace. It would be ridiculous to say that this communication originates from him. Then from whom does it come? When we reflect that in the Sacraments is chiefly fulfilled that promise of our Blessed Lord, that He would refresh those that labour and are heavy-burdened, it is easy to understand how to a Catholic no spot of the Holy Land, no scene of the Passion, can be more impressive than a real church of the Church Catholic, the chief theatre on earth of that incomparable sacramental dispensation without which Christianity is not the Christianity of Christ.

But the supreme gift with which our Heavenly Father's love has enriched and consecrated the churches of the kingdom of His Son, is the presence within them of the Blessed Sacrament. It seems to me that we could hardly help expecting that in the churches of the new and great covenant there would be some visible presence of the

Godhead. To one who studies the Scriptures, it would appear that God was always longing to lift a corner of the veil which must needs hide His glory from mortal eyes. In Paradise there was a wonderful Presence and speech. In patriarchal times we read how God came down ; we read of the rainbow ; the holocaustic fire; the voice; the visitation. Afterwards there is the cloud ; the fiery pillar ; the constant visit of him who is called the angel of the Lord ; then, we see the permanent portent in the Temple which was called the "glory of the Lord." The Incarnation— the presence amongst men of the Word made flesh— was at once the strongest proof of God's anxiety to reveal Himself, and the most stupendous fulfilment of this loving wish. For many reasons, that bodily and sensible Presence could not be perpetual on the earth. What device, then, would the love of our great and best Friend find out, in order to be tangibly and strongly present to the end ? The answer was given when He said, " This is My Body—this is My Blood. Do ye this in commemoration of Me."

I do not deny that His Eucharistic presence re- quires the exercise of faith. It is certain that the Blessed Sacrament is so mysterious, so true a veil and concealment, not only of the divinity, but also of the humanity of our Blessed Redeemer, that unless there be faith—unless there be instruction in Chris- tian doctrine, childlike obedience to the word of Christ and of His ministerial teaching body, and the supernatural help of the Holy Spirit—the Eu- charistic presence must be as dead in the world as the glories of sunrise to the blind. But to say that the Blessed Sacrament needs faith to make it work upon the faculties of human nature is not in the very least to lessen its power or depress its efficaciousness. Faith is not blindness, as some would seem to think. Faith does not, it is true, lend acuteness to the eye or the ear ; but it seizes upon certain other faculties just as powerful for making things real and present, and to them it gives an intensity and a retaining grasp which has no parallel in matters corporeal. By faith a spiritual presence often becomes to men a far more overpowering presence than the very things round about which can be seen and felt. And how frequently does it come to pass that sensible things grow stale and unimpressive by custom or repetition, whilst the things of the invisible world are kept always fresh and green by supernatural faith ! In the holy Eucharist, then, there is Divine faith. But it is faith in combination with a visible dispensation—a combination the most marvellous and striking that could be conceived.

For the Blessed Sacrament is left to the Church in the manner of a sacrifice. Sacrifice is the grand religious act of humanity. All the generations of the world have offered sacrifice. Our Redeemer redeemed the world by performing, High Priest as He was, the sacrifice of Himself. The Christian Church has inherited from Him His own perpetually renewed bodily presence, to be made for all generations the great daily sacrifice. It need not be said that it is the same sacrifice as that of Calvary. But it goes on to the end of time, all the world over, from the rising to the setting of the sun—the great act, the great worship, the great gathering together of the people of Christ. O blessed Presence, not enshrined in remote solitudes of the world—not shut up by locks, or guarded by soldiers in the midst of the Christian millions—but put forward, used, glorified, handled, lifted up, every day, in every place, so that no man may be a stranger and no man may forget!

Consider, further, what the Eucharistic Sacrifice involves. It means a Presence more or less continuous. In some ages of the Christian era that presence in our churches has been habitually less constant than it is in these modern times. There are abundant reasons for this and similar changes. But even if it were only during the action of the Mass —even if it were only in the ministration of the Communion—we have a presence long enough continued to furnish the occasion of an engrossing and most striking ceremonial, of a public and splendid observance. The name of this ritual to which the Eucharistic presence gives rise is called the holy liturgy. The liturgy is to the Blessed Sacrament what their court, their magnificence, their heralds, and their officers are to the kings and emperors of the earth.

The presence of Jesus amongst men is still further signalised and emphasised by the ordinance of Holy Communion. It is given to us in such a way that we partake of the Body of Christ, as in the ancient sacrifices there were portions that were given to those assisting. Thus the Christian altar plays a twofold part : it is the altar of sacrifice, and it is also the Holy Table. And thus the presence implies the altar, the roof under which the altar stands and beneath which the faithful gather ; it means a priesthood, with all its degrees, a solemn ritual, a lavish use of things precious and artistic, a grand literature of official prayer, song, and music—all of which go to seize the world's attention and to occupy the faculties of men.

And, most of all, this presence draws together in constant assembly and devout crowds the millions for whom Christ died. It offers them a centre of spiritual interest. It builds a house, and lights it up —and the wayfarers in the night of time are cheered and gathered in. At a certain hour of the day, in a definite place, at the moment when a minister bends over the altar and utters his Master's creative words —the presence occurs and Calvary is renewed. Ever and again there are liftings up, triumphant expositions, joyful processions—which follow from the gift of the presence, and stir the multitudes to acknowledgment, to remembrance of so many mercies. As the ages go on, there are the great words, the ever-growing treasury of the utterances of Saints and Pontiffs, doctors and preachers. And for each Christian's own soul there are the teachings received from childhood, the memories of first Communion, of many communions, the always strengthening feeling of nearness, help, and consolation.

It is no wonder, then, if a church which possesses

so great and majestic a presence, is by excellence the house of prayer. Prayer before the Blessed Sacrament is prayer at once the easiest and most fruitful. Before the tabernacle, the world is shut out, the world's distractions are silenced. Before the tabernacle the mind remembers, the imagination is filled with holy presentations, the very senses are wrought upon, and the will without impediment lifts itself in worship and self-oblation. It is Our Lord's chosen mystery and dispensation. If He is there, why is He there? Certainly to hear and listen; to take hold of hearts; to conquer His enemies; to communicate Himself in love and imperial gifts to His creatures. If He saved us by Bethlehem, by Nazareth, by Calvary, and if heavenly influences seek out the heart that lives in the presence of the crib, the holy house and the Cross—where is it likely that the spirit will find itself nearer to Jesus in His life, Passion, and death, than here, where He dwells in true reality, in virtue of His own command, "Do ye this in memory of Me"? Where—in the language He used of old—where will His eyes be, but here? Where will His Heart be, but here?

Thus we thank God to-day for another house of prayer. And as we think of our many needs and wants—of our own defects, the trials of the Church, the labours of her pastors, the multitudes round about who are yet outside—let us be sure that it is the Blessed Sacrament which can accomplish everything, if Christian believers love and honour it devotedly. For it is in our hands. When the barbarian foe attacked Assisi, St. Clare carried it to the very walls, and the enemy was vanquished. So we must carry it. We must not leave it alone and unvisited ; but we must remember ; we must make its home a second home to ourselves, we must deepen our devotion, and give our very lives to its honour and love—and then it will be known how great is the God of Israel in His own city, upon His holy mount.

And may the ever-blessed Virgin Mother, never absent in motherly solicitude wherever the Blessed Sacrament is—she whose glorious Nativity we are this day celebrating—draw us to the church, and to the presence, and obtain for us the true spirit of prayer !

GOD WITH THE CHILDREN OF MEN.

Preached at the opening of St. Mary's, Liverpool, on Thursday, July 9th, 1885.

" I will open rivers in the high hills, and fountains in the midst of the plains ; I will plant in the wilderness the cedar, and the myrtle, and the olive " (Isaias xli. 18, 19).

WE are assembled to praise God and to give Him thanks for the successful completion and dedication of a church ; of a house and temple to His holy Name ; of a centre of faith and a home of Catholic life to His people. When a new church is built—and this is especially true of missionary countries and of districts like this of Liverpool—it usually means a new flock and a new parish ; it means growth and expansion. But this church, as I need not remind the flock of St. Mary's, is both new and old. In the days when Israel journeyed through the wilderness, they pitched, every night, the great tent which was the Lord's tabernacle, and struck it again in the morning. Each night's halt brought them to a new camping ground, to another rocky shelter, to a new watercourse, to fresh difficulties and strange conditions. But, as they rested in the desert, there were still above them the same stars which had shone on their father Jacob ; there was always the Divine pillar of fire for their beacon and their guide.

So in the midst of this wilderness of interests which
we call the world, of this wilderness of houses and of
men which we call a city, you move the tabernacle
of the Lord.   As the years go on all things change ;
commerce grows, men come and depart ; there are
new conditions and fresh problems, an altered horizon
and strange ground under foot.   But it is not all new.
Move your church where you will or where you must,
there is still God's light over your head.   Men have
only to raise their eyes ; the fires which God has
placed in the firmament of the human reason shine
on, leaving man without excuse ; the light of Divine
revelation, far brighter than the radiance which shone
at night on the dark rocks of the desert, brings comfort to the anxious heart seeking for truth ; comfort
to this age as to every age, to this year as to the years
gone by ; to the children as to the fathers, to the
living as to the departed, and to you, my friends,
now here gathered under the freshness of a new roof
and before the glitter of a new altar, as to those—
some departed, some still here—who all these years
have worshipped God within the hallowed walls of
old St. Mary's.

The dedication of a church—the rejoicing over a
new home of the ·Blessed Sacrament, a new fortress
of Divine teaching in the midst of this vast town—
cannot fail to stir up one great thought, one great
longing in the hearts of the servants of Jesus Christ.
Would to God that all men understood !   Would
that our brethren who feel, so many of them, the
want and the necessity of faith, could see that

nowhere but before this altar can their hearts find
peace ! You hear them say that they find faith impossible. Modern conditions and modern difficulties
have so altered the outlines of spiritual problems that
the old teachings are useless ; the altar has no longer
any power ; the word of preaching is obsolete ; the
sanctuary has lost its holy awfulness. Faith, they
tell us, was a dispensation for the infancy or the
childhood of the race ; man is too mature now either
to accept it, or indeed truly to need it.

It is not my intention to dwell upon the nature or
the conditions of faith ; but, briefly put, our Catholic
view is this—that faith is a light beyond what man's
reason supplies, given by God to enable man to live
for the bliss of God's vision in the everlasting time to
come. The analogy of the word " light " implies two
things ; first, a visible, substantial system of true
ideas, somehow or other given as a gift to the world
by God, through Jesus Christ ; and secondly, a personal power or faculty, by which the human mind is
enabled to see, and, what is far more, to cling to those
saving truths of God. Faith is the light left us
between two great visions. One vision has come
and gone ; the other is to come in the fulness of
time. The first vision was Jesus in the flesh, seen
and heard of men ; mighty, gentle, attractive, and
Divine ; illuminating, drawing, and convincing the
minds aud the hearts of those who humbled themselves to Him ; the God of reason, the God of revelation, the Head of the Church, the author and the
finisher of faith. That vision went away. The

second vision will be on that day when the heavens
shall part asunder, and the clouds roll up their
masses ; when the angel's trumpet shall sound, and
the armies of the host of Heaven shall throng the
upper air of this little world ; when the Son of Man
shall come with the standard of His Cross, and " every
eye shall see Him " as He sits to judge the living and
the dead. Between these visions there is a light ;
not the light which Peter saw, and Andrew, and
Zaccheus, and Mary Magdalene ; not the lightning
which shall bring conviction at the last day to every
mind and heart of every people and every generation ;
but still the light of God, sufficient for the needs of
men. When Jesus went away, He said : " A little
while and ye shall not see Me, because I go to the
Father."[1] But let us understand what He meant
by that. On that very same evening He had said,
as you read two chapters earlier in the same Gospel
of St. John : " A little while and the *world* seeth
Me no more. But *you* see Me because I live."[2] It
is only the world, those who keep apart from Him,
who shall not see Him ; His servants shall see Him
because He lives, and His living power, in word, in
act, and in presence, can be recognised, can be used,
by every man who enters within the magic circle of
Divine faith.

Here, then, we have before us to-day, as in the
days gone by, faith confronting unbelief ; and the
question is, Why do men not believe ? Or, rather,

---

[1] John xvi. 16.   [2] *Ib*. xiv. 19.

we have our Lord and Saviour Jesus Christ offering
belief and life to every man, and the problem is,
Why do so many stand apart? It is well for us, who
have our altar which we hold so dear, and our Divine
oracle to which we cling with firm conviction, to be
very gentle with those who do not believe or who
only half believe. It is true, no doubt, that thousands of men, in their fallen nature, reject faith
through passion or through pride. With such as
these argument is useless until their passion has
been exorcised and their pride extinguished. But I
would rather speak of those who are not led by pride
or passion ; to men whose pride is not their tyrant,
whose passions have not blinded them ; men who
are not unwilling to believe, and who, if they did
believe, would on the whole live the life of believers.
Are there not many such? And is there not, in such
countries as this, a widely-spread feeling, quite distinct from that hatred of religion which we find in
other countries? In too many countries men, marked
with the sign of holy Baptism, rage wildly and furi-
ously against the Name of Christ, until the day when
the near vision of death drives them to seek His
pardon—if haply they are allowed to find it. But in
countries like this you have men who think faith is
not needed for virtue and for well-being. You have
men who live contentedly in the sterility of a natural
life ; in a barren land, a land of stony soil and in-
clement skies, of stunted trees and sour fruit ;
because they do not believe in any other. To them
the life of faith is not, what we believe it to be, a

realm of fertility, of luxuriant development and glorious results ; but rather a dream of priests, a philosophic system, a complication of the simplicity of human existence which is unnecessary, and therefore mischievous.

To lead to Christian belief such souls as this is a task which is very dear to the heart of every priest, of every Catholic. I would like to take hold of that very human nature in which they entrench themselves, and let them see, as if I showed them a wounded man on a battlefield crying out for water, that there are clamours and longings of their nature which they have let go too long unnoticed. It is difficult to make people reflect. It is difficult for a man to make himself reflect. Work, human interest, and the perpetually changing show which we call existence, distract the mind from itself. But if we could get this heart of ours in some secret and silent place, and let it hear its own beatings, then truths would be revealed. There have, probably, been moments—not many, perhaps, but some—in which we have seemed to hear the voice of our very being. It may have been in the darkness of the night, when sounds were hushed, and brain and faculty were resting, like some sea-cliff when the tide is out and the waters are murmuring far in the distance—resting from the beating of those surges of sensible emotion which fall all day, wave on wave, upon the tired sense. Or it may have been when the night was rather in the soul itself—when pain, disappointment, or loss had clouded the light of day in those outer chambers of the spirit where dwell imagination and her train. It is then that the spirit sees itself. Distraction departs like a mist, the noise of outward existence ceases like a huge machine run down. And in those precious moments of insight one sees what one is, and what one must have—what is one's destiny, and what is one's deadly peril—better than if a hundred wise men had talked for a hundred years. It is then that a startling revelation is made ; then something asserts itself, as if a hidden man had sprung out upon us. This something is ourself; yet not that self that we have any power over, not the self that we can direct, rebuke, or rule like a master. It is a self which says, " I am not content, and I charge you to satisfy me." It is an imperious self, which sees far into dim distances, and has instincts which cannot be argued away. It is a self which spurns this world as a folly, and seems to wither it, all in a moment, into insignificance—this world which is so pleasant, so satisfactory, so engrossing. Terrible questions come up, which nothing on the earth's surface can answer. What are we living for ? Are we right in using the world as we do ? Why do so many suffer ? Why are beautiful lives cut short ? Why must immortal souls spend themselves in hard, degrading labour ? Why must the rich drop their riches just as they have grasped them, and the poor live from day to day in insufficiency? Nothing can answer these questions but a voice from some other world than this. But at these moments answers do come ! This spirit of ours answers. It is a spirit which has tremendous convictions, just as the frame of nature has tremendous forces which man cannot cross and live. Your spirit believes, first of all, in the right and the good. Some things are right to it and some things wrong. On this matter, it has one or two clear rules which are as much a part of its essence as instinct is a part of the animal. And as right and wrong imply a standard, being only the approach to or departure from an apprehended ideal, therefore your spirit sees, holds, and has, a standard of right and wrong, altogether independent of human law and human accidents. But next, it cannot acquiesce in the failure of the right, or the final success of the wrong. You may argue, and you may seem to prove, the possibility that evil will triumph. But your spirit revolts at it. Things were meant to be right. Justice was intended. There must be law—or prayer—or personal interference, or some power that will straighten what is crooked, punish the guilty, and help the innocent and oppressed. This is your heart's conviction, rooted in it, or shining from it, evidencing itself like the bird's song or the diamond's light. And, thirdly, your spirit proclaims that there is no such thing as annihilation ; no final and complete death. "Surely," it seems to be crying out, "I shall not be extinguished. Even when worlds crash together, surely some refuge will be found for me ; when time tries and changes all, still that which I call myself will surely survive." Reasoning has no place here. My spirit, left to itself, resists the thought of dying and holds on to perpetual existence. It is not a blind instinct of self-preservation, as with the animals; but it is a deliberate intuition, part of its nature, only not innate because it springs up at the contact between the spirit and its environment, as the falling star bursts into flame when it touches the atmosphere of the earth.

These convictions, or instincts, of the spirit of man —the conviction of good and evil, or right and wrong; the conviction of the final triumph of the right, and the conviction of immortality—are part of the essential nature of the soul. They are often obscured, covered over by prejudices imbibed in childhood, warped by wrong education, hidden out of recognition by the eruptions of passion or the mists of pride. But reflection brings them out as they are. The spirit of man has recognised and recorded them in every age and country; the lives of your philosophers witness them, the careers of your heroes embody them, your books are full of them, the speech of the people rests on them, the little child, brought face to face with them, takes them in as if he knew them. And now, what are they? They are the spirit's native light, a light which in every spirit is the same; whence is that all-pervading light? When a traveller has lost his way in the night, and has sat down to wait for dawn, he at last sees, in one quarter of the heavens, the pale light of morning, and he knows it is the east, and that the sun is climbing there. And when man finds, in the universal world of the human spirit, a light which he cannot control or banish, as he could not produce it, it does not take many steps to prove the existence of the Sun of all existence, the radiating Mind of minds, the everlasting One and only God.

And then, at the vision of God—even His dim and imperfect vision—there breaks forth from the human spirit, as the eagle breaks its bonds when it feels the desert air, the whole of its longing and its want—its worship and its love. Speculation is only half of the nature of man. He has intuitions which, the more he interrogates, the faster they stand ; he has fountains of intellectual light which, the deeper he digs, gush out with the greater force. But he has also that immense, that mighty, that glorious power and necessity which we call worship, or attraction, or simply love. No sooner does he see that the light of his instincts is but the reflection of the ever-shining light of an Eternal Being, than that Being becomes to him the beginning and the end. The Infinite explains all. He is the ruler of good and bad. He is the power which will finally make all things right. He is the loving Father Whom my nature longs for, to cherish me in elemental war and in the vicissitudes of universal being. Above all, He, and He alone, can fill the capacity of this spirit of mine, whose vision and reach keep slowly, but surely, overtopping every horizon of created things. He alone can satisfy a heart which has been made to such a startling likeness to Himself.

These truths affect every man. Those to whom they are new are either those who have lived in them

unconsciously, or those who have never taken their
spirits to task. And now, let us bethink us where we
are.   We are in God's own house, surrounded as
honoured guests by evidences on every side of the
wealth, and the benevolence, and the affection of the
Master to whom the house belongs. That is to say,
that God, Whom the instincts of the spirit prove, and
Whom the instincts of the heart must worship here,
and must possess hereafter, has brought Himself
down to our very doors. This is the true, the real
Christianity. Christianity means God given to our
human faculties. Some revelation, some Divine condescension, some kind of incarnation, we may justly
say, was necessary—necessary, seeing what man is,
and what God is. For God is very far away ; very
high up, wrapt in a light which is very difficult of
approach. Or, rather, the atmosphere of this created
world is so thick and heavy that His Divine light
penetrates with difficulty, and His never-extinguished
voice is easily passed by unrecognised. And yet our
immortal souls must have Him near. And, therefore, He has come near us. That He has taken flesh
and dwelt amongst us is the sum and the short
abridgment of a long history of Divine skill and
contrivance. The Almighty and Infinite God has a
human story, and a human name, to seize and to fill
our fancy and our thought. The immovable God of
Heaven has passed through the vicissitudes of a
human life, bearing the burthen of it ; He has taken
a human heart, with all its sympathies and its com-
passions, that we might feel Him nearer to us. He

has taken up suffering—sought her out, lived with
her, died as she stood over Him, in order that the
fountains of our hearts might be unsealed by the
sight of His pain, and that suffering might never
stand beside us, in our turn, without whispering to us
the secrets which she has learnt beside the Cross.
The attributes of His divinity are now translated
into every picture made by human speech ; into
literature and into art, into law and custom. And
there is a living presence of Him in this earth which
is a real, a strong, and a persisting fact, giving solidity
and efficacy to the image of His attractiveness left
by the Incarnation. The reason why this church
and altar are here, is that Christ still speaks ; in no
figurative sense ; but because He guards and protects
from mistake the pastorate which He has left. This
church is here because His hand still falls upon the
sinner and the innocent, healing and giving life as
only His hand can do, in the Sacraments. This altar
is here, because, in a way that stupendously combines
the strength of faith with the impressiveness of
sensible experience, He has left us His Real Presence.
And, lastly, this church is here, and the clergy and
the people are here, and ministers minister and a
voice speaks, because, amid all the turmoil and the
distraction of human life, we know that Christ has
said, " The charity of God is spread abroad in your
hearts by the Spirit of God which is given you ";[1]
and that every man may have in his being, if he will,

[1] Rom. v. 5.

the intimate presence of that Divine and supernatural grace which is the very shining of the Divinity itself. These are the rivers in the mountains—the springs in the plains, opened by the hand of God. These are the glories—the cedar, the myrtle, and the olive, planted by God in the wilderness of this world.

And now we turn to Him, Whose presence is the light and life of the Church. Now the ranks of the sacred priesthood close round the altar, and the people join their prayer and praise. Now the Lord of Heaven comes down, and the greatest act that this world knows is about to be accomplished. Pray that the power of this Royal Presence may spread and be widely felt, in this flock, in this city, among those who believe, and among those who believe not yet. And as I speak these walls seem to vanish, and this roof to dissolve into the sky; and the spirits of the just seem to gather silently to this altar, joining themselves to the faithful people here present in the body; the spirits of those who have lived their Catholic lives in this ancient district of St. Mary's, keeping their faith amid many trials: the spirits of the good and faithful priests who have ministered to so many generations passed away, who have spent themselves in work and zeal, and even died martyrs of charity for their flock; these gather here to-day. And there join them—for there is only one altar and one Sacrifice—the spirits of all the faithful departed who have lived in this north-western land, and of all who, from other lands, have gone to Heaven, and still love those who bear their name; the men and

women, the priests, the martyrs of Catholic Lanca-
shire and of Catholic Ireland.   Nay, the hosts of the
heavenly courts themselves are making ready to
sweep down with countless legions, with banner and
with canticle, to receive Him Who prepares to make
this new-built church His home.   May the day be
prosperous, and the moment auspicious!   May He
Who wearies not, but delights to dwell among the
children of men, diffuse His knowledge and His love
from this place, henceforth for many peaceful years
to come, till we meet again, where to know Him is to
see Him, and to love Him is to rest in our life's term
and our being's perfect bliss!

LIFE EVERLASTING.

Preached at St. Alban's, Warrington,
March 12th, 1893.

"The Jerusalem which is above is free; which is our mother" (Gal. iv. 26).

THERE is no page of Holy Scripture which does not contrast the visible with the invisible, the temporal with the eternal, the earth below with the heavens above. In this passage of St. Paul we hear him compare the city of this world with the city of our everlasting hopes; this world, in its narrowness and its slavery, with Heaven, where there is to be freedom, peace, and happiness, such as it is very difficult for any human heart to picture or even to conceive. Let us follow the Apostle in the contemplation of this great theme, and let us lift ourselves up to the thoughts of heavenly bliss. Whatever raises the heart above these distracting and engrossing scenes below—above the common and poor elements of our daily life—makes for the advantage and the happiness of men. For it is for the future that we are made; and to keep the eye upon the future, and to restrain the affections from the present, this is our human end and purpose; and if it is what we are made for, it is what we should glory in.

There is no truth more clearly taught by Our Lord

than the dogma of " Life Everlasting." There is no truth which is more explicitly a part of our own belief. " In the world to come, everlasting life," is the promise of Jesus to those who have followed Him.[1] " He that heareth My word hath life everlasting."[2] This word " everlasting " is especially a word of the New Testament. It is not exclusively so, as I shall mention later on. But the frequency with which Our Lord uses it shows that He lays great stress upon it. It was the word which was required in order to complete God's holy revelation as to the state after death. For that revelation had been increasing in clearness all through the Old Testament. There are some learned commentators on the Bible who pretend that even the Jews, in the early period of their history, did not know of a future life. Nothing could be more misleading. What was the primitive revelation? It was this—that those who had committed the primal sin of disobedience should " die the death."[3] Adam and Eve did not understand this of physical death. Doubtless the death or dissolution of the body was a part of the punishment of the original sin. But, if you observe, there is another, and a quite distinct, result of that sin most explicitly mentioned in the sacred narrative. After the verses in which the respective punishments of the serpent, of the woman, and of the man are described, the last words of which are, " Dust thou art, and unto dust thou shalt return,"[4] there comes this mysterious an-

---

[1] Luke xviii. 30. [2] John v. 24. [3] Gen. ii. 17. [4] *Ib.* iii. 19.

nouncement : " And God said : Behold Adam is become one of us, knowing good and evil ; now, therefore, lest perhaps he put forth his hand and take also the Tree of Life, and cat and live for ever. And He cast out Adam and placed before the Paradise of pleasure cherubims and a flaming sword turning every way, to keep the way of the Tree of Life."[1] It would take us out of our way to explain how it is that the sacred writer expresses himself in these phrases. But there can be no doubt that the passage comes to this—that the being driven out of Paradise meant much more than bodily dissolution : it meant the loss of everlasting life. This was, therefore, the belief, not of the Jews only, but of every nation of the world from the beginning, that a certain state which, under happier circumstances, would have been the lot of men, and their unchangeable lot, was not to be—on account of sin.

Now let us observe how this absolutely proves that they believed in a future state. The loss of life everlasting was due to sin. But sin was not destined to finally triumph. At the very moment when the Divine anger announced to our first parents their doom, the Divine compassion promised them a Saviour. The offspring of the woman was to crush the head of the serpent. The knowledge of this promise—the hope of their final redemption—was a part of the inheritance of the human race ; it was certainly a part of Jewish tradition. Is it not evident

[1] Gen. iii. 22, 24.

that this very hope implied the knowledge of a future
state ? The loss—the punishment—regarded a period
beyond the grave. And therefore the redemption
regarded the same future period. The race of man,
therefore, had a future after physical dissolution.
That future could no longer, after the Fall, be named
by the glorious name of "life everlasting," or even of
"life" at all. But it was *existence ;* there was no question of ceasing to exist ; the dissolution of the body
was not the end, because in God's good time the
Redeemer was to come Who should once more bring
back that "life"—yes, that "everlasting life"—which
had been destroyed by sin. This belief must be
absolutely read into every page of the Bible. It
explains how the Patriarchs, the priests, the Prophets,
and the people both believed in future existence, and
yet, at the same time, had in early times no more
than an obscure knowledge of what that future life
would be. It explains, moreover, those passages of
Holy Scripture which seem to say that when a man
dies he lives no more ; for it was true that, until the
Redeemer came, he "lived" no more ; because he
waited for life—for the "life" which the Redeemer
was to bring. His existence, until that redemption
did come, was no "life"; it was a darkness, a sleep, a
dream ; but it was existence ; the existence of the
germ that lies beneath the soil whilst the winter's
storms darken and buffet the earth, awaiting the
warmth of the spring days and the power of the life-
giving sun.

For the revelation of life everlasting depended

upon the revelation of the world's Redeemer ; and as the latter was given gradually, and became more and more explicit as the generations went on, so did the former. In the earlier days the Redeemer was promised ; but the way in which the fulfilment of the promise was to be brought about was not made clear. Therefore, the believers in God went through their mortal career trusting in God and keeping His commandments ; and when the end came they passed, not without dread, into the land of shadows, still trusting in Him Whom they had learned to call the strong God, and the God of every generation. There is a phrase which is used in the Old Testament at the deaths of the Patriarchs—of Abraham and of Isaac and of Jacob : it is said "they were gathered to their people."[1] They passed away from the earth ; but they were gathered to another company, existing somewhere, guarded in the care of God. The phrase cannot possibly mean only the grave—the cessation of life. Look at the death-bed of the wise and patient Jacob. He lies there in the land of Egypt, with his sons around him, and with Joseph, the powerful and splendid minister, by the side of his couch ; he blesses his children with those prophetic and poetical blessings which we know ; and then he passes away— is "gathered to his people." It is the phrase used at death, not at burial. In an instant, Joseph, who had been watching with tender anxiety, falls upon his father's face weeping, and kisses him.

[1] Gen. xxv. 8, xxxv. 29, xlix. 32.

Then he is mourned for seventy days, and at last buried in the tomb where Abraham lay, and Isaac ; but the "gathering to his people" had taken place the moment the breath was out of his body. During the long years of Israel's wanderings, the future Redeemer was symbolised by God's never-failing protection ; and the faithful Israelite, after he had spent his life in serving God, and had felt at every instant that God was with him, fell asleep as one who is about to be led into the nearer presence of his Captain. Death, therefore, to him, as holy David says, was the certainty that he would " see the good things of the Lord in the land of the living."[1] As we come to the prophetical writings, the Person of the Redeemer becomes far more distinct. We explicitly hear of the approach of a kingdom, not earthly, but everlasting, when all the friends of God shall rejoice with the angels in glory and happiness. This certainty, growing not more absolute, but more definite, lighted up the sombre tombs in the ravines of the rocks and on the slopes of the hills, where the Israelites laid their fathers and mothers to their rest. The day of that hope might be far off, or it might be near ; but no generation and no individual would be cut off from its fruition by the envious hand of intervening bodily death. The God of Israel was the God of the living ; and, as Job said, deriving his knowledge from a tradition altogether independent of the law of Moses : " I know that my Redeemer liveth, and that at the last day I shall arise out of the earth, and in my flesh I shall see my God."[2]

When Our Lord came, the name of Life Ever-lasting was already familiar to the Jewish people. His mission was to startle them with the announce-ment that *He* was the Life. Long had they looked for it. The eyes of kings and prophets and just men had grown dim in trying to discern the coming of that Life when the promises should be fulfilled, and the souls of the servants of the Lord should pass into His kingdom. The living generations, as they suc-ceeded one another, had longed and prayed, and the dead generations had waited in the dim realm of their peaceful rest ; when would the day-star appear and the day break in the East ? And Jesus had stood amongst them and said : " I am the Resurrec-tion and the Life."[1] The life was given now. The hope which had been their inheritance in the past was revealed to be the kingdom of the Lord Jesus Christ ; and that kingdom was at hand.

It was described by Him in two words : it was "life," and it was "everlasting." It was "life"—that is, a living, conscious state, where faculties would act and powers display their energy ; where the eye would see and the heart rejoice ; where all that a human being was made for would be found in its complete development ; and where death and the shadow of death would be known never more. And it was "everlasting"; for that life was to be fixed and final. No more fears, no more changes. It was Jesus Who said so ; it was the Truth Who uttered this

[1] John xi. 25.

last and complete revelation. Let them accept Him, let them believe in Him, let them follow Him, and theirs was the kingdom—a kingdom such as the Prophets had foretold, and yet a kingdom which even those words which He so often repeated—even those words "life" and "everlasting life"—were quite inadequate to describe.

I am not going to try to put into words the state of the soul of a man who has won his life's crown and entered into the possession of the promises of God in the house of his Heavenly Father. There are few things that words cannot paint; but among those things are the joys of the Blessed and the woes of the lost. The reason is that both heavenly bliss and everlasting punishment have an element in them which is beyond human grasp; for they both depend on what God is to us, and what we are to Him.

And yet there is much to be said—and profitably said—about the state of the Blessed. If we cannot bring it completely within the comprehension of our faculties, we can at least make out its bearing upon our own lives. We can point our telescopes at it, and, standing on this earth, feel the awe and inspiration of that world which floats afar off in the infinite space of God's almighty power. We can compare it with all that we know, and can realise, at any rate, that nothing in time or space is comparable to that which is to be revealed. Even the weak words that we use—words borrowed from sense and imagination, words tinged with the stains of the earth, words which aim at the essence of things and fall back ineffectual even before the mysteries around us—even these human words have a power of suggesting the wholly spiritual, the incorrupt, the unchanging, and the infinite. For human language is the laborious expression of the human soul ; and the immortal soul of a human creature has in it a participated likeness of the Divinity itself.

What is the life, then, that my Saviour promises me in the kingdom which is to come ? For a " life " it is to be. It is not to be mere existence—a changeless state, without movement or emotion. There are pictures, in the poets, of a fairyland where the sun always shines and the winds are hushed, where the blue sky never alters, and where mortals sleep, or dream day-dreams, through ages of time unmeasured and unmarked. Heaven is not to be like that. Life means movement ; life means the activity of the whole being with all its powers. Life means the shock of impressions, the reaction of comprehension and of fruition, the stir and the swift succession of scenes, of events, of experiences. If Heaven is " life," Heaven must be this. But how ?

St. John the Apostle writes thus in the third chapter of his first Epistle :[1] " Dearly beloved, we are now the sons of God ; and it hath not yet appeared what we shall be. We know that, when He shall appear, we shall be like to Him, because we shall see Him as He is." This is the well-known passage of the New Testament which states the fact

---

[1] Verse 2.

of the Beatific Vision. The bliss of Heaven is to "see God as He is." Now we see or know God as in a glass, darkly, to use the words of St. Paul,[1] but then "face to face." "Now I know in part," or partially; "then I shall know even as I am known"— that is, by direct and immediate vision. This is the striking and magnificent teaching which, as by a stroke, describes the life of Heaven.

Do you doubt that this vision—this possession of the Infinite — will be most truly and excellently "life" in its fullest sense? Think of some creature which is lifted up out of a state of suspended animation—some winged insect, let us say, which has been lying bound in fetters—to which at last the day comes when it can shake off its shroud and soar into the air. What has happened to it? It has taken possession of a *universe*. The wide spaces of the air belong to it; for it the sun shines, the trees grow, the flowers bloom, the brooks and rivers run. Its freedom is boundless, its wings are strong, the world is wide, and it may roam from joy to joy as long as its day shall last. This is "life," and all that belongs to life. *God is a universe.* His being contains, within the one pure spiritual essence which He is, all things that are, all things that will be, or can be, or that have been—not in their created natures, but virtually and as they derive whatever they have of being or perfection from the inexhaustible fertility and abundance of the Divinity. For there cannot be anything

---

[1] 1 Cor. xiii. 12.

in the Heaven above or the earth beneath which does not exist in a more excellent manner, in a more noble way, in a more interesting way, in the being of God. God, then, is a universe ; and it is to be our bliss to possess this universe.

But first let us observe how it is that we can possess it. Whence the power, whence the capability of seeing God? The eye can only see what is visible. Sights, not sounds or touches, are the objects of our bodily vision. So it is with our intelligence—that magnificent power by which we share, in a sense, the intellectual nature of God. We are intellectual, and God is intellectual : but the likeness stops very soon ; for God is the Infinite ; and, as far as we are concerned, the Infinite is further off than the furthest star of the starry spaces. Nay, it is as far out of our sight as the sounds of music are out of the ken of the eye of the body. What we must have, then, before we can possess the Beatific Vision, is the power to see God's face.

A power of this kind is of the very highest order of powers. To look upon God's face is God's own prerogative. No created being, not even the highest of the cherubim or seraphim, could by the powers of his own nature look upon God face to face. Nay more—it would be impossible even for the omnipotence of God to make a creature with *natural* power sufficiently elevated to see God with this direct and intuitive vision. Nothing can avail here except an endowment coming straight from God, and in its nature altogether *supernatural*. The truth is, that

for me and for you to see God as He is, God must
Himself possess, as it were, our powers of intelligence. He must take hold of us, lift us up, strengthen
us—as it were pass into us—or we shall not be able
to look upon Him. This, if you will observe, is what
St. John himself says. "We know that, when He
shall appear, we shall be *like to Him.*" And there
is a beautiful passage in the 35th Psalm[1] which
shows what the Apostle's meaning is: "They shall
be inebriated with the plenty of Thy house, and
Thou shalt make them drink of the torrent of Thy
pleasure"; these words refer to the bliss of Heaven;
then the Psalmist proceeds: "For with Thee there
is the fountain of life, and in Thy light we shall see
light." That is to say, the only way by which the
soul can live with the "life" which is life everlasting,
is to receive that "life" from God Himself, the
only source thereof; and the only light by which
the intelligence, in that happy land of Heaven, can
look upon the light of God's countenance, is the light
that bursts forth from the Divinity itself. This light
is called by theologians and the Fathers the "Light
of Glory." It corresponds to the light of faith, which
it is our privilege to enjoy here below—that light
which illuminates this puzzling world, which reveals
to us our heavenly destiny, and brings near to us our
hidden God and our hidden Saviour. When the end
of our mortal struggle comes, the light of faith goes
out, like the light of the pilgrim's lantern when he

---

[1] Verses 9, 10.

reaches the shrine he is bound for, and the light of glory comes instead. Happy are those who cling to their holy Faith! For them is prepared that other great and glorious light, which is to shine, not over the dreary spaces of this world, but over the plains and the hills of the heavenly country. A little light is the precursor of a great light. A feeble and dim light, held fast and faithfully, through temptation and through anxiety, in simplicity and in obedience, is the pledge and promise of that Divine effulgence which will make error impossible and banish the darkness for ever. For in the Jerusalem which is above there is neither sun nor moon; "for the glory of God enlighteneth it, and the Lamb is the lamp thereof."[1]

Thus, after the short struggle of earthly life, after the judgment, after the purifying flame of Purgatory —thus does the redeemed soul present herself, burning with the supernatural capacity of the Beatific Vision. Her own nature is not destroyed. It was said of old to the leader of the Hebrew hosts, "Man shall not see Me and live."[2] But that which nature cannot endure, the supernatural power of God can meet and bear. The natural intellect and will of the human soul are not destroyed; but they are so elevated and strengthened by the new Divine capacity that they can stand even the fiery shock of the uncovered face of God. The ancient of days, in the Prophet Daniel, is seen seated upon a throne; His

---

[1] Apoc. xxi. 23   [2] Exodus xxxiii. 20.

garment is white as snow ; His hair as white wool ;
His throne like flames of fire ; the wheels of it like
a burning fire ; and a swift stream of fire issued
before Him. Fire and whiteness ! Whiteness and
fire ! Awful purity and tremendous energy ! Holiness, power, and flames ! Dread sanctity which
withers mortality into dust ! Omnipotent life which
annihilates all that is not itself by the mere lightning
of its approach ! Can human powers look upon this
mighty Godhead and yet live? Yes, in Heaven ; for
it is that very Godhead which throws its own
splendour like a garment round mortal frailty, and
transfigures the human spirit, with human flesh and
blood, until each redeemed servant of Jesus shines
like the stars of a new heaven whose light is of
God.

Thus the Beatific Vision becomes possible to the
children of Adam. And with that vision there comes
the essential happiness of the Blessed.

Happiness is a word that every man understands ;
and yet absolute happiness is what few indeed have
ever experienced. Perhaps, in the unspoiled years
of our childhood, it may have chanced that for a few
moments the tide rose till the waters closed above
our heads, and we were happy. But how soon the
waters went down again, and left us to our troubles
and our work ! Our experience in life is that pleasure
comes sometimes ; that if it is slight it fails to satisfy
us, if it is intense it intoxicates us ; and that in any
case it quickly passes away, leaving more frequently
than not a very bitter taste behind. Our experience

is that we are rarely quite satisfied ; that we sometimes attain what we strive for, but have not held it
for many moments when reflection, always restless,
shows us something further, something better, something different, that we have not. Our experience is
that we have known what joy is ; joy, that song or
psalm of the spirit under the pressure of happiness—
but that joy, like happiness, has always been shallow,
always transient, always followed by its very opposite. "Laughter," says the Wise Man, "shall be
mingled with sorrow, and mourning stands on the
skirts of joy."[1] This is human life. Yet we do
know what happiness is. With care and thought,
as a man puts together the pieces of a puzzle, we
can make out what the happiness of Heaven will be.
For, first of all, in Heaven we shall be satisfied.
Satisfied ? Have you ever held a tiny drinking
cup under the downward rush of a water-fall ?
The human spirit is the little cup, and the Godhead is the mighty rushing river. Satisfied ?
Nay, filled to overflowing — drowned in satisfaction—lost in an ocean of all that the heart can
desire ! There will be no failing or diminishing
for the ocean-springs are in the bottomless depths
of the Infinite. There will be no weariness, no same-
ness, no cloying, for the cataract runs with full flow
for ever. No fretting thought or restless memory
will be able to suggest anything that is wanting.
Pleasure will thrill through all the powers, each

[1] Prov. xiv. 13.

finding its most delightful exercise; and the strain
of joy will rise, as rises the spontaneous song of the
bird, showing that the heart is full. All this is what
must be—and must be without interruption or cessation. For the evils of the earth will be far away.
You cannot have a Paradise here below. You cannot
make its wall high enough or its gates strong enough
to keep out the influences whose work it is to blight
its flowers and to lay waste its pleasant places. But
our inheritance in Heaven, as St. Peter has said, is
"incorruptible, and undefiled, and cannot fade."[1]
There shall be no more sin. There shall be no
more death, for " Death is swallowed up in victory."[2]
" And God," says St. John, " shall wipe away all
tears from their eyes ; and death shall be no more,
nor mourning, nor crying, nor sorrow shall be any
more ; for the former things have passed away."[3]
These things shall not be able to enter there. They
may prowl outside, but they cannot get in. O blessed
state of unchangeable happiness! Is it not worth
living for! Nay, what is there to live for but this
Paradise of God !

As it is with all human ideas, many words are
required to impress upon the mind the thought of
Heaven. And this, in one respect, is a misfortune.
For Heaven, after all, is God—the sight and fruition
of God ; and it is essential, both for our instruction
and for our spiritual life on earth, that we should
thoroughly understand this great truth. We may

---

[1] 1 Peter i. 4.   [2] 1 Cor. xv. 54.   [3] Apoc. xxi. 4.

not see it very clearly in the dust and distraction of life, but it is none the less true that these hearts of ours were made for God, and for God alone. Moreover, the day will come when we shall be forced to understand this great truth. For a time we are able to shut our eyes, to intoxicate ourselves in one way or another, and to bar out all warning sounds. But the day comes when we shall be forced to see and to hear with sober senses. Because that is the way we are made. Reason and free will ; a time when reason has to guide us and free will to be exercised (both of them assisted by the grace of God) ; and when that time of probation is over, then we are brought face to face with what is final, what is radical, what is absolute, what is everlasting. Turn as we may, we must all face this at last. Our immortal souls are made for God, and unless they attain to God, they must be wrecked—and like wrecks in mid-ocean must float for ever on the ocean of eternity. But if they attain to Him, then it is He Himself, and no other thing, Who fills and glorifies them. Cannot every understanding see what this means ? Perhaps you have seen, in a country of lakes and mountains, a lovely lake lying in the hollow of hills. Its waters have found their level at this spot ; the hills on every side slope down to the peaceful water and hold it safe and tranquil, whilst the slow course of ages has rounded off the promontories and smoothed the little bays all round its edge, where the bushes and flowers grow, and the green turf comes to meet the tiny ripple ; and the hills are mirrored in its depths.

That water may have come down many a rough channel, and foamed and leapt from stone to stone ; but now its wanderings are at an end ; it is at peace, just where it ought to be, clear, deep, and undisturbed. Has the soul no resting-place? Is my immortal spirit, of all the grand forces which make up this universe, alone to have no native country, no home ? Yes, God is her home. She is to rest in Him. However unquiet her course may have been during the years of her trial, she is meant to rest in Him. In Him, and in Him alone, she finds what she must have. With His arms about her she is safe. With His infinitude her mighty powers have more than room to play. With His inexhaustible Being her unresting vision is never disappointed. If she must have a Father, He is her Father; if she feels the innate need of a friend, He is that friend. If she would bow herself in worship, He is her God ; if she would nobly serve, He is the Master ; if she would possess and enjoy, He is the King, the Sovereign, the bounteous source of all that can bring joy and satisfaction. Above all, if she would love—as she must love—He is the abyss of the good and the beautiful. Thus, being with God, it is well with her. And no exercise of human power on earth can be more noble, more human in the truest sense, than to live for that God, to lift the soul in acts towards Him, and to long to see that face whose glorious vision in eternity is to fill all her capacity and give her ever-lasting rest.

The Saints tell us that one grand way of securing

Heaven is to long for Heaven; and that, putting grievous sin out of the question, the reason why many souls have so long a Purgatory to undergo is because they have not desired to look upon the face of God. And it is true. Our faith and intelligence may tell us that Heaven is happiness inconceivable, but for all that our hearts too often remain cold. Pleasure, as we know it, seems different from the pleasure that is promised. The interests, the occupations, of eternity, described as they are in human words, seem to forbid us to expect to find, when we are at the feet of God, those things which undoubtedly occupy us and interest us here below.

This is a temptation which may make itself felt, at times, in the heart of any one. Our own baseness makes it more importunate; for there are pleasures and satisfactions that our fallen nature is too easily content with, which are incompatible with the very idea of the Beatific Vision. But it is, after all, only a temptation. The least reflection will show that God cannot deceive us; and that if He promises beatitude, beatitude we shall have. We may not understand how; but we can trust our Heavenly Father. We know that we shall be changed. Our immortal souls will be in their proper sphere, no longer subject to the passions and the frailties of fallen nature, but strong in their angelic strength, ruling as they are born to rule, and with fair play for their development. Moreover, they will be transformed by the supernatural gifts of God into beings whose every throb and instinct will be in harmony with the holiness of the Divinity. Our flesh itself, after the resurrection, will be changed with that ineffable change of which the Apostle speaks[1]—when the corruptible shall put on incorruption, and the mortal immortality—when that which is corporeal shall be endowed with many of the gifts of the spiritual world.

But, beyond all this, there is a law in all the living and breathing universe, that a more intense experience swamps and drowns out one that is less intense. Pain will neutralise all a man's bodily satisfaction : a greater pain will nullify lesser sufferings ; an intense joy will make us forget even the severest anguish ; and sometimes the mere excitement of news, of interest, or of strong passion, will render us utterly insensible to acute physical torture. Place yourself, in imagination, in the presence of the supreme God, the supreme Life, the supreme Love, the supreme Beauty—given to you, meant for you, poured out for your bliss, all your powers filled by it and strung up by its presence to the intensest energy of living reaction. Where then will be the capacity for feeling baser things ? As well could the eagle, when he cleaves the skies, desire to crawl like the worm in the slime of the earth below! As well could the lion, in the ecstasy of battle, think of his food or his den ! In Heaven the great tide of the ocean will be full, and all the sands of existence covered, and the tiny streams which trickled across the beach at low water will be obliterated for ever.

But though all this is true—that the vision of God is all that we need, and that His vision is and must be man's total and overwhelming bliss—nevertheless we must not be led to think, either that these beings of ours cease to be conscious, or that the powers of human nature become useless in Heaven—like old tools that are thrown away. The Christian Heaven is not like the Heaven of the Buddhist. It is not cessation—absorption—annihilation. It is " life." To see God is to live. For to see God is to see what there is in God, as far as the finite intelligence can be made capable of seeing. It is to see God and His attributes—to see the Holy Trinity, the three Divine Persons in their unity of nature. It is to see the wisdom, the justice, the mercy and omnipotence of God. It is to see the Incarnation, the Blessed Sacrament, the economy of Divine grace, and all that kingdom of mysteries which on earth we know by faith. It is to see the Sacred Humanity, the Blessed Virgin, the Angels, and the Saints. It is to see the past, the present, and the future. " What is there," says St. Gregory the Great, " that they do not see, who see Him that seeth all things ? "[1] It is true that the Blessed cannot be said to know all that God has done, does, and can do. · That would be to comprehend God ; and to comprehend God adequately is impossible. But it is taught by Catholic tradition that whatever in any special way concerns themselves, that the Blessed will see in God, whether it

[1] *Dialogues*, Book IV., 33.

be past, or present, or to come. "O vision," exclaims St. Bernard, "in which we shall then most perfectly know all things on earth and in Heaven, drinking draughts of knowledge at the fountain of wisdom!"[1] The records of the universe, the depths of the ocean, the distances of the starry spheres, the grand generalisations of science, the possibilities of discovery, the splendid and varied evolution of human history—all that God has made will be the field of the joyful knowledge of His blessed ones. They will take with them to Heaven the loves, the affections, the pure solicitudes, of the earth. The father and the mother will know and follow the steps of their children, the pastor of his flock, the ruler of his people, the sovereign of his nation, the Bishop of his diocese, the Pontiff of the universal Church, the religious founder of his Order—every man and woman there of his own circle. They will hear prayers and read thoughts— each in his own degree. They will follow with ecstatic delight the working of God's decrees, as one follows the lightning of a distant storm. They will even read the awful and most wonderful pages of possibility—a mystic scroll that dwarfs to littleness all that God has done yet, except as regards the mystery of the Incarnation itself. What do we want, my brethren? What do our most advanced thinkers claim as the noblest exercise of man's being? Is it knowledge? Is it investigation? Is it freedom? Is it truth? Prepare for Heaven, and you will find it all

---

[1] *Serm de trip. genere Bonorum*, nn. 7.

there. But do not spoil your chance of the supreme development of humanity by chaining it down to the earth, to seek knowledge with purblind eye, to investigate only the narrow circle round your kennel, to call that freedom which is only the license of ignorance, and to claim the name of truth for what is but the mirage of the desert of this world.

It is the glory of the canonised Saints to have understood " life everlasting." And there is one Saint—he whose feast we keep to-day—St. Gregory, Pope and Confessor, called the Great—St. Gregory, who is called the Apostle of England, because he sent St. Augustine and his monks to our shores—who has spoken so truly and beautifully about Heaven that I must quote to you a passage from his writings, and so end these words.

He was once preaching[1] in St. Peter's, at Rome, on the Gospel of the Good Shepherd ; it was the second Sunday after Easter, which is the Sunday of the Good Shepherd. He quotes the words of Our Lord, " He shall go in, and he shall go out, and he shall find pasture,"[2] which are a little higher up, and he says : " He entereth in by faith ; he goeth out by the vision of God, passing from faith to sight, from believing to intuition . . . and his pasture is the everlasting joy of the ever-green Paradise of God ; the revealed face of God ; the satiety of eternal delight ; the choirs of the angels ; the companionship of the heavenly citizens ; the sweet festivity of pil-

[1] Hom. in Ev. 1. 14.   [2] John x. 9.

grims returning from their weary pilgrimage ; the
far-seeing Prophets ; the Apostolic judges of the
world ; the innumerable host of the martyrs ; the
patient confessors ; the men faithful and true, whom
the world could not corrupt ; the holy women, who
have overcome at once the world and their own sex ;
the children, young in years but rich in merits. O
my brethren," he exclaims, " let us seek these pastures, and long for the joys of that solemn festival
of the Blessed ! If we celebrate an earthly festival
—if, for instance, there is the dedication of a church
to be kept—there is not one of us who does not
wish to be present—who would not be sorry not to
join in the common rejoicings. Behold, the citizens
of Heaven hold high festival, and yet we feel no
ardour to belong to their happy company." These
words might have been addressed to us this day.
The very joy of this meeting should remind us of
the Jerusalem which is above, which is our mother.
We dedicate an altar ; and the altar is Christ. The
altar is the light and the joy of this church, as of the
whole Church on earth. Around it gather in their
places the Pontiff, the ministers, the flock. There is
the Lamb. There are the fountains of the Saviour.
There is the pledge of life eternal. You have made
sacrifices for this altar ; you rejoice to see it in its
place, to the honour of God and of the holy Eucharist ; and for many a day, let us hope, your pastors
will stand before it, and you and your children will
kneel around, whilst the blessings of the heavens
above and the earth beneath rain down silently, and

radiate, invisible but beneficent. This is right ; but there is one thing more. I will put it to you in the words of the great Doctor of this day's feast. He continues thus : " Stir up your hearts ; enkindle your faith ; and long with ardent aspirations for the Heaven above. To long for Heaven is to travel to Heaven. Let no difficulty hold you back ; let desire smooth the roughest way. Turn not aside to the pleasant places of this fleeting world. Fix not your hearts on the things that you must one day leave behind. You are the sheep of a heavenly shepherd, and His pastures are above ; and it is to your heavenly country that you must lift your hearts."

CHRIST'S CHRISTIANITY.

Preached at the Church of Our Lady, Birkenhead, at the first Pontifical Mass of the Right Rev. Francis Mostyn, D.D., September 15th, 1895.

"God hath visited His people" (Luke vii. 16).

IT is impossible not to look upon the ceremony of which this church was yesterday the scene, followed by that which it witnesses to-day, but as a sign of one of those special interferences of God our Father which the New Testament calls "visitations." It will not be out of place, therefore, to speak of this occasion ; nay, according to one's poor ability, it is a duty to do so ; for there is nothing more fraught with calamity to man or to peoples than not to know the day of visitation.

We persist—the Catholic Church in England persists—in claiming to be the one true Church, outside of which, unless there is the excuse of pardonable deficiency of information, there is no salvation. It is in this light that we offer ourselves to the English and the Welsh peoples. It is this view which impels the Roman Pontiff to write Encyclicals of invitation, to organise prayer, and to appoint bishops. It is this that makes the Catholic body in this country— bishops, priests, and laity—work so anxiously ; and it is this profound conviction which makes them seem at times to be uncharitable in their judgments and aggressive in their behaviour.

For it cannot be denied that this attitude on the part of the Catholic Church does imply a severe judgment on the Christianity of the English and Welsh peoples. It implies that she considers their Christianity defective and inadequate.

These words are not used in any railing sense, or with any intention to insult or irritate. To refuse to a man the title of Christian, if he reverently claims it, is far from the wish of any Catholic. Rather do we respect the spirit and the piety which urge him to cling to so august and powerful a name. But it should not be taken amiss that we endeavour to show how far short of complete and historic Christianity is the belief and the practice of the religious bodies outside. To impeach the Christianity of races whose clinging to Christ is expressed by so many observances and by the churches and chapels which cover the land, seems, no doubt, at first view, to be unwarrantable and even insulting. One reason, however, why it seems so, is that Christianity has now very largely come to be identified with kindness, and the practice of those virtues which are connected with brotherly love. To question one's Christianity seems as much as if one judged him dishonest, uncharitable, and heartless. Another reason is that Christianity, in this country, has substituted for definite beliefs, a vague trust in Christ ; and, when you say that a man is not altogether a Christian, you appear to deny that he is sincere when he makes use

of the holy Name of Jesus, when he follows the
prayers of his minister, or joins in the hymns of his
church or chapel. But it is not with either of these
two points that we are really concerned. There is no
wish to deny or extenuate the charity, the active
philanthropy, or the kindness of heart towards other
men, which are so conspicuous everywhere in this
country, and among all ranks of men. These good
gifts have followed on the preaching of the Gospel ;
they are, without doubt, the fruits of Christianity.
But there is much more in Christianity than this ;
and without complete Christianity even these fair and
gracious virtues are in danger of turning into mere
outside show, without real merit in the sight of God.
Neither need it be disputed that the non-Catholic
may be drawn to Jesus, may sincerely adore Him
(though this is not really common), may praise His
Name, and invoke Him. Even with these admissions,
it may be reasonably maintained—as Catholics maintain—that there are certain definite revealed views
about our Blessed Lord which only Catholics have
hold of ; and that, besides, there are revealed views
about remission of sin, sacramental help, spiritual
conduct, and many other things which the Catholic
Church alone teaches ; and that one is not only bound
to accept these things as the Christian inheritance
given to us by a loving God, but that to renounce
them, or to do without them, with open eyes, is to
renounce the lights of the new covenant, and to
refuse the helps without which weak human nature
must remain in imminent danger of perishing.

There are two great features of Scriptural and
historic Christianity which are virtually non-existent
in English and Welsh Protestantism.   The first is
the principle of authority in doctrine and in government.   It is difficult to understand how any one who
is acquainted in the most superficial way with the
New Testament can help seeing that Christ's religion, as it was understood by Himself and His
immediate disciples, was to be a system of doctrine
authoritatively taught by the living voice.   The prophecy of Isaias foreshadowed this.   A marked
feature, according to that great delineator of what
he calls the " latter days," was to be "a path and a
way, called the holy way,   .   .   .   a straight way, so
that (even) fools could not err therein."[1]   " All the
children " in those days were to be "taught of the
Lord," and great was to be their "peace."[2]   The
new covenant, as described by that very name,[3]
was to be this—that God's words were not to depart out of the mouths of men " from henceforth and
for ever."   And in these same "latter days " there was
to be, as it were, a great citadel, planted in a mountain top, visible far and wide, to which the universal
race of man were to throng in order to receive
the word and law of the Lord.[4]   Now, a path, to be
clear and straight for every generation, implies a
never-failing guide ; if the fruit of teaching was to
be " peace," there must be always at hand the means
of settling controversies ; and that great visible house

[1] Isaias xxxv. 8.   [2] *Ib.* liv. 13.   [3] *Ib.* lix. 21.   [4] *Ib.* ii. 2.

of the Lord could be a symbolical expression of
nothing but a teaching ministry. Hence Our Lord
said—referring to these very prophesies—"Go and
make all nations your disciples, . . . and I am
with you all days to the consummation."[1] Hence
He spoke of wolves in sheep's clothing—by which it
is impossible He could mean anything but teachers
of falsehood ; and consequently there must be always
a way of distinguishing the false from the true.
Hence He looked forward to a never-failing Church
—a Church grounded upon a rock ; and as this
was not a church of stone or brick, but meant
never-failing Christian doctrine, it meant a never-
failing supply of Christian teachers—teachers perpetually upheld by Christ. For a mere gathering
or assembly of men is not a Church ; it only
becomes a Church when it is united in belief and
in worship ; and no such union is possible for any
considerable time, much less for all ages, without
continuous and authoritative teaching. Therefore
our Blessed Redeemer's ideal—and all His ideals must
come true—was perpetual divinely supported authoritative teaching. St. Paul's ideal was the same. He
looked upon the elders or bishops whom he met at
Ephesus, at that memorable leave-taking, as men who
had a Divine commission to "rule the Church of
God."[2] He warned them against "ravening wolves"
—not persecutors, observe—but who "will enter in
among you, not sparing the flock"—and he con-

---

[1] Matt. xxviii. 20.   [2] Acts xx.

tinued : "Of your own selves shall arise men speaking
perverse things, to draw away disciples after them."
Why were false teachers called "ravening wolves,"
and why were the Bishops warned to watch the men
who wanted to draw away disciples—unless false
teaching was a supreme calamity, and unless there
was the possibility of distinguishing the false from
the true? What, again, does St. Paul mean by the
"form of sound words" which he exhorts Timothy
to hold?[1] We can only construe it as "orthodox
dogmatic teaching." What does he mean when he
says that Hymeneus and Philetus have "erred from
the faith" and have "subverted the faith of many"?[2]
Why does he say to Titus, the Bishop whom he
had appointed in the Island of Crete, "A man that is
a heretic, after the first and second admonition avoid,
knowing that . . . such a one is subverted and
sinneth."[3] It follows from these and similar passages,
that to hold a wrong belief was sinful ; that it was
possible to know what was right from what was
wrong ; and that the Church's pastorate had the
charge of declaring what was right, and expelling,
as far as they could, what was wrong. This is the
Scriptural view of Church authority in teaching.

The other feature which we find wanting in Protestantism is the sacramental system. It seems
clear, in the face of the New Testament, that the
ministry of the new, or Christian dispensation, were
to possess a power of imparting spiritual grace by

---

[1] 1 Tim. i. 13.   [2] 2 Tim. ii. 17.   [3] Titus iii. 10.

outward acts.   Such a power is undoubtedly supernatural, and very wonderful.   But if the human hand
which touched the eyes of the blind man nigh to
Jericho was the hand of the Everlasting God, it is
not very much to believe that the hand of the
Christian minister, used under certain conditions, by
the will of Christ, can carry with it Christ's own grace.
This is the sacramental idea.   That spiritual regeneration comes by Baptism cannot be reasonably disputed by those who believe the New Testament.
That a certain spiritual grace is imparted by the
laying on of hands is clear from several passages.
That sins are forgiven by ministerial absolution, and
that the dying are strengthened by the anointing
with oil and prayer, prejudice alone can dispute.
That the Eucharist of Christ's Body and Blood, under
the forms of bread and wine, is a real Presence, is
sacramental in its effect, and constitutes, in the very
doing or making of it, a perpetuation as well as a
memorial of the Sacrifice of the Cross, is evinced by
the sixth chapter of St. John, and by St. Paul's most
striking expressions in 1 Cor. xi.   The important
influence of the sacramental view (or faith) on
worship, on personal religion, on ritual, and on the
visibility of the Christian Church need not here be
pointed out.

As far as history goes, it testifies in a quite un-
equivocal way that these two principles—authoritative
teaching and the dispensation of Sacraments—are
the very foundations on which Christianity rests.   I
am aware that we are told that, in certain documents

of most ancient date, neither Pope nor Mass nor even
Sacrament is named. This may be perfectly true.
But that absence, as far as it goes, can be readily
accounted for; and the absence of the names that
are familiar to ourselves is a very different matter
from the absence of the things themselves. Here are
the broad facts, undeniable, easily capable of verifi-
cation, stated by every non-Catholic writer. Within
half a century from the death of the last of the
Apostles there is evidence that the rule in religious
disputes was to refer to the Bishop. Within the
same period there is evidence of a Eucharistic
liturgy, of the universal and essential practice of
Baptism, and of the excommunication of the dis-
obedient. A century or so later, when the Christian
records become more abundant, we see elaborate
Eucharistic liturgies in Rome, Milan, Constantinople,
Egypt, and the East; we find all the great Church
writers appealing to authority as decisive in matters
of Christian belief; we find the clergy credited with
the most stupendous powers; we find a most unmistakable method of branding and dealing with
heretics; and, as to heretics themselves, we find that
they rise and then disappear, that they are without
influence on the mass of believers, and that they
agree only in contradicting the universal Church.
Then, as the ages go on, with their wars and disturb-
ances, with the destruction of the Empire, the rise of
new nations, and the gradual development of Christendom, we see a Church, one in faith and practice,
obedient to episcopal authority, magnificent in its

Eucharistic liturgy, assiduous in its sacramental observance, expressing all its beliefs and aspirations in
the most splendid architecture and marvellous paint-
ing that the world has ever seen, occupying undisturbed the whole ground of earthly Christianity.
Is this Church, or is it not, the legitimate successor
and representative of Apostolic Christianity? If it
is not, where has Christianity been? Did it cease to
exist when the last of the Apostles left the earth?
Was it hopelessly corrupted somewhere about the
fifth century after Christ? Something like this has
been said and maintained by some Protestants.
But this hypothesis of the prevalence, for a thousand years, of a Christianity corrupted in vital
Christian faith, is too blasphemous to be held by any
but those who do not know what they are saying.
That this Church of Christ, purchased by His Blood,
against which hell should never prevail, and which
was to be the very pillar and ground of truth, should
not only die out of visible existence, but be replaced
by an aggressive, specious, and prosperous system of
lies, lasting ten centuries and commanding all that
time the willing and childlike allegiance of the masses
of the poor for whom Christ died—this is too pre-
posterous to be argued against. But even if we
could let that pass, I would boldly affirm that there
are in the New Testament points of doctrine and
practice, germs, if you like, but quite plain and unmistakable, which demand us to recognise Catholicism
as the only adequate Christianity. For example:
Our Lord promised perpetual assistance of the most

effective sort to the preachers of His kingdom ; where is that idea to be found as a Church principle except in Catholicism ? No Protestant body dares to proclaim it, for the principle of private judgment practically destroys it ; to have a right to form your opinion and to be even generally right in your opinion, might be found joined together in a scientific professor here and there, but it could not possibly be verified in miscellaneous tens of thousands and through twice ten centuries. Or consider the doctrine of St. Paul—that a person who takes the Eucharist, when in an unworthy state—a state of sin —eats and drinks judgment to himself—in other words, damns himself by his eating ; it is undeniable that no Protestant body dares to teach this. Or, finally, take the principle of the ministerial forgiveness of sins—"whose sins you shall forgive, they are forgiven"; whilst Catholicism in all its periods is seen to be striving and contriving to give effect to this promise of Our Saviour, in the development of the great Sacrament of Penance, the very idea has dropped out of the formularies, the exhortations, the ritual, and the practice of nearly every Protestant body now in existence.

It is on these broad facts—which require no special pleading to bring them clearly out—that the Catholic Church holds the Christianity of a Protestant nation to be defective and inadequate. There are other mistaken ideas and errors besides what have been pointed out. There is the great Protestant mistake as to grace and righteousness ; the view, that is to say, that by regeneration the soul's sinfulness is not taken away, but only covered, Christ's righteousness being imputed ; the consequent view that whatever one does, in grace or out of grace, is equally bad and corrupt. The practical consequence of these errors is the conviction that good works are useless before God, and that repentance does not consist in turning away from sin, but only in some vague confidence in Christ. Ideas like these, which are widely and deeply held by all that enormous class of Protestants who range between High Anglicanism on the one hand, and Agnosticism on the other, must (it is not too much to say) result in a morality which is distinctly different from that of Catholicism. It must result in indifference to such evil thoughts and desires as are merely internal ; in making humility of heart, mortification, and chastity "dead virtues," as many Protestants call them ; in making Christianity consist solely in kindness to others, or the promotion of man's physical well-being ; in the abolition of all creeds or beliefs except the vague trust in Christ, before referred to ; in a complete darkness about the world to come ; and in a general inclination to make as good a thing as possible of the present earthly life, leaving the future to take care of itself.

When did this change begin ? When did the current begin to set in this direction ? At the time of what is called the Reformation. Or rather, as far as Wales is concerned, not till fully one hundred years after the Sacrifice of the Mass had been by law abolished in this country. It is related that when the

Catholic Marquis of Worcester, who was fighting
for his King against the revolutionists of the Common-
wealth, marched through Carmarthenshire and Cardiganshire, he came to the once famous Abbey of Strata
Florida, the burial-place of the princes of South
Wales. The church and cloister had been lying in
ruins for the whole of a bad and calamitous century,
whilst the blood of Catholic priests and laymen had
been lavishly shed in England. But it is related that
a woman who was a hundred years old was presented
to the General — a woman who remembered the
monks in the Catholic times, and had lived above
three score years in "great regret for the loss of the
public service of the altar." He promised to take her
to Raglan Castle, where she would find a priest and
might hear Mass every day. But she died, of sheer
joy it is said, before the next morning.[1] What had
happened in Cardiganshire had happened over the
whole of North and South Wales. Catholicism died
in slow agony. First, the clergy gradually disappeared. Religion in Wales, before the so-called
Reformation, was dependent in large measure on
the monastic houses. The thinly populated regions
of mountain and forest could be spiritually served
best by men who could work from central stations.
There were something like fifty monasteries in
Wales and Monmouthshire at the time of the
dissolution, besides a far greater number of convents of friars. When these were put down the
wilder parts of the country were almost with-

[1] See Alban Butler's *Movable Feasts and Fasts*, p. 74.

out religious teachers. The few parish priests, isolated and without resource, were helpless. When even these died out, the people, left to themselves, retained the outward forms and practices of Catholicism, until the great Methodist movement one hundred and fifty years ago. Their churches had been Catholic churches, like the other churches of Christendom. Their rites had been Catholic; the great Eucharistic Sacrifice had gathered them to altars only less splendid than these of the grandest fanes of England. The land was covered with the names of Saints, like the blue heavens with the host of stars. Catholic Sacraments had been their spiritual life, the mysteries of our Blessed Lord's life, and the story of His Blessed Mother had occupied their thoughts and directed their prayers. Their bards and monastic poets had produced hymns and odes in Welsh breathing the truest and deepest piety, of a type which only men who cling closely to the Incarnation could have conceived: such as the following by Gruffydd ab Yr Ynad Coch, written about the time that Edward I. and his Queen went on pilgrimage to the shrine of St. David:

> The Blood is as fresh
> As the day He was crucified ;
> And His hands were spread out
> When the deed was done.
> And the blood was in streams
> About His breast ;
> And His wounds
> Are unhealed.
> And the crown of thorns
> And His lifeless body,

And His Head encircled
With the thorny ring.
And the mark on His side
Of the scourge,
Which took away His life
And gave Him pain.
And all to purchase the son of man
From the everlasting fire ;
By the enemy
In whose hands he was.[1]

Of this ancient religion of Wales—Catholic, hier-
archical, sacramental, devotional—there are yet in
existence a few monuments which themselves would
prove what it once was. I do not speak of the old
Catholic practices, such as seem to relate to the holy
Eucharist, to devotion to the Saints, to the use of
blessed water, etc.; but chiefly to the old Welsh
literature and the old Welsh churches.   Such a
treatise as the *Gemma Ecclesiastica* of Giraldus
Cambrensis, written as it was by a censorious critic,
though a devoted Welshman, shows us the Blessed
Sacrament of the Altar as surrounded with that new
enthusiasm and devotion which spread all over Europe
during the thirteenth century, and culminated in the
festival of Corpus Christi.   The bardic writings of the
Middle Ages, the more they are known and studied,
the more they excite the surprise of scholars by their
ardent religious feeling, and by the evidence they
afford that religion entered into the whole life of
the Welsh people.[2]   As for the churches, you have

[1] Newell's *History of the Welsh Church*, p. 336.
[2] See Newell's *History of the Welsh Church*, p. 335, and
Stephen's *Literature of the Kymri*, p. 392.

only to leave the railway at any point, and walk
through a white-washed village, or follow up a pic-
turesque valley, or climb to the ridge of a grey mountain, to find some small, dark church that may have
been standing when Archbishop Baldwin made his
famous progress, or even in the age of St. Teilo, St.
Iltyd, or St. David himself. Not one of them can be
mistaken for an Anglican temple or a Dissenting
chapel. There is always the sign of the Eucharistic
altar—the chancel ; small generally, but always distinct, with its arch, its lower pitch of roof, and its
narrowed walls—marks that have come down from
the days when the great mystery was more or less
shut in from the gaze of the people. There is often
the presbytery also, and the Ladye chapel. It was
in these churches—in the small but beautiful cathedrals, in the monastic and parochial churches, which
became more numerous as each century passed by—
that Wales kept up that Christian worship and
Christian piety in which she was at one with the
Christianity of the whole world.

Is it a dream to think that these missing elements
in their Christianity can be restored to the people of
Wales ? And are we, who pray and labour for this
object, mere benighted visionaries, who feed our
fancy upon echoes of the past ? We do not think
so. First of all, it is impossible that Christ's Christianity can ever die out, or can ever irrevocably ebb
away from a people or a race. But Christ's Christianity is the Christianity of definite religious teaching, of Eucharistic sacrifice, and of sacramental

ministration ; and as it must prevail, on the whole, and must always cover by far the wider part of the area which the world agrees to regard as Christian, so it is not only possible, but probable, that the day will come when the shores, which now are dry and unvisited by the tide, will once more feel the grace-bearing waters of the true and complete Faith. If this is to be long delayed, and is not to happen in our time, our work and our prayers will even so be far from useless or in vain. The labour that is for Christ and in Christ is never thrown away. As sure as hearts pray—as sure as there is the cross to bear—as sure as the word is preached and the Apostolic office carried on—so sure and certain is it that not a sigh or a syllable, or one step of conflict and sacrifice, falls to the ground in the sight of our Heavenly Father. "Thou hast numbered all my steps."[1] God's plan is wide and spacious, working itself out in wide revolutions which seem like immobility, but are real, recognisable, and irresistible. The time comes when the work of God's servants has its result ; and the more hopeless that result has seemed, the more it has been hidden from earthly divining, the greater its call upon our faith in invisible powers—the more complete and glorious it is when God's hour strikes. It is not the triumphant prince, who rides in glory up the Capitol, to whom the victory is due, but to the soldiers who have left their bones on the battlefields, and the leaders whose hardly remembered graves have been dug where the fields were bloodiest and the fortunes of the war least secure.

[1] Job xiv. 16.

Little, indeed, little can bishop, priest, or layman effect when souls have to be won—unless God visits His people. Vain is labour, vain is eloquence, vain is learning or wealth, unless the Lord gives the increase. Rather must the secret be humility. Who am I, may the pastor say, that I can hope to reach these intelligencies, to move these hearts, to win these living thousands, so long estranged, so deeply distrustful, so busy with their own thoughts, customs, and prepossessions? This may any man say, and with deep conviction, when the work before him is religious conversion.

But there are, in these days as in the past, times of the " visitation " of God. This newly-consecrated chief Pastor, whose brow bears now for the first time the mitre of Divine prerogative, has his mission from the great Catholic Church and her Sovereign Pontiff. He takes up his pastoral staff at a moment when men are full of religious inquiry; when the preachings of the preachers are running as dry as a summer water-course—long lengths of sand and gravel, but very little of the stream that flowed from the right hand of the Temple ; when the non-Catholic bodies are growing more and more perplexed how to reject the principle of authority and still keep a roof over their own heads ; when the old bare walls and black gowns are disappearing in a rising of waters which will undoubtedly, if they are not beaten back, bring the very Altar of Sacrifice, like a second Ark, to the threshold of church and meeting-house ; and when thousands of good men in all the land have been

moved to pray for that blessed " union " which Christ
begged for His disciples.   Let us hope ; let us lift up
our hearts on high.   And that our hope may not be
confounded, let us implore upon the newly-consecrated Bishop, during this his first Pontifical Mass,
and often hereafter when we think of his work in
Wales, that blessing, that strength, that endurance,
and that " mouth and wisdom " which God gives to
His chosen Apostles.   May the power of the Holy
Cross, on whose day he was consecrated, defeat the
adversary and bring the victory; and may the intercession of Mary, whose blessed name is commemorated
to-day, be ever with him.   " May the Lord guard his
entering in and his going out, from henceforth now
and for ever ! "[1]

[1] Ps. cxx. 8.

CHRIST HEALETH OUR WOUNDS.

Preached in the Church of Our Lady and St. Joseph, Kingsland, on the Sunday within the Octave of the Immaculate Conception, 1894.

"Tell unto John what you have heard and seen : the blind see, the lame walk, the deaf hear" (Matt. ii. 5).

THESE were the miracles by which Our Lord proved His Mission. They were necessary in order that the Jewish people might believe in Him. They were not to cease with His ascension. Signs, and even (as He had foretold) signs that seemed greater than any He Himself had wrought, were to be shown to the world, for the world's conversion, by His Apostles and the first preachers of the Gospel. But, in truth, it was not the bodies of men that Our Lord came to heal, but their souls. His tender mercy was always ready to alleviate sorrow and suffering, and He has taught His followers to be of His spirit. But the prophecies, and His own words, point to a far wider field of wonder-working compassion than was offered by the blind and the lame who gathered round His progress through Judæa and Galilee. Let me recall the thirty-fifth chapter of Isaias. It speaks of the day of the Lord's coming. It foretells how the wilderness should rejoice and flourish as the lily ; it speaks of blossom and beauty and glory ; of strength

for the feeble and courage for the faint-hearted ; the
eyes of the blind were to be opened and the ears of
the deaf to be unstopped ; the lame man should leap
as a hart, and the tongue of the dumb should be
free ; there should be fertilising streams, and " holy
ways," and safety from every mischievous beast, in
all the land of the redeemed.

This is a prophecy which was to be realised, and
which has been realised. Our Saviour Himself proclaimed its fulfilment when He said, " Come to Me
all ye who labour and are heavy burdened, and I will
refresh you."[1] He came to lighten, to lift from the
backs of men, the burdens of humanity. He came to
open our eyes and to heal our infirmities. Do not
imagine that because we are here dealing with the
spiritual order that we are not dealing with realities.
The spiritual is as real as the material. Mind and
will are as real as your hand, your eyes, your nerve,
or your muscle. Nay, were it not for mind and
spirit, what human reality would there be ? The
wondrous organs of a man's body would be only
lifeless tissue, common matter. There would be no
pain or pleasure—because there would be no vitality.
There would be no human burdens—because there
would be no human sensitiveness to feel them. The
infirmities of the flesh are the infirmities of the spiritual
soul. And if the spirit have burdens and weaknesses
of its own—just as its spiritual endowments are its
own—these must be even more real, more momentous, touching more deeply the essence and substance

[1] Matt. xi. 28.

of things, than anything it can bear or suffer through
the flesh ; just as some monarch, who feels for the
troubles of the poorest of his subjects, has to carry,
in addition to all else, the solicitudes, the fears, the
weakness, and the anguish of his own heart.

To heal the spirit of man, to redeem him, to restore him, to set him once more in his place in this
creation, with the beauty and the dignity that are his
by God's wish—this is the office, the perpetual office,
of Him Who, as He once passed through Palestine,
so now passes to and fro throughout the ages till the
consummation come.

Is, then, the world smitten with disease ?   Is
human nature sick and languishing ?   There are
many minds to whom it seems unreasonable to say
so.   They will tell you that it is an insult to the
Creator to assert that the creatures He has made,
with infinite wisdom and infinite love, should be in any
way imperfect in their adaptation to their end, or de-
ficient in such knowledge and such strength as their
nature seems to require.   But to say nothing of revelation, are not facts against them ? You may argue
that an all-powerful Creator must have made all
things perfect.   There is a sense in which that must
be true.   But evil exists, ignorance exists—in spite
of all abstract argument.   And not only do evil and
ignorance exist, but unless they are counteracted they
decidedly do interfere with the doctrines of human
nature.   That is easily proved.   Put the destiny of
human nature as low as you please.   Do not say it
is Heaven or God — but say it is society, peace,

culture. Is it not true—nay, evident with unmistakable clearness—that it is only by a moral struggle and by hard effort that man can prevent his ignorance and his passion from making these things impossible? When we inquire as to human nature's destiny and possibilities, we have a right to interrogate the noblest whom our race has produced—its philosophers and its thinkers, its men of mercy, its men of faith, its men of prayer. What have been the careers of the earth's Saints and sages?. An uphill labour; a constant fight; a battle against overwhelming odds. And the contest has been not only with outside evil, but with evil within their own breasts. Had the race of man been only another tribe of beasts or animals, this kind of conflict would never have taken place. Beasts fight; but no beast fights to make himself better, or to make another beast better. Animals are urged hither and thither by their appetites; and so is man; but it is only man who comes to loathe his appetites, and who sets himself to bridle them and tame them into submission. But surely this means that man is spoiled, hurt, injured, maimed, in some way or other? His nobler powers should rule his lower, and should guide and control his whole being. They do not do so. In some important respects, they cannot. These are the facts. You cannot argue them away. But you can seek to explain them. The explanation lies in the "original sin" of the human race.

It is not necessary to endeavour to probe to its depth the mystery of this Original Sin in which we are all concerned. We need not seek to describe its exact nature, nor to explain how, because Adam sinned, therefore in him we all fell. It is sufficient to say that the race, by that primal sin, became turned from God, and despoiled of God's sanctifying grace. The moment that any member of that race, by God's mercy, is baptised, or turns to God, desiring to do His will, in that moment grace comes back, and he becomes once more a child of Heaven. So that although individual human beings who have committed no personal sin may, in some cases, be excluded from a bliss to which they have no claim of justice, it is only in that sense that they can be said to be punished. And thus it may truly be said that no man is punished in the world to come except for his personal sin. But in this world there are consequences—hard and rigorous consequences—of that original sin, which look like punishment, and which are indeed punishment. Whether they necessarily continue always to retain the nature of punishment, is a question to which I hope to give the answer before very long.

The first consequence of Original Sin is darkness. It is not true to say that men even now are born without mental or moral light. History and experience testify that even the lowest savage, if he has opportunities, can recognise whence he is, who and what he is, and for what he ought to aim. Human darkness or blindness seems to be rather an inability to hold truth fast, than the failure to see some rays of it. In this the savage and the civilised man are not so far asunder,

as long as they are left to the natural light. Man,
when he reflects, easily recognises a certain mental
consciousness and spiritual activity within himself,
which he calls a Soul. But he recognises it, too
often, like a man recognises a friend in a noisy
crowd. He no sooner sees his soul than he loses
sight of it again. It greets him, calls to him, chal-
lenges him ; but the sound is lost in the clamour, the
rush, and the turmoil of a hundred different powers
and appetites, all of them more pressing and more substantial than the subtle essence of his inmost being.
And in the stress of attending to lower wants and desires—to the requirements of the moment—to the
things that he can feel and see—the consciousness of
his spiritual nature lies neglected in his heart, like a
pearl that is dropped by one who dances at a feast.
It lies forgotten—yes, and too often it lies trampled
out of all shape by reckless indulgence, by unreflecting
leisure. This is true of the cultured citizen of an
age like the present, just as strongly as it is of the
ancient or modern heathen. Men, in these days and
in these countries, may have many more notions of
their spiritual nature than were possible to barbarians.
But the darkness is very similar in the one as in the
other. For the darkness of Original Sin is not precisely the absence of knowledge. Man would certainly have known a great deal more had he not
fallen in Adam. But there is still the possibility of
knowledge quite sufficient. The darkness is in our
own eyes. It is in the inability to keep a hold on
the very truths that we cannot get rid of. There is

something the matter with the eyes of the spirit. There is a haze, a dancing and elusive atmosphere, a heaviness, a painful smart—some of these, or all of them—that keep our very knowledge outside of us. This is a peculiarity of a rational nature. It can know, and yet not apprehend. It can work out thoughts, even elaborate thoughts, as a weaver weaves his webs of cloth, and then stores them away in storehouses and forgets all about them. The knowledge that I have a soul, and that I am bound to pursue the good and decline from the evil, may be, in the man of education, like the electric light which illuminates a city, in the poor savage like the thin candle that lights up a cabin of mud ; but a man may lose his way in the blaze of the streets as easily as he may stumble and fall in a miserable hovel. If his infirmity prevents him from using the light that he has, his darkness is darkness wherever he is. No education, that is merely natural, can make a man hold to his spiritual consciousness in the conflict of life. Education too often neglects the spiritual side. But even if you teach a man that he is rational, that he is responsible, that he is immortal, and that his Father is God, even then you teach him very little indeed unless you can also teach him to keep this precious knowledge clear, vivid, active, operative, right in front of him ; unless you can beat off the distractions that will push it aside ; unless you can silence the interests that will turn the heart away from it ; and unless you can infuse into the human mind that peculiar grasping power, which, like the hand of the drowning man, must hold on to spiritual truth, or drift away and be suffocated in the turbulent river of human error and human passion.

Thus my reason, and probably my education, give me light; yet the grasp of my weakened and wounded intellect is unable to make it effectively a light of my being. My soul, my good desires, my higher convictions, and my God, they appear and disappear—they reappear only, perhaps, to vanish again—and my life is like a rudderless ship, the plaything of the winds and the waves. Who shall heal me? There is only one healer, and He is my Saviour.

Let us briefly consider the other wounds of human nature. They are all, in a certain sense, the consequences of this inability to hold fast the natural light of the soul. For it is from this darkness of the mind that follows the malice of the will; that deadly propensity to seek self first and always, which is at the root of personal sin. From darkness also proceeds that sloth and cowardice which fears the least difficulty, and is intimidated by all that seems arduous or troublesome. There are moments when the consciousness of spirituality, of immortality, and God, makes the heart of a man despise the whole world, and long to trample all its seductions under foot. But there are not many such moments in the life of the man who is left to his nature. Why is this? Because, as St. Augustine says, the glimpses of truth and reality are quickly lost; the clouds and mists again roll over hill and valley, and the poor heart is left with its darkness, with no spirit in it to fight the fight of life. And it is left, moreover, with that other propensity which thrives and lives in the darkness. The mind ought, in the fitness of things, if not by actual right, to rule the senses and the appetites. In the state of original justice this was the spirit's prerogative. But we know how different is now the condition of humanity. There have been men, left to their nature, who seemed to have the mastery of their sensuality. It has been very often because they were rather proud than sensual ; the one disease or weakness being in them more pronounced than the other. In a few men lofty aims or pure ideals may contribute to make them pass by, or even loathe, the attractions of self-indulgence. And if we take the vast multitude of the human race, there is hardly one who, at times, does not feel disgust, or satiety, or remorse, at the thought of certain sins and excesses. But concede as much as you please to this spiritual consciousness, what do facts and history prove ? That for the most part that spiritual insight is silent and dark; and that then the lower nature has nothing to hold it in but external law, the pressure of society, or personal inconvenience. Original Sin has left human nature at the mercy of its most animal part. Human nature is a captive, a bond-slave. Was it made for this? And if not, will God not redeem it !

These wounds and disabilities are either in the spirit, or they are within the spirit's active sphere. But there are others which more affect the body and

the temporal life. There is first, death. By death is
meant the separation of soul from body, and the consequent dissolution of that union which goes to make
what we see and know as a human being. This is a
punishment of nature for the transgression which has
affected nature. And a punishment it is—in the un-
certainty of its coming, in the dread that it inspires,
in the oppressive horrors which surround it, and also
in the very act itself when it comes. Next, there is
the liability to disease. Man's frame should be as pure
and flawless as the crystal spheres where the orbs of
Heaven rush through space with melody and gladness.
No star, no serene heights of ether, no inviolate
depths of the tranquil ocean, have a better claim to
absolute soundness, rightness, and loveliness than the
material sphere which is pervaded and informed by
the immortal spirit. Dust we may be, and from the
earth have we sprung; but when the spirit was
breathed in, there was mere dust and earth no longer,
but the spirit's habitation. Ah! the noble and pure
and beautiful bodies that the Lord God gave to the
first parents of mankind! O sacred body of Jesus
Christ, holy, lovely, absolutely perfect—will it always
be that we shall be as we are? When shall we
behold our Healer and our Redeemer? Finally, all
suffering comes upon us as a punishment for Original
Sin. For suffering is either the trouble of the mind
or the pang of the flesh : and these come from sin.
Where there is suffering there is something out of
order. Suffering is like the creaking and the jarring
of some grand machine ; some spring is broken, or

some wheel no longer does its work.   When the male-
diction of the primitive sin fell on man, the symmetry
of his glorious nature was disturbed, the harmony
of part with part was destroyed, and the perturba-
tion which in things inanimate would have only
have occasioned confusion and disorder, in man, with
his faculties of touch and brain, brought the mysterious
dispensation of pain and sorrow.   And with man, as
the Apostle says, all creation seems to be in travail
and suffering ; the living creatures have more to bear
than there is any need, and the very earth with its
elements is gross, harsh, and unkindly.   We are all
waiting, waiting—soul and body, the earth and all
that is therein ; there is expectation over all ; for
death, and disease, and pain cannot be the condition for which we were intended by the Lord Who
created us.

You know well that redemption, healing, and salvation is not intended to be completed on this earth.
Even had there been no Original Sin—even had we
all been as our first parents—earth, although heavenly,
would not have been Heaven.   And now, when the
primitive justice and dignity have been forfeited and
have to be restored again, our Healer and our Redeemer must be allowed to heal us and redeem us in
His own way.   It is a way which cannot fail to be
the best for us.

First, then, He does not re-establish here on earth
man's dominion over his passions and his sensuality.
No doubt, the gift of Divine grace, which we shall
consider just now, does, in some way, justly claim

such a power. But the power is not given to us. The effect of grace is so far suspended, at least with the multitude of men. Neither has Christ's grace abolished death, or taken away disease and suffering. The truth is, that none of these things need prevent that union of the spirit with its God which it is the purpose of redemption to bring about. These things are not necessarily a curse or a punishment. They all contain the possibility of good. To fight against sensuality is to win a more resplendent crown in the end. Death and suffering are a fire in which the acts of the spirit are heated to a white heat—a heat they can never derive from any other source. Therefore these things are left.

Of the other disabilities of the spirit—darkness, malice or selfishness, and sloth or cowardice—it is also true to say that they are left with us. But here we have to make a most important distinction. These wounds of the heart are left; but their condition, or, if we may so speak, their virulence and their danger, are so diminished by something that is given us that it is perhaps more true to say that they are taken away.

I am not going to speak at any length on that sovereign balsam of our souls, won for us by the Blood of Christ, poured upon us by Sacraments or otherwise, which we call the Grace of Our Redeemer. It is sufficient to say that we *are* redeemed; and that the work of redemption takes place—although not fully or completely—upon this earth. And if we are redeemed, we are healed; and if we are healed, the wounds of Original Sin must be healed.

We saw that the worst of all the effects of Original
Sin was that of "darkness"; the soul's incapacity
to hold fast to its natural light. And the chief
effect of redemption has naturally been to restore to
us this very power. It is true, also, that our sphere
of light has been increased; we have the gift of
revelation, and know many more things about God
and the spirit and the world to come than we could
have known only by the light of nature. But whether
we speak of the light of our natural intelligence, or of
that supernatural revelation bestowed upon man by
his merciful God, the grand effect of the redeeming
grace of Christ seems to be—that wonderful power of
holding fast, of clinging to, of realising our spiritual
light, which is called Divine faith. It may not be
an adequate description of redemption, or of Christ's
grace, to say that it is faith and faith only. We
might speak of it as life, as strength, as purity, as
charity. Neither do I say that faith is always the
first of graces; much less do I assert, as you well
understand, that a man can please God and be saved
by faith without charity, that is, by dead faith.
But I take faith in its wider sense—in the sense in
which it is used in the eleventh chapter of the
Epistle to the Hebrews; as that gift, endowment,
and transfiguration of the mind for which all pre-
vious graces are a preparation and which finds its
normal and complete bloom and fruit in charity.
It is called faith—a word that denotes, not purity, or
strength, or mere affection, but a certain insight combined with adhesion, a certain clinging combined with

realisation. It is called faith because the deepest and gravest wound of our fallen nature is its blindness to the things of the spirit. It is called faith because the healing of human nature means the living attention of the human faculties to God. It is called faith because a man cannot be healed without being brought to live for an eternity that is out of sight. It is called faith because belief in Christ, loyalty to Christ, adhesion to Christ, is the only remedy for fallen man.

Faith, then, is more than information, more than education, more than study. It is more than philosophy, more than theology, more than the study of the Bible. A man may know much or he may know little ; he may be educated, or he may be rude ; he may be a genius, or he may be of humble abilities : if he has faith he will cling to, and keep before him, the light that he has, and he will be a redeemed man. And this is what his Redeemer has specially come to give him. He gives it to him—when it is given— as really as He gave sight to the blind man on the way to Jericho. That is, faith is not a mental attitude merely, but a mental endowment—a healing, a strengthening, a faculty, an alteration of the intelligent nature, a new power. This is mere Catholic doctrine. As a gift, it does not make us acquainted either with things naturally knowable, or with Divine revelation. And a man might even hold certain revealed truths without having faith at all. What it does, is to furnish us with a conviction, an adhesion, a mental security, which finds its food in the matters which God has revealed, or in those natural spiritual truths which, in a wide sense, are also a part of God's revelation ; and which are also, every one of them, illuminated by revelation strictly so called.   This is the faith of which Jesus spoke when He said to the sick, the blind, and the paralytic, " Be of good heart, thy faith hath made thee whole ! "   This is the faith which was to bring " the justice of God," that is, God's redemption, to the nations,[1] as it had brought that justice to Abraham in the ages long before.[2] This was the faith of which it was said, " He that believeth and is baptised shall be saved."   " Believe and thou shalt be saved."   This was the faith that giveth life, by which the just man liveth, by which even he that was dead was to live.   This was the faith of which Peter spoke[3] when he said, at the primary Council of the Catholic Church, " God, Who knoweth hearts, hath given to the Gentiles the Holy Ghost as well as to us, and put no difference between us and them, purifying their hearts by faith."

The world, then, is healed by the gift of faith.   For faith first brings with it the strong adhesion of the heart and being to the Divine light, which is abundant on every side.   Then, in the vividness of this supernatural enlightenment, the cultivation or worship of self becomes infinitely less constant and intense.   Movements, nay, transports, of generosity, are the natural accompaniment of faith ; and where

---

[1] Rom. iii. 22.   [2] *Ib.* iv. 3.   [3] Acts xv. 8, 9.

there is generosity self must die, and the malice of the natural will must be healed. Further, faith rouses courage, by the sight of the world to come and the world of grace; "by faith the Saints have conquered kingdoms."[1] And thus darkness, malice, and cowardice, if not taken away, are so healed that the heart is sound again, and the whole being is restored and redeemed.

When will the world seriously turn to seek Jesus Christ and His faith—the only medicine, the only balm; the true oil and wine of the Good Samaritan? Shall not we, at least, who are Catholics and who understand, do what we can to spread faith and to deepen faith?

To-day we celebrate the festival of her who knew not Original Sin, and whose glorious nature the wounds of Original Sin never touched. It might seem, to those who look at these things hastily, that Mary's immaculateness and entire freedom from pride, passion, and concupiscence, were of little comfort to the race of men who are born in sin and must fight all their lives in the dust and noisomeness of sinful propensity. There could not be a greater mistake. Whence came our Blessed Lady's stainless birth and sinless life? From the unction of the Holy One; from the Blood of Jesus; from that very grace of which we have been speaking. If grace—if faith and charity—can do such a work as this, what is there they cannot do? Mary,

---

[1] Heb. xi. 33.

because she was the Mother of God, was redeemed
in this transcendent way ; but redemption is intended
for all of us, for each of us.   The whole world is
redeemed.   Every individual soul is redeemed if it
turns to Christ.   We are not redeemed mechanically,
it is true.   That is, if we have the use of our reason,
we must use our faculties in contrition, obedience, and
love.   But, in comparison with the bounteous healing
which Jesus is ready to visit us with, how little have
we to do ourselves !   What we have to do is not so
much to ask for faith, for we have it, but to give our
faith free play.   The magnificent gift of faith—faith
living by charity—is poured upon us ; but it remains
too often like a flood pent up among the hills.   Down
with the barriers, and let it rush and roar into the
valleys !   The child, the man, the priest, the layman
—what we all want is that we should earnestly guard
and exercise our gift of faith.   All who have anything to do with children know well how mere
knowledge or instruction will leave their conceit, dis-
honesty, and animalism untouched ; and how, on the
other hand, they respond to the word of piety, to the
example of a holy life, and to the sweet suggestions
of the altar and the sanctuary.   It is because they
have the gift of faith.   When do we find that the
poor—the poor, with their temptations, with their
hard lot, with their scanty instruction—when do we
find that they serve God and keep the commandments ?   It is when their hearts can be attracted to
their church, and their lives impregnated with supernatural and sacramental influences; because then their

gift of faith has free way. What is it, think you,
that will keep our people good—our people who are
more or less educated in the public schools, who
read the cheap literature, and frequent the free
libraries? None of these things will. Their teachers
may be Christians, their lecturers moral, and their
reading harmless ; but unless they have time and space
and opportunity for exercising their faith by daily
prayer, by Mass, and by religious observance, all
their increased facilities of cultivation will bring
them no nearer to the healing and the redemption
of Christ. One of the gravest and most characteristic perils of this present time is the persistent
substitution of information for faith. There is plenty
of talk in this country about religious things. Ministers of religion discuss religion, professors prove it,
journalists approve it, statesmen profess it, the ordinary citizen observes its forms. There is no healing
in most of this—no redemption. The inward, childlike, intense, and devout clinging—which is the mark
of living faith—is hardly known outside the Catholic
Church ; and even with Catholics, faith, in too many
cases, is choked and strangled by heretical surroundings, by free opinions about mysteries, about Scripture and the Church, and by ignorance about the
mysteries of revelation. O Healer and Redeemer
of mankind! of what avail is it to know, to doubt,
to inquire, to discuss, unless Thy power and gift
makes me hold fast with loving constancy to Thy
light and Thy attraction! Where shall I find this
blessed healing of my dark and perverse nature ex-

cept in greater attention to Thee, Thy presence, and
Thy Sacraments! And if we mourn for the unbelief
of the land—if we sigh for the conversion of our
brethren—let us be sure that it is not controversy—
above all, not biting controversy—not even argumen-
tative discussion, which will bring souls to the Church
but rather exposition touched with piety, explanation warmed through with devotion ; the presentation
of faith, not as a system to be accepted, but as the
holding lovingly fast to what God has taught. The
non-Catholic, who has surrendered his own pride and
who prays like a child, is near to healing and redemption, though he be as yet ignorant of two-thirds of
the Creed.

It was the faith of Mary, Mother of God, that was
the great solid foundation of her august sanctity.
Beata es quæ credidisti. The healing of her nature
—which was never wounded—began with the preven-
tion of darkness, and the same gift produced the
sanctification of the will and the subjection of all
passion. Any one who truly recognises and understands the Blessed Virgin must needs learn many
things about the faith of Christ ; for her greatness is like a chapter in the book of the dispensation
of Christ. And to read that chapter leads the heart
to turn over many another of these pages, until the
heart becomes familiar with Jesus, with His work,
His intentions, and His holy will. It is by this nearness and intimacy with Our Lord and Redeemer that
the soul of a man partakes more and more of His
miraculous healing. It is by this seeking, following,

and touching Christ that blindness departs, and all
our infirmities are cured.   May God give us inward-
ness, the spirit of prayer, and the love of heavenly
things, that all our life we may never be far away
from that Master and Saviour Whose whole desire
is to heal us here, that He may crown us with His
perfect redemption hereafter!

MINISTERS OF THE NEW TESTAMENT.

Preached at St. Peter's, Lancaster, August 25th,
1895.

"God hath made us fit minister of the New Testament"
(2 Cor. iii. 6.)

GOD Almighty requires no ministers. Yet the
pages of both the Testaments are full of the name
"Ministers of God." The angels are His ministers ;
kings and warriors are His ministers ; the inanimate
things of the earth, the fire, the winds, the stars—these
are all ministers of His who do His word. We find
men in primeval times gathering round the patriarch
who offered sacrifice and called upon the Name of the
Lord ; and when the Covenant had been given, we
behold a chosen tribe standing in their ranks, with
the robes of their priesthood, before the altar of God
in the wilderness, and in holy Sion. "You shall be
called the priests of the Lord," said Isaias, " ministers
of Our God shall be your name."[1]

Then, when the old Covenant had passed away,
the Apostle speaks of himself and his associates as
"ministers of Christ and dispensers of the mysteries
of God."[2] For, although the God Who made these
souls and bodies of ours is near to us, and within us,

[1] Isaias. lxi.   [2] 1 Cor. iv. 1.

and is even more truly and essentially present to our
beings than are our own hearts, yet He hides Himself
from our faculties.   Although He has His own secret
way direct to our spirits, yet He has placed Himself
at the mercy of a hundred barriers and obstacles.
Although He has a voice that can be heard—yea,
that can make mortal ears tingle, and can pierce the
very marrow of existence—yet He keeps that marvellous silence which sometimes seems to discourage
His servants and to make the wicked presume.
Although it is within His omnipotence to make Himself not only known to all His creatures, but to
possess every sense, to dominate every power, to
overwhelm every faculty, yet He will not stretch out
His hand and display His glory, but leaves the
universe to the forces which He has primarily set in
motion.   Because only thus was rational creation
possible, and the probation of mankind.

It is because of the barriers which a state of probation has raised, that the God Who made us must
use ministers to keep Himself before our faculties.
Yet even in the state of the perfect there will be—
there is—a ministry.   Among the angels there is no
seraph or cherub who can gaze upon the wholly-
revealed Godhead.   The beatific glory, although it is
the vision of God face to face, is not God's own
immensity or infinity.   There are grades, ranks,
hierarchies, and choirs.   And though all enjoy the
vision, yet that mighty universe which is made up by
what we are fain to call the knowledge and the will
of God, is imparted from choir to choir, the highest

nearest to the throne, the lowest being august and princely beyond all comprehension. So it will be with men, as we cannot doubt. The spirits of the just will minister one to another, and convey, repeat, reflect the infinite riches of God, each in the rank to which his merits, by the power of his Saviour's redeeming blood, have raised him. " Dost thou know the order of Heaven," cries out holy Job, " and canst thou set down the reason thereof?"[1] We know it not—and its glories are hidden from us. But order there will be, and ministration, and the God Who can do all things by Himself will be glorified afresh throughout eternal duration by using as His instruments and means the creatures whom He has called out of nothing.

No one will doubt that of all spiritual needs, the deepest and the most vital that men have is to respond to the ever-present God. Only the unbeliever will deny this—the unbeliever, and the man who in these days wraps his unbelief in a new cloak, and says he does not know. To a Christian, God is a Father, a Friend, a Teacher, and a source of spiritual strength. It would be as wise, therefore, to ignore God as it would be to shut out the sunlight, to have no friends, or to starve oneself to death. What is deadly sin except the turning of one's back on God? What is coldness, worldliness, indifference, except a certain deadness to the unseen presence—a preoccupation with other things than Himself? Such

---

[1] Job xxxviii. 33.

states are common.   They are as perilous as they
are common.   It is the complaint that runs through
all Holy Writ that "My foolish people have not
known Me ; they are foolish and senseless children."[1]
"The kite in the air," cries out the Prophet, " hath
known his time ; the turtle, the swallow, and the
stork have observed the time of their coming ; but
My people have not known the judgment of the
Lord."[2]   The creatures who have no intelligence or
free will—all the birds and beasts—have an instinct
which draws them, in beautiful conformity, to obedience and fixed law.   They seem to feel their Maker
and to rejoice in carrying out His will.   Only man,
with his power of looking before and after, of penetrating the depths and piercing the heights, of
throwing beams of spiritual light into the darkness
of things and seeing in the universe more than ever
came by matter and its laws—only man seems so
often to have no sense of Him in Whose image he is
made !   Of the primeval world it was said, " They
knew not, till the flood came and took them all
away."[3]   Had it not been for the goodness and mercy
of God Our Father, of how many generations of the
human race would this have come true !   In spite of
their intelligence and their rational powers, which are
amply strong enough to enable them to know God,
and the justice and goodness of God, how many
generations would have lived as if there were no
God !   It seems as if the fate of humanity would

have been to eat and drink, to marry and give in
marriage, to let the invisible pass unregarded, to take
no account of Heaven and futurity—and then, when
the time was full, to be swept away by some more
awful deluge than the first, into eternal and irreparable
destruction.

But, as you may well suppose, God, being who He
is, would not—could not—leave His children to such
a fate.   He must make His people know and feel
Him.   Although His own absolute spirituality might
be, in its own nature, so far out of the reach of
human faculties, and although the waves of influence
which stir human pulses must be of a coarser matter
than the ether of the heavens—yet God could not be
baffled.   He must use the ministry of men, and,
through men, the ministry of all created things.
There is a striking Messianic Psalm, the forty-ninth,
which describes the action of God when He had determined to make Himself better known.   " The
God of gods, the Lord hath spoken ; He hath called
the earth."   It was to be impossible for the earth to
mistake that call.   "God shall come manifestly ;
Our Lord (shall come) and shall not keep silence."
The eternal silences were to be broken ; God was to
be heard.   " Hear, O My people, and I will speak ;
O Israel, and I will testify to thee ; I am God, thy
God."   And after many glowing verses, which describe God's wishes and His ways, He says, at the
end, " Understand these things, you that forget God."
To forget God was to be henceforth impossible—
impossible except to the absolutely perverse.   At

their peril, men were to " understand " the plan of
God for making Himself seen and felt.

What that plan was, you know.   Men could never
have foreseen it.   They would have perhaps expected
Him to proclaim Himself with some mighty sign ; to
repeat, or to multiply, Sinai, and to let His thunders
speak.   Or they might have looked for letters of light
in the heavens, that from morn till eve, and through
the night, these unresponsive hearts of ours might
see His revelation of Himself.   Or there might have
been messengers from the Heaven of heavens—angel
after angel—to every people, to every generation.
But none of these things were enough for the love of
God.   In certain degrees, times, and places, He has
used them all.   But in order to take hold of all
people, and all generations, so that none could miss
Him and none could lose Him from their sight, He
had another counsel.

You know what it was.   For us men and for our salvation, He descended from Heaven—and was made
man.   God became His own messenger—His own
minister.   He spoke, He acted, He suffered—but, in
one sense, it was enough that He should have taken
human nature.   I will not say that the Incarnation
absolutely tells us what we might not in substance
have known before, by our reason, of the solicitude of
God for our immortal souls.   But henceforth God is
not a mere demonstration, an idea, a truth of science,
dry, abstract, and hard to grasp.   He fills the world
that our very eyes and ears take note of.   He warms
us like another sun; He chases away the darkness and

lights up and colours all creation; He touches a hundred fibres in every human heart; He is bound up with the world's history, and He has Himself a new story, incidents, speech, and a Name, which draw men, and interest men, and make it impossible for men to lose sight of Him. No wonder that the Incarnation is described by seers and psalmists of the olden times by every beautiful and gracious epithet. It is the dew that drops from Heaven; the gentle rain upon the parched earth; it is light; it is fertility, flowers and fruit; and it is mercy, grace, life, and salvation.

I have said that Our Lord and Saviour Jesus Christ was the grand and sovereign "Minister" of God to men. You will remember that this name was given to Him, in prophecy, more than once in the ancient Testament. "My Angel shall go before thee," said the Lord to Israel.[1] "Behold I will send My Angel . . . and My Name is on him."[2] St. Clement of Alexandria and St. Athanasius see in these passages a prophecy of Christ the Son of God. And Malachy, looking more nearly to what was to be, cries out, "And presently the Lord Whom you seek, and the Angel of the Testament, whom you desire, shall come to His temple."[3]

It is not necessary at this moment to insist and to explain how Our Lord, in His Incarnation, is the Angel and Minister of God. He was, it need not be said, much more. But He was the "Minister" of

[1] Exodus xxiii. 23.   [2] *Ib.* 20-21.   [3] Mal. iii. 1.

God by bringing God home to the intelligence, the feelings, and the needs of the human race. Through Christ we adore God more easily, more fervently, and more continuously. Through Christ we realise the world to come and the awfulness of the destinies of immortal spirits. Through Christ the mercy and grace of God are applied to us ; for we receive mercy through Bethlehem, through Nazareth, through Calvary ; and that the Divine grace should be given us thus, through Christ—through one who first merits it by humiliation, obedience, and death, and then beckons us to the foot of the Cross that the stream of His Blood may fall upon our heads—this plan or, counsel of God is indeed worthy of the supreme wisdom and the supreme love. For grace, which, if God had so willed, might have come in an awful silence that would have puzzled the understanding to make sure of it, and would have left a score of human powers and human affections cold and unresponsive, now comes with surroundings of emotion, with the touch of a hand and the sound of a voice, and thus seizes hold of man's nature by all its clinging tendrils—its spirit and its flesh at once. "Come near Him—come near Him" is the prophetic cry of one who saw what was going to happen. "Come near Him—taste and see that He is sweet—you shall be illuminated ; you shall fear no rebuff; for the Lord is near"—ah ! so near—"and none that trust in Him shall trip or stumble."[1]

---

[1] See Ps. xxxiii.

There can be no idea of the Christian ministry more true, and at the same time more striking than this—that its office is to continue Christ in the world. Our Blessed Saviour has not remained among men in bodily and sensible presence. He is out of sight— until He reappears at the judgment. Just as the Divinity, being spiritual, was to be brought close to human faculty by the Incarnation, so the Incarnate Word, when He withdrew to the heavens, was to be kept in the world and before the world by a certain wonderful dispensation. It is true that, whether Christ is visible or invisible, the facts of the coming, the living, and the suffering of Jesus can never be altered. Even had there been no invention of Divine love for keeping Him always with us, yet still the fact of the Incarnation and the story of His life would have always been the means of bringing the Godhead near. But He has not been content with this. What did He promise by Isaias? " Thy eyes shall see thy Teacher, and thy ears shall hear the word of one admonishing."[1] It was not angels that He was to send to represent Him. He had resolved to do a wonderful thing ; to bring about, in this earthly universe of ours, a prodigy which is only surpassed by the Incarnation itself. He wished that Jesus Christ should be known and felt by every generation and in every region of the world. He took, therefore, that which is found always and everywhere—He took the human race

[1] Isaias xxx. 20, 21.

itself, and He set men apart, and He "ordained" them, in the original sense of the word, to prforme for Him a certain office. He left them in their human nature ; He left them on the road of pilgrimage, on the field of struggle and conflict ; He left them with their temptations and their weaknesses. But He gave them certain gifts, endowments, powers ; He gave them—not His own sinlessness, or His own miraculous dominion over nature—but those of His prerogatives which were best adapted to win the human race to remember Him and follow Him.

He gave them His power to teach. There could be no Divine ministry without the gift of sure and certain teaching. Men can attain by their reason to the fact of God's existence. But from that point their limited yet always busy brains will diverge this way and that ; they will dispute about His goodness, His justice, and His judgments. If He should give a supernatural revelation, they will ask a thousand questions on every phrase of it, and being unable to agree upon the answers, they will tear it to shreds in a single generation. Should He even take human flesh, human speech, and teach them Himself, they will never agree as to who He is, or what His grace is, or how sin is to be blotted out, or what is to be expected of the human soul, or what is its destiny in the world to come. Therefore, through the genera-tions, if God, if Christ, is to be seen and felt by men, they must be taught. In the words of the Prophet, all the nations, all the multitude of men, in the last days were to say to one another, " Let us go up to the mountain of the Lord, and to the house of the God of Jacob, where He will teach us . . . for the law shall come forth from Sion, and the word of the Lord from Jerusalem."[1] This mountain—this house, this Sion—is the teaching ministry, with the gift of infallibility or inerrancy, enjoyed by it collectively and in its Head, and the Divine protection which unmistakably guards even its humblest member.

Next, He bestowed upon His ministers His own gift of exhortation ; the gift of speech which touches the spirit and moves the heart ; the gift of the word of God. Speech is the natural and the most powerful means of making felt that which is not seen. Christ's ministers were to have the use of a speech like God's own word—living and effectual—more piercing than a two-edged sword ; a word that was to be a fire to burn and a hammer to break ; a word that was to penetrate as the rain and the snow sink into the earth ; a word that was to convince and cow governors and kings, to refute the gainsayer, to turn the sinner from his evil way, and to bring strength and comfort to the hearts of God's little ones. Their word was to resemble the word of Him Who spake as never man spake.[2] For the priests of the Church, the ministers of the word, are not mighty, or rich, or philosophers, or men of science. They hold themselves, indeed, bound to learn as much as they can, and to prepare themselves with all diligence and humility. But they

---

[1] Isaias ii. 3.   [2] John vii. 46.

will never be able in any generation to compete in earthly advantages with the world's rulers, the world's great soldiers, statesmen, orators, or discoverers. Yet they will always move the world and, in a sense, control the world. Their word will, in the future as in the past, be stronger than armies, and more persuasive than the eloquence of those who seem to shake nations with their speech. Men will come from councils and parliaments to hear the Gospel explained by a poor priest ; the learned and the cultured will listen without dispute to the setting forth of principles which are not proved or demonstrated except by the authority of Christ. Keen men of business will pause in their calculations and their schemes after money, to be instructed and checked by men who come forth from the dimness of the altar and speak of things which are out of sight. The young, full of the vehemence and recklessness of youth, will recognise an authority they cannot sneer at, and a warning which they fear to set at nought. And the multitude, the poor, the workers, the untutored masses, those in whose interest God's love must be shown most strikingly, and for whom Christ's death and resurrection must be most emphatically proclaimed, when left to themselves and not seduced (as they are here and there in the world's history) by error, by flattery, or by fallacious promises, will crowd round the minister of Christ's word, and press close to him, as to one who can explain to them this difficult world, and show them where alone to find direction, satisfaction, and peace.

Before the word of the minister of God every man
will be equal. The Prophet Jeremias was ordered to
proclaim : " Hear the word of the Lord, O King of
Juda, that sittest on the throne of David, thou and
thy servants, and thy people who enter thy gates."[1]
And at the thought of that mighty and far-reaching
word, the minister of the Lord's threatenings cried
out at the end of the same message, " O earth,
earth, earth, hear the word of the Lord."[2]   For the
word of God's minister is truly God's own.

Thirdly, our Lord Jesus Christ conferred upon
those whom He sent the ministry and gift of bringing His own most sacred personality in contact with
those whom He had redeemed ; of personating Him,
if we may use the phrase, till the end of time. " For
your sakes," said the great Apostle, once, when he
exercised a well-remembered act of jurisdiction, " for
your sakes have I done it, in the person of Christ."[3]
The sacramental power is the continuance in the
world of the touch of Christ's hand.   It is nothing
less.   It is a tremendous claim to make.   The religious bodies which have been generated by Protestantism have come by degrees to shrink from such
a claim, and to repudiate it.   At the beginning they
carried with them the sacramental vesture, the sacramental ritual, and they kept in their formularies some
kind of sacramental phrase.   But the sacramental
claim can only live with the spirit of faith.   As these
churches and sects more and more fully reduced to

---

[1] Jer. xxii. 2.   [2] *Ib.* 29.   [3] 2 Cor. ii. 10.

practice their principle of criticism and revolt, they gradually ceased to believe in a priesthood and to care for Sacraments. But the Catholic Church believes that every rightly ordained priest possesses certain stupendous supernatural powers, which come into play when certain conditions are complied with.

We do not pretend to inherit from Christ the power of working miracles, properly so called. Outward miracles are not part of the economy of the Redemption. They were necessary to prove the mission of Christ. They were necessary at the first preaching of Christianity. They are, in varying degrees, necessary always to the missionary, to the enforcing of the ideal of sanctity, and to the upholding of the Providence of God. But they are not within the ordinary ministry of the Church.

What we claim is the bestowal of invisible spiritual grace by outward words and signs. We claim that Christ has instituted this marvellous dispensation of mysteries. As He said, "Thy sins are forgiven thee," and "Receive ye the Holy Ghost," and the souls of men thereupon were cleansed from sin, or had the grace of Heaven infused into them, so He also said to His Apostles, "Baptise," "Impose hands," "Consecrate," "Loose from sin." These things, under certain conditions, the Church claims to be part of her daily ministry for the souls of men. It is as if Jesus still passed to and fro—not in Galilee or Judea alone—but over the universal world. Wherever the light of the Gospel has so far penetrated, there is to

be found a man who acts in the person of Christ.
There is no difficulty in recognising him. You find
him standing by his altar—the altar of the New Testament. It may lift itself up under the vaults of a
great church, or it may be humbly laid amid poverty.
You find him in the garb of the levite, the evangelist, the prophet—whether in the mystic robes of the
great sacrifice, or in the habit which marks him out,
even in the ordinary life of men, as one who is set
apart for the grave ministry of man's most solemn
destiny. You find that he has functions of his own
that occupy him—functions very different from the
observances or the ceremonies of the world. You
find that he seems to go into some holy of holies and
to be face to face with Him Whose minister he is ;
that he seems to turn his back upon all men, even on
the flock which is gathered in attendance. You see
mysterious rites, and you hear words that have come
down from the beginnings of the Christian Church.
And the power of those words and rites is as the
power of the uplifted Hand which gave peace and
grace on the Lake of Genesareth and in the courts of
the Temple.

   But with all this, you find a shepherd, a father, and
a healer. He is not one who sits immovable in a
dim shrine--who wraps himself in his pride—who
is the mere mechanical instrument of one greater than
himself. He watches the flock committed to him
by day and by night ; he goes into the deserts after
them, or into crowded haunts that are more repellent
than the wilderness. He leads them to the altar ; he

enlightens their ignorance and prepares their hearts ;
he has comforting and healing words for them ; and
he brings them by many persuasions within the circle
of that power which Christ his Master has given him.
For the sacramental prerogative is great and wonderful, and greatest of all is the power of the Eucharistic
consecration, which truly and really makes Jesus
Christ Himself present under sacramental forms.
But how is its effect upon the souls of men en-
hanced and multiplied by that gift which belongs to
the priest, of making himself, in love and solicitude,
in word and deed, the image of what Jesus was when
He trod the ways of this earth of ours ! For it is
not to the priest that the priest's word and life lead
the sinner. The priest is the veil of the Temple
which thinly hides the glory of the Lord. Nay, the
veil is now rent in twain, and Our Lord is seen and
felt only at a little distance away. That ministerial
power combined with that fatherly solicitude—that
mystical ritual and that most human watchfulness—
the words of awful dispensations mingled with the
voice of pleading and of encouragement — these
things present the living Jesus. And that most sweet
Name, whether invoked in the might of its grace-
giving office, or urged in the ears of the sinful, the
wavering, and the indifferent—it is to that Name
that the priest always returns, and it is that Name
that he takes care the redeemed world shall never
forget. This is the Ministry of the New Testament.

It cannot be denied that, in the present temper
of the world, it is hard to persuade it that there

does exist in our midst an order of men endowed with the supernatural powers represented by the Sacrifice of the Mass and the ministry of the Sacraments. This is a subject which is well worth considering, and it is a difficulty which must be faced. Yet it is plain that no one who accepts the New Testament can refuse to admit, in principle at least, that in Christianity supernatural results are bound up with external rites. The institution of Baptism, and the words of Our Lord and of the Apostles on that Sacrament, are simply conclusive. Baptising is, beyond contradiction, an outward, physical, sensible act or rite. When it was first used in the world need not now be discussed ; but it was in use before Our Lord adopted it. It was then nothing more than one of those symbolical and initiatory ceremonies which have been found in all religious associations. It does not seem to have signified washing or cleansing ; but rather, perhaps, drowning. It was probably taken up to denote the consecration of a being to some special purpose ; just as fire was used with a similar intention. Hence it came to signify the entrance upon a new state. Our Lord deigned to submit to this ceremony at the hands of John. To His most perfect human soul it could not bring any additional glory, grace, or gift. But the symbolical apparition of the Holy Spirit at that moment showed what the rite was to become. We find that Our Lord adopted the ceremony of Baptism. In doing so, He distinctly stated that, henceforward, it was to confer interior grace. " Unless a

man be born again of water and the Holy Ghost, he
cannot enter into the kingdom of God."[1]   And, in
His last charge to His Church, He commanded them
to baptise the whole multitude of those whom their
preaching was to make disciples of His holy law.[2]
This they proceeded to do.   When St. Peter, after
his first great sermon, is asked by the Jews what they
must do to be saved, he replies, " Be baptised every
one of you "; and on that occasion no less than three
thousand received Baptism.[3]   It is quite clear, then
that all must be baptised ; that our birth, in the order
of grace, is attributed to the baptism of water and of
the Spirit, and to nothing else ; that the effect of
Baptism is, in St. Peter's words, the remission of sins.[4]
" Rise up," said Ananias to Paul at Damascus, "and
be baptised and wash away thy sins."[5]   And St. Paul
himself, later on, says, " He hath saved us by the
laver of regeneration and renovation of the Holy
Ghost . . . that being justified by His grace
we may be heirs of life everlasting."[6]   And if there
is anything certain in the history of Christian doctrine, it is that for sixteen centuries after the Day of
Pentecost all Christian people—differ how they might
on some points—agreed in believing that spiritual
regeneration and inward grace followed on the ad-
ministration of the rite of Baptism.   The same thing
can without difficulty be proved of the laying on of
hands, and of the anointing with oil, and of the Eu-

---

[1] John iii. 5.   [2] Matt. xxviii.   [3] Acts ii. 38, 41.
[4] *Ib*. 38.   [5] *Ib*. xxii. 16.   [6] Titus iii. 5.

charistic consecration, and of the absolution of the penitent sinner. The New Testament view, the primitive view, the traditional view, and, therefore, the genuine Christian view, is that these things are more than outward rites, more than ceremonies, more than signs and symbols ; they are the touch of the hand of Christ—that hand which can reach even to the innermost substance of the spiritual and immortal soul.

It need not be said that this most striking doctrine —this faith in the existence of supernatural power in a human ministry—is a distinguishing note of the Catholic Church. True, there are Churches or sects who in name uphold sacramental efficacy : although it is to be observed that even the Article of the Church of England on Baptism seems to have been studiously made ambiguous in its language, in order not to offend the school of Geneva. And there are undoubtedly, here and there, in the Anglican communion at least, individuals who believe in baptismal regeneration, in the grace and character of holy Order, and in the real Eucharistic presence. But these are the minority ; and no religious body in the country has the sacramental view in any of its formularies. The Catholic Church, then, whether as regards theory or as regards facts, may justly be called the only sacramental Church.

It is a distinction of which we may well be proud ; a distinction which goes very far to settle the question as to where the true Church is to be found. For the sacramental ministry is the only effective and adequate continuance of the redeeming and reconciling work of an Incarnate God. The sacramental ministry is worthy of the God of the Incarnation; and it is difficult to see how the promises made, or involved, in the taking of human nature by the Infinite God, could be otherwise carried out. It must never be forgotten that Jesus Christ was promised to these latter times, not as a passing vision, but as a permanent possession. He was called, from the beginning, the Expectation of nations. In Him the earth was to be blessed. He was to be the King and the Ruler of a kingdom, spiritual and visible, who should execute judgment and justice in all generations. "In those days," said Jeremias, "shall Juda be saved, and Israel shall dwell confidently; and this is the Name that they shall call Him, the Lord, our Just One."[1] This prophecy, it need not be said, refers to all the latter times. He was to be a shepherd—a physician, He was to draw all things to Himself; He was to refresh all generations and make their burthens light. It was to be a time when knowledge was to abound—which could only be by teaching; when grace was to be close at hand—which could only be by new dispensation and external observance, for in other ways it was always close at hand; when peace was to be abundant— which could only be by the preaching of the Cross, for there is now as much to suffer as ever there was; and when there was to be a certain fruitfulness in heavenly achievements, an abundant harvest of sanc-

---

[1] xxiii. 6.

tity and holiness—which could only be by men becoming more completely saturated with God's nearness, in memory, fancy, feeling, sensibility, so that holiness might thus be more intense, deep, and continuous.   It was to be a time which St. Paul calls " mystery ";[1] a time when things were to be given which neither eye had seen nor ear heard, nor had they entered into the heart of man to conceive.[2]   It was to be the " dispensation of the fulness of times ";[3] a time in which believers were to be signed with the Holy Spirit of promise ;[4] a time of inheritance, of acquisition.   Christ's body the Church was to be the fulness of Him Who was utterly filled with all abundance.[5]   And this Church was to be made a living force by and through men who were to exercise a ministry of reconciliation—who were to be ministers of Christ, ambassadors of God, dispensers of mysteries, witnesses, fishers of men, God's coadjutors, and priests of Him Who was for ever a High Priest.

Conceive, for one moment, how or in what sense all this could have come true had there been no Christian priesthood !   Christ gone from the earth ; men at variance as to what the story of the Gospels meant ; religion asserted by the learned to have sprung from the gross dreams of savages, to have taken the colour of every generation and every climate by turns, to be perpetually altering by growth or diminution, under analysis, or by force of advanc-

ing thought, till it was likely to result in something
as thin and unsubstantial as the blue shreds of mist
that linger among the hills after the sun is high in
the heavens.   Is this what was meant by the promise
that in the latter days the wilderness should blossom
as the rose?   Was the Incarnation to make no
deeper prints upon human affairs than some myth of
the ancient Greeks?   Why, the pagans of old were
better off.   Their gods were fictitious and often vile ;
but there were rousing names among those gods, and
there were glorious temples and many august rites,
which drew the multitude at least to believe in higher
things, and to live a life that looked forward to beyond
the grave.

And as for the Old Testament, there would have
been more force, more efficiency in Judaism than
in Christianity.   The Hebrews of the chosen people
had scriptures and priests and levites ; they had
their great Temple of Sion ; they had the most
splendid ritual that the world has ever seen ; they
had the most impressive sacrifices, and they had
ceremonies which can hardly be distinguished from
true and real Sacraments ; in one word their religion
seized upon every sense and every association, in
order that God might be brought close to the mind
and heart of man.   Yet how does St. Paul speak of the
Old Testament?   He calls the law of Moses a law
of poor and infirm elements[1] ; he goes very near to
calling it sin.[2]   Yet it was neither.   It was powerful,

not infirm ; rich, not needy ; a law of blessing and
not of death. What then does St. Paul mean ?   He
means that if you compare it with the law of Christ—
the new dispensation—all its efficacy seems to shrink
to nothing, and, like the belated moon when the sun
has risen, it hangs in the heavens pale and ineffectual.
But would St. Paul have said this of a Christianity
without a priesthood, sacrifice, or Sacraments ? Do
not say that the glory of Christianity is the spiritual
grace of Christ. There never was a time, since Adam
and Eve first stood in mourning outside the gates of
Paradise, when that grace could not be had in an
instant by any one who lifted his heart to his God.
God has always been God ; and the great fact of
redemption was valid in the Old Law as in the New.
The difference is a difference of application and dispensation.   Just as the Incarnate God did not simply
utter a decree of forgiveness, or merely merit forgiveness (as He might have done) by a single act,
but took a Name, and a Mother, and lived a career,
and spoke to men, and touched them, and went
through the Red Sea of His suffering—so He was
to continue through all generations to speak, to
touch, and to be near. No longer in the world in
bodily presence, He was still to be with us by His
Spirit ; and this Spirit, seizing upon men, setting men
apart, was to carry on by ministerial agency nearly
all of that gracious dispensation which those witnessed
to whom it was given to hear and look upon Jesus
Himself.   Above all, men were to be empowered to
do certain ritual acts, and in the doing of them were

not merely to instruct, or to edify, or to stir up faith,
or to comfort the contrite heart—though all these
things were to come to pass—but so to exercise the
very power of Christ as to pour Christ's own grace—
grace of regeneration, of strength, of light—into the
duly prepared soul of the Israelite of the New Testament. One can see in a moment the far reaching
effect of an ordinance like this. The ministers of
Christ—the pastors of the Church—are men unlike
all other men in power and responsibility.

I do not stop here to reflect on what the result
must be, or ought to be, upon themselves. But upon
the vast and wide flock of our Redeemer Christ there
must come an awe and an observance far beyond that
which was commanded when it was said to the Hebrews, " Fear the Lord and reverence His priests."[1]
The times and the moments when that august
ministry is to be exercised must be times of holy
fear, of strict preparation, of earnest spiritual acts.
The sacramental ministry will lead to the building
up of a beauteous and touching ritual, full of the
inner spiritual meaning of the grand actions of that
stupendous ministry. There will be gatherings of
men, and solemnities, and pomp, such as men always
have recourse to in order to express intense emotion
and appreciation. There will be altars, and sanctuaries, and the raising of walls and roofs, that symbolise, each in its place, that universal Church and
kingdom to which these great prerogatives belong.

[1] Ecclus. vii. 31.

There will be a hierarchy of ranks and orders, culminating in one who is the special Vicar of Christ. Music and the arts, poetry and eloquence, all the genius of believing men, will be turned to embody it and honour it, and to lift it up to a place in man's thought and veneration worthy of a faith which puts religion before all things, and which sees in the sacramental dispensation the very heart and life of Christianity.

This grand ministry is built up on a basis of supernatural power, and it is true that the asserted presence of the supernatural seems to excite the resistance of human reason. But how inconsistent men are! I presume that they accept the fact of the Incarnation; that they would have adored Jesus as the Infinite God, and would have implicitly believed in the power to heal and to forgive of the Man Who was the Son of Mary and the foster-child of Joseph. Or would they have refused to see the presence of the supernatural even in our Blessed Redeemer? For a supernatural ministry is a very small prodigy in comparison with the Incarnation. If you believe in the divinity of Him Who stretched out human hands and said, " Receive the Holy Ghost," it is no great thing to believe that those who now say similar words have a share in the Divine power. If you believe that God was made man, it is not much to believe that God, in order to keep Himself effectively amongst us, endows certain chosen men with the gift of inerrancy and the prerogative of communicating spiritual gifts. Once accept that mingling of the human with the

Divine, that lifting up of human nature, that plan or counsel of what the Psalm[2] calls " fitting a body " to be the vehicle and instrument of God's direct operation—and all this is implied in the revelation of the Incarnation—and it becomes easy, reasonable, and delightful, to see beneath the commonplace exterior of the duly ordained minister the stirrings of the very winds and fires of Pentecost.

Thus, the ministry of the New Testament is a divinely devised means of leading men to Christ and to God. And yet there are those who will assert that every priesthood must necessarily come between a man and his God. " No priests for us," they will say, " we go straight to Christ." This is one of those specious but flimsy fallacies which fall to pieces when you touch them, or disappear when you approach them. The very reason of all external religion, the very purpose which God's supreme wisdom has had in His external revelation and action, is precisely to bring man into nearer relations with his God. What is the Incarnation itself, as planned and carried out by God, except a Divine effort to arrest man's attention, to hold his powers, to make him approach his Maker?

Can you conceive a man who would say sneeringly, " I want no Babe of Bethlehem, I want no Man of Nazareth, of Galilee, or of Calvary ; I go straight to God " ? Straight to God ! with your blindness, with your weakness ! with your interest in this world !

[2] xxxix.

with your instability, your difficulty as to things out
of sight, your natural callousness to the supernatural,
the spiritual, and the eternal ! Let us not deny that
a man *may* go straight to God. Let us not deny that
there is, in the heart of the least of us, a strong and
natural turning to our Father and our last end. But
is it not the experience of all ages and races, that there
is no human heart but may in this regard be led, and
drawn, and helped ? God knoweth our frame—and
He thinks so. Therefore hath He spoken by the
Prophets and by His Son ; and therefore hath He
willed that until the very consummation His Son
should live and act among us by a visible ministry.
By that ministry the invisible becomes visible ; the
things of the soul take rank among earthly interests ;
our salvation becomes a matter that may be fixed and set
down by earthly time ; our relations to God are made
so much the more certain and secure because we can
walk to the church to attend to them and can have
recourse to a minister for Divine gifts. Time, place,
and visible presence make men remember ; they are
exhortations ; they rouse many touching associations ;
they fight against that sloth which is so natural in
things of the spirit. And therefore it is in the church,
and when the priest is prepared for his work, and
when the moment of a Sacrament draws nigh, that
you see rapt forms, and bowed heads, and the silence
of the occupied heart. It is then that sorrow for sin,
love and union with God, and Christian charity are
hottest and most alive. And what means this, except that men are, in reality, never so truly drawn to

God as in sacramental dispensation ?   The priesthood, as an institution, operates precisely in this direction ; that is, in joining men with God.   To the man
who rejects the help of a sacramental system, and
says that he seeks God directly, I say, let that man beware ! To stop outside a church is not, in itself, to
seek God ! To rest and idle on the Sunday, when
other men kneel, is not to seek God ! To gaze up in
empty vacancy to the skies, to entertain stray good
thoughts, or utter pious sentiment, to substitute work
for prayer, none of these things is a true seeking
of God ; and those who protest against a sacramental system are too often such as are here described. If I found a man in good faith who really
prayed, who prayed frequently, who habitually lifted
himself up to God in belief, adoration, petition, and
contrition, and did all this caring nothing for external
ministrations, I would say that, in all probability, he
was rightly seeking God ; but I would try to teach
him that humility and obedience to Christ's dispensation would certainly deepen and intensify his prayer
a hundredfold. And I would say that for one who
might, perhaps, by temperament find it easier to
approach God without a ministry, there are a million
who could or would hardly approach Him at all
And God legislates for the multitude—for every soul
is dear to Him, and He loves all that He has created.

I do not forget—we are not allowed to forget—
that the ministers of the New Testament are weak,
frail, and short-sighted mortals. I do not forget the
possibility that they may, in many instances or in a

few, neglect that warning of Holy Writ, addressed to the priests of an older covenant, and solemnly repeated to them by the Bishop who ordains them ; " Be ye clean, you that carry the vessels of the Lord."[1] It is a warning that rouses an answering thrill and resolve in the breast of every man who is in any degree worthy of so high and awful a vocation. It is a warning which is impressed upon the Catholic priest even in his tender years, by all his training, by masters and venerable books, through the long courses of his preparation, by the rules, the practices, and the prayer which guard and consecrate his whole life. For the " vessels of the Lord " which his hands are privileged to bear, no longer contain the wine of the old libations, or the bread of proposition, or the blood of victims symbolical ; but the power of Christ, and the gifts of the Holy Spirit, and even the true Body of Him Who died for us. " Think what the hands should be which thus minister !—what the tongue which utters such words !" said St. John Chrysostom fifteen hundred years ago in Constantinople.[2]

All this is true. And there are some who are scandalised, or pretend to be scandalised, that priests are not better men. No one longs or prays that priests may always be an honour to their great ministry more than those who believe them to possess the prerogatives they claim. And it is certain that, on the whole, the priests of the Catholic Church

---

[1] Isaias lii. 11.   [2] *De Sacerdotio*, VI., cap. 1.

walk in the footsteps of Christ, exhibiting in their ordinary life a virtue, a self-denial, and a zeal which go far to prove their Divine mission. Yet there is no desire to claim for the priesthood angelic perfection. The great Bishop whom I quoted just now, and who, after his life of devotedness, of burning speech, and eloquent writing, died under the tyrant's hands, used to say that if priests were allowed to be subject to the passions and to sin, it was to make them sympathetic and merciful. An angel, he said, would have been unable to make any allowance for the sinner ; had a sinner come to him he would, in his zeal and amazement, have killed him on the spot.[1] This is a startling thing to say. But see how Our Lord trained Peter. He made him the Head of the Apostles, and then He allowed him to deny Him thrice. It was to give him the essential—the indispensable—lesson of compassion and kindness.

The most august ministry of Jesus Christ is intended before all things, and above all things, to draw mankind to God. A priest, seeing his own failings, trembles, and redoubles his patience with the ignorant and the sinful. A priest first uses the Sacraments himself, through the ministry of other priests, and then goes out to seek the lost sheep, or stands by the altar to receive the wanderer. Let me persuade you of this. Pride is the last vice of a priest. Priests have been tempted to pride, by power and by wealth. But it is a rare temptation, especially in our

---

[1] *Hom. on Peter and Elias.*

own day. Could you but read the hearts of the large
body of priests who minister the ministrations of the
Church in this country, you would recognise that
they were oppressed and humbled by the thought of
their dignity compared with their imperfection, and
that they were burning with the desire to do something for that Master Who had so chosen and
honoured them. Believe this, my brethren--and
then you will understand to some extent why the
Incarnation lives and lasts in the priesthood ; for you
will pierce and transcend all the littleness, the weak-
nes, and the foolishness, and you will find the compassion of Christ, the voice of Christ, the hand of
Christ. You will tread upon your own pride ; you
will put the curb on your own censorious judgment ; you will call upon your faith--and you will
find yourself near to God. For it is the childlike
spirit, as Christ has so emphatically told us, which
alone leads to the kingdom of Heaven ; the spirit
which makes nature bow the neck ; the spirit which
is not afraid of unpromising appearances, and which
is not ashamed of the shame and lowliness of Christ;
the spirit which does not trouble itself with questions,
is not fastidious and is easily satisfied. " Fit ministers of the New Testament ! " Fit, because God
has furnished them with such wondrous gifts ; fit,
because no dispensation could better suit the manifold
nature of those whom Christ came to save ; fit, not
least, because the poverty of Bethlehem, the weakness
of Nazareth, the obscurity of the thirty years, the
humiliations of the ministry, and the apparent failure

of Calvary, still live to the end of time—the victory of grace and the triumph of redemption ; and because the souls who in faith and humility make resolute use of such ministry, are like those who, once, under the garb of poverty and lowliness, recognised Jesus Christ the Son of God.

THE DIVINE UNION.

Preached in the Church of the Servite Fathers, London, on the Feast of St. Juliana of Falconieri, 1898.

" I live, now not I ; but Christ liveth in me " (Gal. ii. 20).

THE oldest of the world's wonders, and the oldest of its mysteries, is life. This earth seems to be inert, hard, and cold, and yet from its bosom springs the soft and tender plant, ever renewed, with its flower and its fruit. The animals which people its plains and forests are without reason, inarticulate, strangely silent, straitly limited ; yet within their veins there flows an intangible force, in the framework of their tissues is diffused a subtle power, from their eyes there leaps a hidden fire, and in their movements there is evidence of a strong invisible essence, far other than the earths and the vapours into which science can resolve their bodies. Whence came upon this planet the strong seed of vital force, the first kindling of self-motion ? And when there was life, why or how was there death ? What stifles into ashes so ethereal a flame ? Or whither does it betake itself? And where does it lurk while its work is interrupted ? There are answers, doubtless, to these speculations ; but no answer which is capable of lifting all the veil of mystery, or of sweeping away the sense of awe from the heart of man.

And the wonder of the fact of life, as witnessed in the plant and the beast is only the beginning of wonder. For the human spirit turns its eye upon itself, and is conscious of a power, an activity, a self-movement, as remote from the impulsion of the animal, as the planetary ether is from the slimy bed of the ocean. Whence comes intelligence? Whence comes the power to look before and after? What essence is it that summons into being forms and modes which do not exist in nature? which tears things asunder that neither steel, nor lightning, nor alchemy can affect? which creates the worlds of science, of mathematics, of literature, of art? We know, my brethren. But because we believe in a spiritual soul we are not out of the land of mystery. Yea, rather, we soon come to understand that the God on Whom life and movement and intelligence and free will all depend, being infinitely good and infinitely merciful, and being our Heavenly Father and our great and only Friend, has resolved to use the mystery of life and spirit as a starting-point for a mounting scale of marvellous life whose lower end may be on earth, but the top of which is hidden in the heavens far out of the sight of men or of angels.

The two great certainties to which we look forward —eternal existence after earthly dissolution, and the Beatific Vision of God's face—give to the word "life" a significance which it would never have had from plants, or animals, or even from the nature of man. Life

everlasting—life for ever—life without failure or decay
—what primitive vital force can be strong enough and
full enough to carry it on? and whence the gift or
endowment which makes such a life possible? And
the power which is to see God face to face—a condition of blessed activity and fruition which no created
nature, however sublime, could realise by its own
endowment—what kind of vital principle must that
power live in? What kind of a soul must that be a
function of? What kind of a spiritual or glorified
nature must be implied by such a grasp, such a re-
ceptivity, such a capacity for breathing the air of
God's heights?

We know that a man does not acquire a new or
different soul when he crosses the river of death,
when he enters upon his eternal duration and (if God
grant it) his eternal happiness. This could not be—
for it must be the same " person " who lives here and
lives hereafter—who is tried and who is crowned. But
we also know that a most wonderful alteration or elevation of man's soul has to take place before he can
enter into bliss. He undergoes, in his soul, a change
or transformation, brought about by the infusion of
sanctifying grace. This state is generally called the
" state of grace "; but it is also called the "new
birth," " spiritual birth," " regeneration "; by the
holy Fathers, it is called frequently by the word
" deification "—the making the human soul divine."
And their strong language is by them justified from
the text of St. Peter, where he says that by redemption, man has become a partaker of the Divine

nature.[1] He does not, and cannot, mean that man
becomes a part of God ; but he does mean that God
enters into and permeates the human spirit by a
special, proper, and transcendent visitation and
inhabitation. It is interesting and moving to hear
St. Athanasius and St. Cyril arguing against the
Arians that the Son and Holy Spirit must necessarily be true God because their indwelling in man's
spirit "makes man Divine." It is touching to hear
another St. Cyril, when speaking of Our Lord's own
illustration of the vine and its branches, assert that
the justified soul lives by the life of Jesus Christ
Himself ; Our Lord's Divine force pulsing through
the spirit which abides in Him. But most impressive
of all is that phrase of St. Paul, calling Divine grace
Divine life, and that life the life of Jesus within us :
" I live, now not I ; but Christ liveth in me."[2]

This august life, this far-reaching life, this fertile
life, this inextinguishable life—there can be no doubt
whence come the seeds of it. There can be no
hesitation in seeking for its source. The Saviour of
the world is its author, and it is by it that His salvation takes effect. The overflowing unction of Christ's
human soul is the fountain whence it pours into my
soul and into yours. The Blood of Calvary is its
cause, its price, its explanation. The human race
must gather it like manna at the foot of the Cross.
Men must lift their eyes for healing to the figure
which, like the serpent of old, is set up before them.

[1] 2 Peter i. 4.   [2] Gal. ii. 20.

The generations must come to the stream of the rock which the Prophet has struck. The journeyers of all ages towards the promises must first assemble round the slain Lamb. Thus only can there be healing, renewal, health, and life supernatural, life beatific, life eternal.

But here, my brethren, the inevitable inquiry springs to the lips, to which every soul, conscious of what its being and destiny are, must find a true reply. No soul of man can use a redemption that is past and done with. Where is Christ at this moment ? Where is the wonder-working hand ? Where is the Precious Blood ?

Christian faith answers with a comforting assurance. Christ died once for all. The power and merit of His Blood are infinite. Although He is in the heavens now, and earth knows Him not, yet distance is no barrier to His mighty grace, nor earthly time and measurable space any needful condition of the swift action of His loving mercy. Bethlehem is where you stand. Nazareth is your own dwelling. Calvary is the spot where you kneel and pray for pardon. The fountains of the Saviour always flow ; of His fulness we can at any time receive, when properly disposed. So that the life of grace, which, when God pleases, is to pass into the life of glory, is within the reach of every human being that is born into this world.

But true as all this is, it does not exhaust what has to be said of the gracious mercy of Our Saviour's dispensation. Redemption, however full and final, would be of little benefit to the sinful and infirm souls of men, unless those souls were made to use it. And as Jesus Christ came to make men realise God, so Jesus Christ has instituted visible and perpetual monuments of His power and love to help us to take hold of Himself. A sacramental system is the pride and the joy of the Church of God. By a Sacrament the heart awakes, the mind bows down, the whole of the soul is moved, and then the supernatural influences which have their native home in the Heart of Jesus burst like a torrent and flood the spirit of the creature, making it live now no longer with its own merely natural or spiritual life, but with the very life of Jesus Christ. Thus, the preoccupation of all that fear God under the New Law is to use to the utmost the dispensation of the Sacraments. As in the ancient days the people of God went up to Jerusalem on the great festivals of the year, and thronged the halls of the Temple, and joined in the great sacrifices, so in these times since Christ, the duty of the Christian flock is to live near the altar, to love to be within reach of the priestly power, to put first among the interests of their lives the devout frequentation of sacred rites, which are far more than mere ceremonies, and are indeed the very touch of the healing hand of Jesus.

You do not need to be told that among the Sacraments there is one which possesses, far more fully than any other of the great seven, the prerogative of filling the soul with the life that is in Jesus. The Blessed Eucharist is the living Bread. It is promised that if any one eat of this Bread he shall live for ever.

It is threatened that, unless we eat of it, we shall not
have life in us. Why is there this close relation be-
tween the Eucharistic Bread and the soul's life ?
Because the soul's life can only be the presence of
Jesus's life, and because when we partake of the
Eucharist we live " by Jesus," that is, by having
His life poured into us. As Christ "lives by the
Father," so we, through the Blessed Sacrament, " live
by Christ." Thus does Our Lord Himself teach.
Thus have the Doctors and the Saints taught. The
Divine life of God pours through the Sacred Humanity of Jesus ; that same life, from Jesus, pours
through the souls of the faithful. This is the new
law. The sources of grace supernatural — the
sources of holiness, the springs of merit — how
remote they seemed to the men of ancient dispensations—to the seers and the Prophets, who
saw the Lord " from afar,"[1] to whom His " name
came from far off,"[2] who lifted up their eyes to
distant mountains,[3] in order to catch a glimpse of
that " glory " which signifies the soul's supernatural
life. But the horizon is nearer now. The very
heavens are bowed down. He that is the light of
of the heavens—He that is the living heaven of
heavens itself—has come with mighty bounds over
the eternal hills, and now is on the earth's great level,
near and easy of approach to you and to me. Still have
we to bestir ourselves in order to save our souls. Still
are these souls of ours the only treasure worth labour-

ing for. Still have we to beware of spiritual death, to cherish spiritual life, to aim at life eternal—but the conqueror of death is with us, the Lord of life is among us, the Sovereign of the time to come has built Himself a palace in the realm of the present, where He sits with doors wide open that none may pass Him by. He begins by raising the sinner to life.

Consider the dread condition of spiritual death; the state of deadly sin; the darkness, the horror, and the ruin; a spirit wrecked now and for the eternity that awaits it; a beautiful creation smitten with deformity; a child of God turned against its Father. The work of Jesus is to give that pitiable soul its supernatural life once more. We turn to the Blessed Sacrament. We remember that when Our Lord raised the dead to life, it was only in the instance of the daughter of Jairus that He deigned to touch the dead. The maiden, perhaps, prefigures those who are not really dead in sin, but only imperfect; "she is not dead, but sleepeth." But the widow's son, and Lazarus, symbolise true spiritual death, and the sin that worketh death. And Jesus draws near to the first, as He is carried out to the tomb, but He only touches the bier. He approaches the sepulchre of Lazarus: with His voice of omnipotence He orders the stone to be removed; He bids him come forth; but His sacred flesh touches not the dead. Here is a figure of what His Eucharistic presence does when the sinner, dead in mortal sin, has to be brought back to the life of grace. The Blessed Sacrament does not do it. That is, the Blessed Sacrament touches not the sinner. Were a man, while yet in sin, to receive Jesus as He is received in the Sacrament, that would benefit him not ; but, as you know, it would be death blacker than before. *Vita bonis, mors est malis.* No. Another Sacrament must intervene ; a Sacrament which, although its whole efficacy is from the Sacred Humanity, yet is not so immediate a communication of that humanity. And yet, my brethren, let us observe this—the Sacrament of Penance may, in the truest and most literal sense, be said to owe its power, not merely to the Sacred Humanity, but to that humanity in the Eucharistic dispensation. For you cannot separate the Sacrament from the Sacrifice. Before there can be the Sacrament, you must have the sacrifice. But in every Mass there is offered to God sufficient compensation for the sins of the whole world ; no new or fresh satisfaction, it is true, but a new application called " impetration," and " pro-pitiation." In the words of the Council of Trent, the Holy Sacrifice is offered " for the living and the dead, for sins, for punishment incurred, for satisfaction, and for other needs and wants."[1] Such propitiatory effect follows infallibly, except when and where the human heart itself puts an obstacle in the way. Now, how are we to understand that the holy Mass is a " propitiation " for sin ? It would seem as if sin could not be forgiven except either by our own turning to God in perfect dispositions, or in the Sacrament of

---

[1] Sess. xxii., Can. 3.

Penance. But what does the Council of Trent say? "By this Sacrifice God is propitiated so as to give *grace and the gift of penance*, and *thus to remit sins*, even the very greatest." [1] Thus the Blessed Eucharist sets in motion the Sacrament of Penance. Whenever a Mass is said, the mighty streams of the grace of the Sacred Passion pour with swifter waves and deeper flood, seeking out sinners on the heights and in the plains, bringing recollection, bringing remorse, bringing compunction, bringing the beginnings of good desires and holy charity. Whenever a Mass is said, human hearts, and especially those for whom it is offered, are drawn to the Sacrament of Penance. Have you never marvelled how it is that a dispensation in many ways so hard to flesh and blood—a dispensation in many ways so troublesome, so intrusive in our life, so utterly at variance with human nature's impulses—is kept up and carried on in the world ; kept up, not by Saints merely, but by the indifferent crowd ; by rich and poor, by the refined and the rude, by the idle and the busy, by women and by men. It is by means of the grace which God gives for the sake of the Mass. The Sacrament of Penance in the Catholic Church is a perpetual miracle. True, it is only too sad to think how far it is neglected. But take it as we find it in the history of centuries ; take it as we see it in the world at large at this moment ; can any one deny that it is a miracle in its observance, a miracle in its

---

[1] Sess. xxii., Can. 3, cap. 2.

continuance, and a miracle in the amazing effects of conversion, of amendment, of restitution, of perseverance, which the world itself cannot refuse to acknowledge ? What a stupendous grace is the grace of repentance !—the grace which turns a perverse, selfish, proud, and obstinate heart to sorrow, prayer, and good resolution ! To cover over one's past sin and say, " Let me forget them," is easy enough. To detest them, to twist the sinews of evil activity back to the right, to confess one's self a wretch and wrong-doer before God—is not easy. And the very grace which God has in store for all His children is prevented and turned away, in just punishment, by our sins ; so that we cannot repent without grace, and, in a sense, we cannot have grace because we are sinners. O glorious propitiation of the Eucharistic Sacrifice which seems to force the bounty of God—by a holy violence which our Heavenly Father welcomes—to force the bounty of God to give the graces of repentance in spite of the sins of our hearts ; to bring the graces of repentance surging and swelling over the barriers of our darkened intelligence and perverted will. It is the Mass which converts the sinful It is the Body of Christ that brings the life to the spiritually dead, on his bier, on his way to the grave, in his very grave clothes, shut up in his sepulchre, turning to corruption, past all human help, all human hope—it is Christ's Body offered up that works the miracle. When will priest and people understand that it is by the Mass that " the Lord hath wrought salvation in the midst of the earth " ?[1]

<hr />

[1] Ps. lxxiii. 12.

The soul of the sinner lives, then, by the power of the Sacrament of Penance through the Eucharistic Sacrifice ; and now that soul is ready to receive the Eucharistic Communion. That Flesh which St. Cyril of Alexandria calls "the Flesh of life," "the life-giving Flesh," "the Flesh which brings life to those who partake of it "—that Flesh is to be communicated to the Christian wayfarer, not by mere mechanical contact, which would be of no effect, but by an ordinance instituted by Christ Himself; an ordinance which is outwardly a reception as of food, and efficaciously a means designed by Christ to confer on the spirit that which healthy food confers upon the body. But, my brethren, you will ask, Has not the forgiven soul life already ? Can the Eucharistic food give life where life has been beforehand with it ?

It is true, the soul in grace is a living soul : living to God, the rightful heir to life eternal. It is true also that that soul's grace is not inert or quiescent, but acts and operates in spiritual motion, tending to God by faith, by hope, by Divine charity ; as the living things dart hither and thither, their wings beating and their colours flashing. And does the soul want more than this ? I know not what men might want, or men might plan ; but the longings and the plans of the Sacred Heart of Jesus go far beyond. If it was to be men's duty to lift themselves to God by the whole power of the intellectual faculties of their nature ; if this was to be their glory and their bliss ; if the tremendous transforming power of sanctifying grace, the tremendous motive power of actual grace, was given them for this—then the Saviour of their souls felt Himself constrained by His love, not only to give it to them, but to give it to them superabundantly. If they were to possess this Divine life, they must possess it in fullest measure. If they were to live by His Sacred Passion, He must not only make them so live, but must come Himself to make them live more keenly. His words, His Divine promises, had always pointed to this. Men were to "live by Him"—as if it was to be no longer their powers that did the work, or their energy that carried them to God, but His; as if it were not to be even the Holy Spirit's ordinary indwelling or prompting merely that made them live a holy life, but the special union of His being with their being, making their action His action, their ardour His ardour, their heart His Heart. This is what the holy Fathers and the Doctors teach about the Blessed Sacrament—that it is a most mighty and indescribable union of Christ with man; a union, not of flesh with flesh, although the Sacred Body of Jesus is the means or instrument of it, but a union of the will, intelligence, and impulses of Jesus with the will, intelligence, and impulses of man. It is not merely, as you will observe, that the holy Eucharist increases sanctifying grace. It does so most truly; but the grace that it brings has a specific character of its own; and its characteristic grace consists in a certain quickening and intensifying of the holy activity of the will and heart, causing fervour, devotion, oblation, and immolation. The Holy

Sacrament seems to give the soul a right—I boldly call it a right—to the special assistance of God's continual actual grace to love Him generously with the whole heart. Is it not this fervour of the will, this transformation of the whole being, that we read of everywhere in the lives of the Saints? This is the " liquefaction " of which St. Cyril of Jerusalem speaks —the blending of our will and our emotions with those of Jesus Christ. This is what St. Bonaventure calls " incorporation in Jesus," resulting in " illumination of the mind, strengthening of faith, increase of hope, and intensifying of charity." This is what Our Lord intended to teach St. Gertrude when He appeared to her after Communion, under the symbol of the pelican, of whom the legend says that it feeds its young with the blood of its breast ; the blood signifying the life, and the life of Jesus passing into our lives. And this is what the Ven. Jean Baptiste Vianney expresses most touchingly and originally when he says that the soul after Communion is like the bee that feasts in the chalice of the flower, immersed in sweetness not its own ; so penetrated and changed by what it finds in Jesus that in its words, its acts, its life, you no longer recognise it for the same soul. And it is with this feeling that the holy Fathers dwell upon that marked effect of Holy Communion —the strong resisting power which the soul there receives ; a strength against external tempting which is the clearest proof of the strength of this life within. There is a most touching passage in a letter of the great St. Cyprian to Pope Cornelius, urging that the

Holy Communion may be given to certain of the faithful who had yielded to persecution, but had long ago sincerely repented. Another persecution was clearly at hand, and the great Bishop of Carthage exclaims : " We cannot send them without arms or shield into the dangers of the battle ; they must be fortified by the Body and Blood of Christ. It is the very end and purpose of the Eucharist to guard in safety those who partake of it, and we must shield with the food which is Christ, those whom we would secure against the adversary. We cannot bid them shed their blood in martyrdom, if before the conflict we deny them the Blood of Christ."[1] Here is the voice of Catholic tradition and Catholic conviction. This is what the Church has taught in the beginning, and what she teaches now and to the end. He who worthily partakes of Holy Communion is filled with a life and strength that is not his own. The words of St. Catherine of Genoa are like an echo of St. Paul when she says, speaking of the effects of Communion : " I have no longer any soul, no longer any heart —my soul and my heart are those of my Divine love." So are those in the life of St. Gertrude, to whom Our Lord said : " Behold My Heart !—I give it to thee that it may supply what is wanting in thee."[2] So are those of St. Catherine of Sienna, who prayed that God would create in her a new heart, and to whom Our Lord said: " My daughter, I have thy heart, and I give

[1] Ep. 54.
[2] Mgr. Bougaud, *Revelation of the Sacred Heart*, p. 136.

thee Mine, that thou mayest for ever live in Me."[1] So it was when the Blessed Margaret Mary symbolically received her heart back burning and flaming from its immersion in the Heart of Jesus. Could there be a truer and more exact illustration of what takes place by Holy Communion? What is the heart? It is the will, the desire, the resolution, the emotion, the love. And, according to theology, it is these that are changed; nature sheds her natural impulses, and new and supernatural impulses take their place. But this new energy and operation precisely resembles, and, as it were, reproduces the activity of the Heart of Our Lord Himself, the love of His Father, the consecration, the lowliness, the spirit of suffering, and the ardour for souls, with which that Sacred Heart was for ever consumed. How true then it is to say that, in the Holy Communion the heart of the servant of God is exchanged for the Heart of Christ—the very life of the natural man for the life of the Son of God —"I live, now not I, but Christ liveth in me."

Yes, even while we still walk upon the earth— even while we are still surrounded by earthly perils, hampered by earthly ties, distressed by earthly little-nesses, we may live by Christ's life, move by Christ's spirit, breathe with Christ's breath. This, as far as feeble human words can express it, is what He in-stituted the Sacrament of the Eucharist to effect. The perils still exist; the temptations still oppress and allure; the enemy still watches for our ruin.

---

[1] Mgr. Bougaud, *Revelation of the Sacred Heart*, p. 138.

But we live ; we are robust ; we possess that gift which the Council of Trent calls the " antidote " and the " preservative." We move amid temptation, not absolutely safe, but, if we are only humble, with little to fear. For, first, the Holy Communion brings with it a special illumination, strengthening faith, inclining the heart to the spiritual, and surrounding us with that atmosphere of the supernatural which causes a horror of sin and a shrinking from defilement. We read of Jonathan, when he and the people were faint on that hard day in the forest, and the enemy near, that when he " carried his hand to his mouth " and tasted the wild honey, " his eyes were enlightened."[1]   And when the disciples at Emmaus had broken the holy Bread and eaten, their eyes were opened. Next, the Communion of Christ in the Eucharist has a peculiar power of keeping at bay the demon, and of putting him to flight. " When the demons," says St. John Chrysostom, " see in us the Blood of the Lord, they fear and flee away—and the angels press around us."[2]   Do not suppose that these words are meaningless. The devils cannot make us sin ; but unless all Catholic tradition is mistaken, they can so act on the nerves and sensitiveness of the living being as to lead us into temptation ; and the angels, on the other hand, exercise their office in keeping us in peace and gently urging us to what is good. O Holy Table, which David foresaw prepared in the wilderness, for the sheep of the

[1] I Kings xiv. 27.   [2] Hom. 45 and 61.

Good Shepherd, against those that would harass and hurt them![1] And, finally, even if attacks continue to be made from without, the Presence of Christ's Body has secured the fortress within. Nature still remains human nature, with its passions, its natural propensities, and its acquired bad habits. These things are called by the holy Fathers the "fuel of sin," "the diseases of the soul." You have read how when the Ark of the Lord entered the Red Sea, the "waters feared and stood still."[2] St. Cyril says that the Blessed Sacrament calms concupiscence. There can be no doubt that all Christian antiquity is in agreement in describing a certain powerful effect which, by its innate prerogative, the holy Eucharist exerts upon the animal nature of man. Human beings are proud, malicious, prone to anger, slothful, covetous, sensual ; they are excitable, irritable, morbid, keenly alive to pleasure, unstable, vain, and light of heart. Neither the student of the mind nor the physician of the body can say precisely how much a man's make or disposition depends on the bodily tissues, nerves, and organs, and how much on deliberate volition ; how far a man is born good or bad ; how far he makes himself so; how far he can undo the harm that is done ; how far he can purify and perfect himself by strenuous endeavour. But it is certain that salvation depends on the power of quelling and controlling this lower nature ; and it is also certain that, apart from, and in addition to, the

[1] Ps. xvii. 6.   [2] Ps. lxxvi. 17.

ordinary grace that gives such power of control to
the will, the Body of Christ has been given to us
after the fashion of food, in order to do by its own
power, and most effectively, what many years of discipline and labour would hardly effect—to weaken
evil passion, to clear away evil habits, to diminish the
impulses born in us and leading to sin; to send
coursing through the senses, the fancy, the imagination, and all the regions of animal being, a purifying
and healing ether direct from His own Sacred Body.

And now, my brethren, if we believe all this—as
we must believe it—there remains still the difficulty
—the unsolved puzzle—why, in spite of this ineffable
Sacrament of transformation, there is, nevertheless,
in the world so little of the likeness of Jesus Christ.
In the world, I say; but I mean in the Church, in
the purchased people, in the spiritual Israel of God.
I mean even in those who firmly trust in it, who
venerate it, who partake of it. The attempt to account for this would lead us into some strange questions, and would reveal some curious secrets of our
fallen nature. But whilst we mourn for our own
shortcomings, let us conclude to-day with thanksgiving. For whatever may be the coldness of men
and the miseries of worldliness, yet there is, in the
results and effects of the Blessed Sacrament, a wide
theme for gratitude, a whole universe for triumph.
Who shall count the number of deadly sins prevented, the good desires cherished into blossom and
fruit, the good sacrifices made, the good deaths
brought about, by Jesus in the Sacrament of life?

Who shall count the martyrs, the confessors, the virgins, the holy and heroic hearts of every condition and century, who have expressed and imaged forth, in the very sight of a world which cannot pretend to ignore it, the life and the supernatural operation of the Lord of all grace! If we can see the very likeness of Christ stamped upon holy men and women, the instrument thereof has been the sacramental Communion. So have all the Saints known; so have they all proclaimed. And all this time I have been thinking of that glorious Virgin-Mother, whose heart we venerate here to-day; and of her—the Saint, foundress, patroness—whose special festival it is to-day, in this church of the servants of Mary. You know well what was granted on her death-bed to St. Juliana Falconieri, by a Lord and Master Who is never outdone in love and devotedness. Her illness made it impossible for her to receive Holy Communion. But the Life of her soul's life was carried in His sacramental state near to her dying couch; in some way that He knew, she received Him; and after death the effigy of the Sacred Host was found imprinted on her breast. It was only a symbol, that miraculous impression, although we praise God for it. But it fitly symbolised that true image, that spiritual transformation, which God, in the greatest of His Sacraments, had wrought within her from the time of her first Communion; which He had made more and more true and living as the years of her service went on, and which He had perfected at the moment when death was about to release her soul—to set it free, that it might for ever enjoy in unveiled bliss what it had held fast on earth by faith and love. May the Sacred Heart be praised eternally for this greatest of all His gifts to His Saints! And may we, sinners as we are, confide in Him, trust in Him, more warmly and more absolutely day by day, that if He grant us grace, our life may grow in some degree to be truly His life, and not our own.

THE CONTINUED PRESENCE.

Preached in the Church of St. Dominic, Newcastle-on-Tyne, May 1st, 1898.

"You shall not see Me; and again a little while and you shall see Me" (John xvi. 16).

THIS "little while" is that space of mortal life during which men see not Jesus, but await the dawn of the day of eternity, when they shall see Him, if He grant His help, face to face, world without end. Our Lord calls the duration of human life "a little while." To us who are passing through it, it may sometimes seem long. The world's generations, the world's annals, with their thousands of years, their varied story, their slow revolutions, their growths and their achievement, may appear to human appreciation to be imposing and august. But when it shall be given to the spirit of man to look back upon time from eternity, then will time seem to shrink and to fade ; then shall we begin to understand, with the Psalmist and St. Peter, that "one day with the Lord is as a thousand years, and a thousand years as one day."

But, short as our life is here below, and insignificant as is time with all its pride and turmoil, life and time are profoundly momentous to ourselves. It is on the present that the all-important future absolutely depends. Brief as our probation is, we may fail in it. Short as the passage may be, it is possible to lose our way.

Can it be true, then, that during the space of our earthly journey we must be content never to see Our Lord? Are we so much worse off than those to whom He granted the sight of Himself in the flesh, during His life on earth—during those days of grace and intercommunion, from the baptism of John to the Ascension, which He also designates a "little while"?

He certainly does tell us we shall not see Him. He must go to the Father. His earthly mission will have been accomplished. Bethlehem, Nazareth, Calvary, will soon be names, written for ever on human annals. The thirty-three years have come to an end, and the Son of Man must withdraw from an earth which He has consecrated by His Presence and His Precious Blood. It would seem, in very truth, as if the eyes which were to see Him lifted into the clouds on Mount Olivet were then to look their last upon Him, and that the light of the world would thenceforward shine no more.

But have we so inadequately "learned Christ," that we cannot understand that the impulses of His mercy are never sacrificed even to what seem the plans of His infinite wisdom? Ought we not to know well that the history of God's dealings with His children is a history of His breaking through barriers, annihilating distance, and bending laws to His sovereign will? Is it possible that any one who knows of that stupendous interference which is called the Incarnation, will not feel sure that even if Jesus goes up to Heaven He will still manage to remain on earth ?

The Incarnation had been given to the world as it were to falsify—or shall we say to supersede?—many of the things that God said of Himself in the Old Testament. You know what I mean. God cannot come near the least shadow of falsehood. Yet what had He said about Himself? To the Jews He was the One Whom no man should ever behold and live ;[1] Whose voice one perhaps might hear, but Whose form was ever invisible ;[2] Whom the Heaven of heavens could not contain ;[3] Who looked down from the far heavens and read the most secret thoughts of the just and the unjust ; Who gave His commands to the angels, and moved the foundations of the world. It is true that, to us who now look back through the prophecies and the Psalms, there are, in spite of these declarations, clear indications of what was to come. As far back as the records of Exodus and Leviticus He had promised to set up His tent in Israel, and to dwell in the midst of them.[4] But from these oracular words, in the face of the solemn and awful proclamation of the inscrutable majesty of God, repeated in every chapter of the Scripture, who could have foretold Bethlehem ? Who could have foreseen Jesus, the Son of Mary ? Who could have expected the shedding of the Precious Blood ? God, as it would seem, could not restrain

[1] Exodus xxx. 5.   [2] Deut. iv.   [3] 3 Kings viii. 27.
[4] Exodus xxix. 45 ; Lev. xxvi. 11.

Himself. That, indeed, is what the Fathers and the Saints have said. " Man does not love Me because he does not see Me. I wish to make Myself seen by him, and to converse with him, and so make Myself loved." These are the words which St. Alphonsus puts into the mouth of the Lord God of Heaven. There is a passage in the prophecy of Isaias in which Almighty God shows His Divine solicitude for His people, whom the Chaldæans and Babylonians were oppressing : " And now, what have I here, saith the Lord, for My people is taken away gratis "—led into captivity and no price paid. " What have I here ! " Where, my brethren ? The commentators tell us that the God of Israel is speaking of the empty city and the deserted sanctuary. " My people have left My temple," He seems to say, " and My heart is sad ; therefore will I come down ;" " without payment were ye sold, and without payment shall ye be redeemed." But the Saints have referred this most human and pleading cry of the Eternal Creator not to Jerusalem, but to Heaven itself. " What have I here "—even in Heaven, now that My people are in captivity ? " Therefore shall My people know My name in that day : for I Myself that spoke, behold I am here."[1]

This is the Divine philosophy of the Incarnation. Must we expect that these longings of God, these pressing impulses of fatherhood, these imperative workings of the Creator's breast—for we must use human language here—will cease, die out, disappear,

---

[1] Isaias lii. 5, 6.

as long as there are human souls painfully toiling on
the road between earth and eternity ?   It can never
be so.   He has said, " A little while and you shall
not see Me."   But somehow or other we do expect
to see Him, even before He comes in the clouds of
the judgment.   Men have many faculties that can
know and possess ; they can see, and can hear, and
can understand, with more than one set of powers.
But whether it be with the eye of the sense, the eye
of the mental imagination, the eye of the pure spirit,
or the eye of faith—we do expect, we do promise
ourselves, that despite the plain words of our merciful
Redeemer, He is too merciful, too loving, not to let
Himself be seen, and seen in some very solid fashion
by those whom He has left behind.

The truth is—and you will have readily anticipated
me—that, in the inheritance of the Christian, there
are many dispensations by which Jesus Christ, Who
sitteth at the right hand of God, is visible and
sensible to men on earth.   I wish to dwell on only
one of these.

Everything sacramental—using the word Sacrament in the full Catholic sense—is a bringing of Christ
into contact with the receiver ; for there is, with the
outward rite, an outpouring of supernatural grace,
which, as I need not say, can come from Christ and
Christ alone.   But there is one Sacrament—the queen
of all the Sacraments—which brings Christ so truly,
which stands for Him so intimately, which takes Divine
possession of so many human powers, which so occu-
pies the spaces of man's world, is so felt by the human

senses, and so fills with echoes all the air of this lower realm, that it stands out among the things left us in legacy by Christ, as by excellence the continuation of His sensible presence. You will understand that I mean the Blessed Eucharist.

It is impossible, in one sermon, to dwell upon every feature of the institution of the Blessed Sacrament. But I would point out very briefly and plainly, how that most marvellous and loving gift enables men in their pilgrimage to see that Divine Master Who said " a little while and you shall not see Me."

When God comes down among men, whether He comes in the supreme condescension of the Incarnation, or under any other veil, men can never recognise Him unless He Himself gives them the light or illumination which enables them to do so. He may send His precursors ; He may work His miracles ; He may speak as never man spoke ; He may even rise again from the dead ; but men will never accept Him merely for these things. I do not say that miracles and fulfilled prophecy, and words and deeds, and the great miracle of resurrection, may not convince the intelligence. But if a man is to worship the hidden God under the earthly presentment, there must be other forces brought to bear upon his heart than these. The Divine stranger, Who would be recognised, must make hearts burn ; He must " open the understanding that they should understand ";[1] He must give, in St. Paul's phrases,

---

[1] Luke xxiv. 45.

"the spirit of revelation," the illumination of the
"eyes of the heart";[1] He must anoint the infirm
senses of mortal men with that sovereign eye-salve
of which St. John speaks in the Apocalypse.[2] You
read that these things were done by Jesus Christ.
You read that He said : "No man cometh to Me
unless My Father draw him."[3] You read that
Apostles followed Him at His word, that sinful men
fell down before Him, that harlots repented at His
feet, that heathens came for baptism to His servants,
that Jews and persecutors surrendered to His Name.
You hear St. John[4] explaining the conversion of
the world by saying, "God hath given us understanding."

But what do we find among the treasures that
Christ has left? We find a mystery—a dispensation
—called the Real Eucharistic Presence, which has
this very power of attraction and illumination which
Our Lord possessed upon earth.

It may be said, without incurring any charge of
exaggeration, that there is nothing on earth which,
on the whole, so powerfully draws the heart of men
to God as the grand Eucharistic mystery. The
Eucharist is in the world like a great light set up on
high. The world may strive against it, and blas-
pheme it, but it cannot disregard it. Even in the
very early days of Christianity, when the great mysteries had to be celebrated with closed doors—when
the secret of them was kept religiously as treasures

---

[1] Eph. i. 17, 18.   [2] Apoc. iii. 18.   [3] John xvi. 44.
[4] I John v. 20.

are kept—the world had a kind of knowledge that the Christians professed to have their God very near them in the rites which they practised. The three accusations which were made against the Church assemblies in the first centuries were—Atheism, the slaying and eating of children, and licentious crime. Two of these charges I may pass over. But when the pagans insisted that they put children to death and ate their flesh, it is clear that some knowledge, some undoubted intimation of the Eucharistic mystery had crept outside of the shut-up chambers and out of the sombre catacombs. And the pagan world —masters who had Christian slaves, husbands who had Christian wives, men of the world who heard what men were saying, philosophers who wrote against Christ— all these by degrees came to recognise and feel that there was something holy, august, and powerful going on at their very doors. They observed how a Christian was drawn as by magnetic power to his assembly, how he went there without breaking his fast, how he returned breathing serenity and strength. They noticed how the Christian apologist, whilst he rejected with horror the nefarious accusations made, yet admitted that there was a sacred banquet, and never said that it was mere bread or wine, or other human food ; in the words of Origen, the greatest of them : " Our Gospels are known in the whole world, but we have a secret ; we do eat bread which becomes a sacred body ; we do eat the flesh of the Lamb that was slain."[1] Since the world became Christian, the

[1] *Contra Celsum*, Lib. VIII.

holy Eucharist has been as overpoweringly visible as
the very Gospels.   The earliest church of which we have
details, in the fourth century, had a sanctuary and an
altar of sacrifice.   The earliest Church books are
liturgies which contain the offering, the consecration,
and the communion.   The dispute which ushered in
the Middle Ages gave to the Church the word " tran-
substantiation," and imparted to faith an impulse
which, during four centuries, built the grandest sanctuaries the world has ever known—the great churches
of Christian Europe, all intended, and fashioned, and
contrived for the enthronisation of the Eucharist.
When Jansenism, a plague which threatened to be as
devastating as Protestantism, was beaten back and
trodden out, it was by a manifestation of Eucharistic
devotion which is still growing in splendour, and
which has made it impossible for any thinking man
not to know the tenets of the Catholic Church on the
reality and the use of the Blessed Sacrament.

It will be admitted by all who have either had
personal experience in converting souls, or who have
followed the history of the past and read the experience of others, that it is this visible presence of the
Eucharist in the world which attracts hearts more
than all other gifts of Jesus Christ.   It is the preaching of the Eucharist which makes those to whom we
preach feel that the Blood of Calvary still flows in
very truth for the sinful and the weak.   It is the
thought of the Eucharist which makes the heart of
the seeker for truth cry out, " Oh ! if I only knew for
certain that there was a Sacrament, and such a Sac-

rament as this!" It is the presence in the tabernacle which so often, as we well know, sends non-Catholic visitors of our churches home with their breasts filled with emotion and their eyes running over with tears. It is that presence which strikes like a wave of holy influence on the faithful Catholic as he enters the temple of God. It is that which bows down his head as he sinks on his knees, and keeps him recollected before the sanctuary. It is the Real Presence of our Lord Jesus Christ which invests the mysterious function of the Mass with so firm a hold on the powers of the soul—so that we come to church for the Mass, wait for the completion of the Mass, hear as many Masses as we can, and feel happy when the Mass has sanctified the day, and diffused its fragrance over our lives as they hasten forward to eternity. There is no Sacrament which does not awake and bring into activity this singular power of attraction and illumination possessed by the Real Presence. A Communion, which outwardly seems only a partaking of bread, becomes by that Presence not merely a partaking of the Body and Blood of Jesus Christ, but an inundation of powerful grace, which makes the very inmost citadel of the rational will tremble in the realisation of the unseen Godhead. The penitent, who thinks over his sins in sorrowful meditation, feels the purity of that Presence urging and constraining him to detest them and to turn once for all to the Lord and God Who is so near. Whoever seek's Christ's minister and the consolations of holy Church, in health or in sickness, amid the

troubles of life or in the darkening twilight of approaching death, feels himself wistfully looking also
for a further ministration, a mightier gift—and there
is an instinct in the child of faith which refuses to
be happy or content without the Blessed Sacrament.
The priesthood themselves, whilst they learn from
their earliest years that they belong to the Eucharistic
presence, and are conscious, every hour, that it is that
Presence which gives form to their being and life to
their spiritual labour, well understand, at the same
time, that all their exertions for the good of souls
must be aimed, directly or indirectly, at bringing
their people to the hidden God. The sanctuary is
their home, the altar is their inheritance—and when
they leave the holy of holies to stand in the pulpit
and to speak to their people, whatever be the theme
of the words they utter there is one subject which,
like a text or a chapter-heading or a musical refrain,
comes up again and again, marked, urgent, insistent
—and that is the mystery of love, the Most Holy Sacrament. Thus does the attraction of that Presence
pervade the church, and even the world. Not to all
does it make itself sensible. Always, as in the days
of the thirty-three years, is there an outside multitude
who, for reasons partly evident, partly easy to divine,
partly hidden from our view, are allowed to live in
the same world with Jesus and to disregard Him;
to hear Him and yet not hear Him, to see Him and
to see Him not. But how strong, how wide, how
merciful is His illuminating grace! What would it
have availed had He instituted the Blessed Sacrament,

written the proofs of it in every tongue with letters of
fire, set up a precious tabernacle in every land—had
He not also given to it that power which He alone
can exercise, of persuading, convincing, drawing the
hearts of men and women ?   Do I say " given to it " ?
I should rather say—for it is Himself—deigned to
display, to exert, to put in operation that grace of
Divine " drawing " which belongs to Him and to
Him alone !

We have, then, in the world, notwithstanding the
words of Jesus that, for a time, we should " not see
Him," a sensible Presence of Himself which has a
continuous, wonderful, and inexhaustible power of
taking hold of the heart and the faith of men.   Jesus
Christ, in the Blessed Sacrament, offers Himself to
the sight and sensible experience of men ; and where-
ever He is found by the eye, He is ready to make
the intelligence accept Him and the will surrender
itself to Him.

And now let us observe what is signified by that
phrase, " wherever He is found."   You read in the
Gospel of St. John how Andrew said to Simon
Peter, " We have found the Messias," and how he
" brought him to Jesus."[1]   They found that Lord and
Saviour, then, probably in a hut made of branches
on the banks of the river where John was baptising.
He was nowhere else in the world !   Before that time
there were shepherds who had found Him in the cave
at Bethlehem ; He was there, and only there !   Some

[1] John i. 41.

thirty years of His earthly life He had been enshrined in the tabernacle of the holy House of
Nazareth—there, and only there! Afterwards, He
was to be found in Jerusalem, in Galilee, in the
Temple, by the lake, on the mountain, on the dusty
roads of Palestine—and they that sought Him had to
watch for Him and to wait for Him and to follow
Him. Later still, He hung upon the Cross, and
although He was dying for the whole world, and the
whole world felt the shock and the power of that
moment, yet His Presence was sensible only to those
who stood around, and was shrouded by the darkness
even from them! The huge world with its multitudes
could neither see Him nor hear His voice. Neither
kings nor peoples knew Him to be present in the
world ; and had they known, and had they wished to
find Him, what pains, what journeys, what long
delays would have been needed before they stood
before the Real Presence of God Incarnate !

My brethren, it was Christ's design to give to the
world a Presence of Himself which should break
through all the laws of space, and time, and quantity ; a Presence which should continue through all
the ceaseless march of time, and should be found at
one and the same moment over all the continents and
islands of this orb of the world, wherever there were
men and women. Does any one doubt that God could
do this thing? Does it seem a contradiction, an utter
impossibility, that the Body of Christ, which is a
material Body, being a human Body, should be
so multiplied, so spiritualised, and yet continue the

true Body, born of Mary ever Virgin, crucified, and risen ? The essential constitution of matter, and the laws of matter, are most imperfectly known to us. But there is no contradiction or absurdity in this—that a material thing should be distinguishable from those qualities by which it affects our senses ; that a material thing which, left to itself, would fill space, touch adjacent surfaces, and spread out in recognisable dimensions, should be so isolated, so cut off from the universe, so concentrated on itself, by Divine power, as to be out of the reckonings which have space and time, size, shape, sensible extension, for their elements. We might not be able to say beforehand, and by the mere light of reason, that this was possible ; but when there is a demonstrated Catholic doctrine, an accepted and proved dogma, which requires such a hypothesis, then we have no difficulty in accepting it—for there is clearly no intrinsic contradiction to exclude it from the realm of thought. Thus, just as in the Gospel of St. John, the Body of Christ, after the resurrection, without ceasing to be a true material Body, passes through closed doors, so in the Eucharist that sacred Body is without quantity, without shape, without effect on the ethers of the world and the surfaces of things— but yet possessing all the essential and inherent capability of producing such effect, did not the hand which guided the waters of the Red Sea and which turned the water into wine, forbid it, for the sake of His people, that they might possess Him.

The bread and the wine, then, depart, leaving be-

hind them those qualities which affect our senses;
the Body of Christ (with His soul and His Godhead)
succeeds to them, and is, in a certain sense, like to a
spirit, without immediate relation to our senses.   It
is a great miracle, and must always remain an adorable mystery.   But why has God wrought that
miracle?   Why does He set this mystery in the front
of His redeeming ordinances?   It is in order that
men may not lose sight of their Redeemer, even now
that He has gone up to the heavens.   It was only
in this way, and by such an effort of power, that it
has become possible for Christ, the Word made flesh,
to be in the world, visibly, tangibly, unmistakably, in
every age and in innumerable places.   The "thirty-
three years" could not have lasted for all time without miraculous interferences such as would not have
been compatible with God's dispensations.   Even had
Jesus remained continuously as He was seen by Mary
or by John, He would only have been in one spot of
this earth.   And had we been privileged to look on
His adorable face as they looked upon it, who shall
say that the world would have been any better for
it than those Jews and pagans who passed Him by,
or even put Him to death?

But now every church is Bethlehem, every church
is Nazareth, every altar is Calvary.   No long and
painful journey is needed to come into His Presence.
He is at hand to the poorest and the most infirm.
Every day is the day on which He is ready to receive
His people.   Crowds may come, and a man's individual communings are not disturbed, for each one

has Jesus all to himself. If there are no crowds, if even single visitors are rare, He remains patiently in silence, in solitude, ready when faith and affection move His people to visit Him. And it is not merely a Presence which this stupendous Eucharistic dispensation has made possible. It is a Sacrifice—not a sacrifice as sacrifices most naturally are, with slaying and streams of blood and the mounting of smoky flames to the sky; not a sacrifice of vast labour and huge preparation ; yea, more—not a sacrifice appalling terrible, crushing the heart to think of, as was on Calvary His own one great Sacrifice ; but a sweet and gentle sacrifice, an easy and beautiful sacrifice, renewing Calvary day by day without the awful circumstances which could never be repeated ; a welcome and comfortable sacrifice, in which, with white linen and lights and flowers, is lifted up the Lamb Who desires to dwell always among the children of men. And not a sacrifice only, but a Communion; for by the dispensation of the real Eucharistic Presence it has become possible to use the Body of Christ as the outward sign of a Sacrament ; as food which is really Jesus Himself, and whose virtue it is, when worthily received, to seize the inmost and strongest will of all man's many wills, and to make it like to the will of His Saviour.

And tell me not, my brethren, that all this supposes faith, and cannot be called " seeing "; that Christ is hidden as God is hidden, and that the Eucharistic veils are far more impenetrable than the humanity of Jesus of Nazareth. Far be it from me to deny that

the Blessed Eucharist requires the exercise of faith,
or to explain away the clouds which hide the tabernacle.   It is just these clouds which make the august
dispensation possible ; it is just faith which gives the
Real Presence its penetrating power.   But is there
only faith ?   Is there only mystery ?   Is there only
the hushed coldness of the unknown ?   This is what
I have been coming to—and it is with this I must
conclude.   What I assert, and what you cannot hesitate to admit, is that the Eucharistic presence is a
visible and sensible Presence.   You can see the
Blessed Sacrament ; you can touch it ; you know
where it is.   There is a moment—a moment of
devout lifting up of men's hearts and bowing down
of their heads—when it is there where before it was
not.   It has a house ; it has a dwelling.   It has a
ministry of living men to bring it on the earth,
to handle it, to distribute it.   As truly, though
not in precisely the same sense as one can meet a
friend or describe living men, record men's movements, or seek out their bodily presence, one can find
where Jesus is, and say when He came and what His
surroundings are, and when or how He goes away.
The whole history of the Catholic Church is an illustration of this.   In the catacombs you find the
presence and the ministry.   In the very shape of our
churches you see the part which belongs to the
Blessed Sacrament.   In the lifting up of the great
domes of the basilicas you see a canopy over
Christ's head.   In the exquisite altar-pieces of Gothic
cathedrals you see the ornamentation of His throne.

In the written liturgies—traditional long before they were written—you see the setting of the Eucharistic act in the consecration, the prayer, the communion. In the treasures that faith and love have lavished on the worship of the Blessed Sacrament you have the expressed conviction of a localised Presence ; the conviction that where the golden citadel is, where the precious tabernacle is, where the marble altar is, where the noble arches of the temple spring to Heaven, there is present—not merely as God is present everywhere, but in that new and solid sense which is part of the Christian inheritance—there is present the very Word made flesh.

Here, then, is a dispensation which God has exerted all His omnipotence to bring about—and which we, for whom it is given, must exert all the powers of our souls and bodies to use to the utmost. It is a feature of this mystery of love that it is left in the hands of men. When Jesus was on earth during the thirty-three years, He was not passive and silent as He is in the Eucharist. Even in His solitude and His long obedience He seemed to be master of Himself, as He always is. Only when Mary carried Him in her arms—only when loving hands laid His dead Body in the tomb—did He seem to have no will or spontaneity. But in this continued Eucharistic presence, unless men call Him down, He comes not ; unless men lift Him up, He rises not ; unless men receive Him, He remains a stranger at the door ; unless men visit Him, He abides in silent loneliness. Innumerable thoughts of our responsibilities spring up as we

think on this.   And there is one special thought
which may console all those hearts of sacrifice who
are anxious to help in the building of churches.   As
we celebrated the solemnities of the Mass this morning in the new Church of St. Laurence, I thought of
what those walls meant; of the coming of men to
Jesus, the lifting up of the heart to Jesus, the pressing near to Him, the sorrow for sin for His sake, the
abundance of graces from His nearness — which a
church must bring about.   Happy and thrice happy
is he who has a share in this.   Who can doubt that
the Blessed Sacrament is the grand source, on earth,
of faith, conversion, contrition, amendment, sanctity ?
May God multiply churches, and fill them with wor-
shippers, that the greatness of His mercy be not given
to the world in vain !

THE SUPREME HOMAGE.

Preached in St. George's Cathedral, Southwark, at the Jubilee of the Dedication, July 3rd, 1898.

" My kingdom is not of this world " (John xviii. 36).

THESE are the words of Him Who said by His Prophet in the Psalm, " I am appointed by the Lord King over Sion, His holy mountain."[1] And both declarations are true ; and each of them enshrines a living truth which is one of the great truths on which religion is built. The kingdom of Christ is not of this world ; not a kingdom of nationalities, of territory, of armies or navies, of taxation, of commerce, of house-building, of money-making. The royalty of Christ brought no menace to the emperor ; it carried no pretension to any throne in the East or the West ; it called no nation to arms ; it unfurled no banner of freedom, of vengeance, or of conquest. The vast, the complex, and the irresistible organisation with which His Name was to be associated was not to interfere— or was only to interfere indirectly—with the soldier, the minister, the magistrate, the merchant, the servant, the father of the family, or with any office or profession instituted to carry on human life on this earth. His kingdom He did not inherit from

[1] Ps. ii. 6.

any king of the ancient time, or accept from any vote of the people. His throne was not one that had been won in blood ; His sceptre was not to be subject to the vicissitudes of time, of anarchy, or of revolution. He would never head armies, or dictate codes of justice. The world, with its needs, its ambitions, its passions, and its sins, was to organise itself, even to the end as it had done from the beginning.

Yet the Sion over which He was to reign—the holy mountain where His throne was to be—was not only to be in the world, but was to be visible, tangible, unmistakable among all the world's phenomena and through all the world's career. It was to be, first of all, an empire over hearts, a kingdom of faith and hope, a vast union of souls in the love and adoration of Himself. But as men are not bodiless spirits, it was also to be a kingdom of common worship, of teaching, of hearing, and of sacramental dispensation. As Christ rules in the region of the human intelligence, in all the provinces of the free will, in every department of the spiritual and of the moral sense, so He must reign also over all human activity and all human intercourse. In a twofold way was He to cross the lines of worldly domination and worldly right ; first, His rule was to check and repress sin and evil, and, next, it was to challenge and assert its own right to free play, to welcome, to honour, and to supremacy everywhere. It was to be often in conflict, often apparently worsted—but on the whole to be triumphant. Its history was to fulfil that prophecy of Isaias : " Behold the sovereign Lord of

Hosts shall break the earthern vessel with terror, and the tall of stature shall be cut down, and the lofty shall be humbled. And the thickets of the forest shall be cut down with iron, and Libanus with its high ones shall fall."[1]

It is not my intention to-day to make any attempt to prove the visibility of the Church, or to describe its visible and tangible work in the world. But this anniversary may well remind us, assembled as we are in a home whose walls for fifty years have been the temple of the Eucharistic Sacrifice, and have re-echoed adoration, praise, and thanksgiving, that the kingdom of Christ on earth is not merely a school of faith, or a dispenser of the means of grace, or a teacher of good conduct; but, above all, a great association or kingdom in which the universal human race may, and should, be drawn together in that homage of mind, of will, of heart, and of feeling to Almighty God which is the grand pur-pose for which man was created. Taking the world as we find it, there is nothing which is so badly carried out as the direct worship of God. True, there is nothing that is so readily, so universally, acknow-ledged to be a duty. But the feeling with most of the world is, that it is a duty that can best be fulfilled indirectly, intermittently; that you worship God if you live decently, if you labour, if you help your neighbour, if you vaguely observe the Sabbath. Catholics are better taught. But very few, even

[1] Isaias x. 33-34.

18

among those who reflect, seem to be really impressed with what there is in their Church — what
there is in the dispensation of their Saviour, and in
their own inheritance—which is expressly intended
to make worship easy, to make worship continuous,
to reach all the springs of reverence and love, to
touch all the chords of devotion, to diffuse the sweet
atmosphere of piety throughout a life which so easily
remains cold to God and unpurified by God's nearness.

Let me recall to you a striking passage of the
Prophet, which seems to prefigure the Christian
Church. He bids the people of God realise what
they possess in that holy city of David, which God
so loved and protected : " Look upon Sion, the city
of our solemnity ; thy eyes shall see Jerusalem, a
rich habitation, a tabernacle that cannot be removed ;
neither shall the nails thereof be taken away for ever,
neither shall any of the cords thereof be broken :
because only there Our Lord is magnificent ; a place
of rivers, very broad and spacious streams ; no ship
with oars shall pass by it, neither shall the great
galley pass through it."[1]   These words could never
apply, adequately and finally, to the earthly Jerusalem.   There were no abounding streams, no fertilising river in the neighbourhood of the rock of Sion,
or in the valleys of the hills which guarded her.   But
they are true of that prophesied city, temple, habitation, tabernacle, or tent, which was to be built on the

---

[1] Isaias xxxiii. 20.

highest place of this world of human kind, whose foundations were to last for ever; whose cords and fastenings, driven in by the power of the Holy Spirit, were to be more firm than the living rock. They are true of that house of the Lord whence was to flow the stream of water that should fertilise the spiritual soul and rejoice the child of God. They are true of that dwelling-place where alone Our Lord is magnificent ; wherein He was to dwell, not merely in the miraculous *shekina*, which filled with its shining the holy of holies, but far more wonderfully under the sacramental veils of His love.

When God created a creature like man, to adore Him and serve Him, He foresaw—as even a human intellect could have foreseen—that the chief obstacle to adoration was the absence of God Himself. True, God can never be absent, really. But to be unseen and silent was to be virtually absent. And yet He could not show Himself as He is ! Therefore, the history of God's dealings with men is the history of His inventing ways of speaking to them, and of being seen by them. In the Christian dispensation— the dispensation to which the old history led up, and which is to last till the judgment shall sit—He was to be present, after the fashion that we know of, and which I need not describe, in the Eucharistic mystery. That mystery, once in the Church, once in the world, must dominate the Church and dominate in the world. Naturally, it would be the summary of faith, keeping fresh and living the revelation of God, of the Trinity, of the Incarnation, and of grace. Of

equal necessity it would create a priesthood, with
power over its ministration and over that body of
the faithful which from it derived its chief unity.   It
would by its prerogative be the chief fountain of
sanctifying grace and spiritual life.   " He that eateth
Me shall live by Me."   It would be all this.   But, in
addition, would it not be the centre of Divine worship ? Would not adoration gather round it ? Would
not homage find in it its strength and continuance ?
Where the Sovereign is, there must be the Court.
Always, and in every place, is man bound to pay
worship to his Creator.   But if He came to Bethlehem and Nazareth, it was at Bethlehem and at
Nazareth that those who knew Him would find the
keenest inspiration for their acts of homage.   And if
He has exerted His power to give us the Eucharistic
presence, it is where that Presence is found that men,
if they have the grace to know it, will gather in their
crowds and will feel God near ; it is there that they
will recognise the occasion of public, common, and
solemn worship ; it is there that they will use all their
faculties, all their means, all their art, to respond
outwardly to such a presence of such a King, and
thus the better and the more absolutely to pay that
duty of interior lifting up of the heart which both
their nature and their faith enjoin.

If, in addition to a genuine and striking Presence,
such as is found in the Eucharistic mystery, there is
also ordained by Him Who, when he went up, left us
so much, a rite the most striking, the fullest of meaning, the most intimately related to the God of the

Universe that has ever been, or could ever be, on the earth—I mean the rite of Sacrifice—there is deeper and stronger reason still for insisting that the Blessed Sacrament must be the world's call to worship.

Worship is a very simple act of the human spiritual nature. It does not require a man to study the science of it in any school. When the intelligence and the heart find themselves in the presence of their God, and recognise Him for what He is, there is kindled in the creature, spontaneously, a reverential acknowledgment, and there goes out from the creature, spontaneously, as the flame of a fire leaps out, the act of submissive adoration. I have said spontaneously ; for worship is natural and easy, and even with difficulty repressed, when the heart is unspoiled, and when that heart knows its God. But worship is not the duty of a moment that passes away and returns no more. It is the occupation of a life. It has to contend with darkness, with weariness, with indifference, and with the attractions of sense and of vanity. Worship, therefore, in its adequate sense, depends upon the exertion of the force of the human will, aided by Divine grace. The heart must be kept forcibly to its work, as the ship is strongly held to its course by the steersman's muscle. As the hours and days go on, it must be made to seize opportunities with vigour and alacrity ; to use its various powers in acts and elevations which are suggested and coloured by different considerations and motives, but which all rest finally on its relation to its God ; to turn life's times and seasons, life's joys and troubles, life's work and life's repose, and also the very moods and chequered temper of its own existence, into matter for the praise of God, and to touch them all with the consuming fire of a sacrifice. Worship is very simple; but it has as many moods as the pure unmingled waters of the boundless sea. Spiritual activity is a universe of kingdoms and provinces, too little explored even by the most fervent. How manifold is the soul of man, and how inexhaustible the fulness of God! He finds himself face to face with God's majesty and power, and his spirit pours itself out in that confession, that joy, and that thanksgiving which is covered by the unfathomable word, humility; humility, which is truth, more than abasement, and filial trust, more than destitution. " O Adonai Lord, great art Thou, and glorious in Thy power! . . . Let all creatures serve Thee, because Thou hast spoken and they were made; Thou didst send forth Thy Spirit, and they were created!"[1] He feels the great cloud of God's supreme dominion hanging over all things that are, and over himself—and the response of his spirit shapes itself like the voice of him that cried out of old, " O Lord, Father, and Sovereign Ruler of my life, forsake me not!"[2] He sees his first beginning; he sees his last end—and he is inspired to spurn all things that tempt, to immolate all desires, to order all action, to consecrate all the space between birth and dissolution, to Him, and to

---

[1] Judith xvi. 16.   [2] Ecclus. xxiii. 1.

Him alone, "Who only hath immortality."[1] He realises the inexplicable love, the generous out-pouring, the ineffable fatherhood, the impregnable friendship of the One true God of Heaven ; and he exclaims with the singer of Israel, " Bless the Lord, O my soul, and never forget all He hath done for thee ; . . . Who redeemeth thy life from de-struction, Who crowneth thee with mercy and compassion."[2]

Worship, in acts like these, should rise like the fragrance of incense from the whole earth of God's creation. But now observe what God has provided in the Church of His Son, the Church founded and perpetuated by His Spirit. We have a Presence which by its very reality hushes the spirit into awe, and disposes it to recollection and reverence ; a Presence which is of itself a sanctuary where nothing profane can intrude. We have a Presence, such as necessarily keeps God before our eyes— God with all His mysteries, God with all His reve-lations, God with all His friendliness to men. We have that Jesus Whose Heart, in the days of His earthly life, saved the world by those very acts of worship, intensified by suffering, which it is our sal-vation to imitate, to reproduce, as long as life lasts. We have, therefore, in the Blessed Sacrament, the two possessions which it would have been impossible to find in one Person had there not been the Incarna-tion—God as our worship's object, God as our wor-

---

[1] 1 Tim. vi. 16.   [2] Ps. cii. 2-4.

ship's pattern, model, and promoter. We have Him Whom we adore ; we have Him Who has adored for us, and has made satisfaction for us to the full, and has given to our own poor acts all the merit that they have. This most inspiring Presence we possess.

But we have far more even than this. Had there been nothing futher than this august Presence, human worship would have been all the easier, all the richer for it. Nay, if you will observe, worship, and public worship, is possible even without the Eucharistic presence. We are accustomed to find religious functions bare and dry without the Blessed Sacrament. A non-Catholic church or meeting-house appears to us cold and even repulsive, because it is not there. Yet, unless the superabounding love of Christ had so willed, there might have been no presence possible but the invisible God and the memory of the Incarnation. And worship might have gone on, and well gone on, whether under the lofty roof of a cathedral or within the whitewashed walls of the commonest of chapels. The Christian, even without the Eucharist, has motives of the strongest, and facilities the most abundant, to adore His God. Many a servant of Jesus Christ has been long deprived of that Presence, and yet has been very near to his Master ; and I would fain add that not a few of our separated brethren, without tabernacle or altar, but not having sinned against the light, by God's grace lift up acceptable prayer. No; it is not that man cannot worship without the Blessed Sacrament ; but that the Blessed Sacrament has made worship incomparably more intense and meritorious. It is the character of all low types of Christianity, such as we find in misbelief and in the practical misbelief of indifferent Catholics, to be content with far less than God has been ready to give them. The Incarnation has brought in a lofty and perfect type of spiritual service. Not only a supernatural life, but the intimate union of the Holy Spirit; not only virtues, but gifts; not only grace, but keen, sovereign, and abounding grace—these things are meant to be the characters of Our Lord's religion. And this is verified in Christian worship. It is intended to be, and, thanks be to God, it truly is, in the Church of God, not mere worship, and not merely virtuous worship, accepted worship, or Christian worship; but worship of a certain unearthly character, such as transfigures the worshipper and prepares great thrones, lofty thrones, for a yet higher worship in eternity.

What is that which, in the Church of Christ, makes Christian worship what it is—so perfect, so august, so Divine? Need I say that it is the Eucharistic Sacrifice?

In a certain sense, it would seem to be impossible for men to worship—habitually and in common—without the rite of sacrifice. The heart can always and anywhere, by the help of grace, lift itself to its God. But we speak of general homage, public homage, national homage, homage in its widest form and its highest intensity—such a homage as that which arises from a gathered multitude, where each heart of all those present finds its acts inten-

sified by the communion of numbers. What can a
religious meeting be without sacrifice? True, we
have already admitted the possibility of real worship
even without sacrifice or Eucharist. But, speaking
now comparatively, and having in view what men are
and what man's nature is, worship in its highest form
seems to require sacrifice. What can happen at an
assembly where there is no priest, no altar? First,
there can be preaching and teaching ; but that is not
worship. Next, there can be the prayer of a leader
or a minister. I would not undervalue such prayer ;
but it has this shortcoming, that it does not call upon
my own soul for its efforts. When my pastor prays
aloud and in public, I may be edified, instructed, and
even warmed to devotion ; but, as a rule, my own
worship has to begin when his prayer has ended.
The public prayer of a minister can rarely be common prayer, and therefore rarely common worship
Again, there may be common recitation or singing.
This also may be good and acceptable. But if there
were nothing more, there would always be something
wanting ; there would be missing the strong, definite,
single, and simple impulse which can only result from
a strong and well-defined common purpose or act.
Common praying or singing is like the parade of
an army in the presence of its king ; but is there not
a difference when that army is charging in grim
earnest to save its king from capture? And, practically speaking, what do we find in the religious
assemblies whence the Mass has been banished? Do
we not find that men go to them to be talked to,

rather than to lift up their hearts ; to hear worship rather than to make it ; to be passive rather than spiritually active ; to feel tranquil and good amidst impressive surroundings, rather than to pour out warm affections to their Creator ?

But the Church of Christ has the Mass. That is, in our religious gatherings we have in our midst a most real, definite, and far-reaching act of sacrifice. It is as if the people once more came together after the Flood, upon the side of the mountain, and watched the altar erected, the victim slain thereon, and the fire going up, in acknowledgment of the sovereign majesty and power of God. No need for a leader to pray aloud, no need for canticle or psalm ; every heart in that multitude is joining in an act impressive and significant. Our sacrifice is that of the Cross, not repeated, but continued in order that its fruit may be the more widely applied. At a certain moment, with solemn preparation and impressive surroundings, the mystic nails are driven in and the blood mystically flows again, and the Heart of Jesus offers Himself in mystic immolation. Then, as the Prophet foretold, " They shall come, and they shall give praise upon Mount Sion ; and they shall flock together to the good things of the Lord."[1] It is for this that we assemble ; it is this that fires our hearts ; it is this that draws forth each heart's affections ; it is this that joins us in common adoration. It is not merely that the august Presence makes us realise

[1] Jer. xxxi. 12.

our God, and turns the house of stone into the
house of God and the gate of Heaven. Neither is
it that we only stand around to look on, and to
wonder at the mercies of the Sacred Heart. No—for
it is the time for worship. We know that our life's
duty is worship—our purpose, our merit, our happiness. But what is the act that is going on ? It is
the act of worship which of all acts has been the
supreme one, the superabundant, the all-suffering, the
infinitely worthy. Why is it going on ? That my
acts, that your acts, may be drawn into it, as the
vortices of the ocean draw the ships into their depths ;
and that our acts and His great act may be, if
it may be said, indistinguishable in one grand
holocaust before the throne of the Eternal. Is
not this the worship which the human race has
been aspiring after—dimly praying for even from
the beginning ? A worship which ascends from a
gathering of men, sometimes great, sometimes small,
and which is shared in by every individual heart in
that assembly—by him who kneels at the step of the
altar as by him who hangs on the edge of a multitude far down in the dimness of a mighty cathedral ;
a worship which is gathered into unity, wrought up
to Divine tension, transfigured into the glory of the
Only-begotten Son. At this moment the voice of
the teacher, of the praying priest, of the singer of
canticles, is better hushed. These may help us to
purify the heart and make it ready ; these may unite
to make the holy time a time of joy or of sadness, a
time of attention, of understanding, of concentration ;

but the supreme moments of that incomparable transaction are rather moments of silence—while every
heart is like one heart, all stirred to a grand unison
with the Divine Heart, as that Heart utters its masterful and prevailing voice—the only holy, the only
Lord, the only King most high !

We have, then, in the Eucharistic Sacrifice, the
means and the occasion of a worship of God, of such
a nature as to cause every single heart to exert itself
to the utmost, and at the same time to unite the redeemed
people, the royal Christian people and race, in an exterior and combined demonstration in which every
human power may take its part, every human
resource may be called into play, and the whole outward life of a community may be shaped and
coloured as if a nation had its king in its midst. To
rejoice in His Presence, to surround Him with honour,
to hold the august Eucharistic Sacrifice as the principal act of religion, and the greatest act of all human
life, and to throng to the celebration of it, making all
times and seasons bow to it—this is natural to a
believing people. And would not a world in which
the Mass was given its true place be a world in
which Christ was really King on the holy mountain
of Sion ? Would not this realise the kingdom of
God upon earth ? Would not obedience be more
thorough, love more loyal, service more adequate,
when all hearts habitually joined in a public act of
sacrifice—when that solemn rite sanctified every day
as it began—when men were never deeply moved by
religious or by national feeling without making the

solemn Mass the expression of their triumph, their
thanksgiving, their affection, or their intercession;
when the Eucharistic mystery was first in estimation,
first in love, first in honour, the lord of human time,
the disposer of earthly seasons; to which all business
must give way, at whose feet must lie all the fulness
of the earth?

Ideals, you will say! Pictures that cannot be
realised! I know not, my brethren. In some places
and in some centuries this most true and solid conception of what the Eucharistic presence and Sacrifice should be to men has, to some extent, been put
into actuality. In the Catholic centuries of Europe
the Blessed Sacrament was lodged in the noblest
palaces which man's art has ever erected, and it possessed altars whose material riches can hardly be
exaggerated. At a great church like the Cathedrals
of Canterbury, London, and York, the solemn High
Mass of a great festival was an event which nobles,
knights, magistrates, and civic dignitaries, with crowds
of the people, joined with the Bishop, the chapter,
the clergy, and the choristers, to make the most dignified, the most triumphant, the most resonant, the
most sumptuous of any that the age could produce.
And was not the solemn Papal Mass in St. Peter's,
speaking with human proportions in our thoughts, a
fit and worthy embodiment of the vital Christian
persuasion, that Christ, in the Sacrament of His love,
should be the King of all this world? Christendom
has not everywhere, even yet, suffered the modern
spirit of apostasy to suppress the touching, the con-

soling, the most salutary demonstrations of religious pomp. But what more concerns ourselves is this— that, during the century now drawing to its close, the Catholic clergy and people, having witnessed the overthrow of nearly all that Christian civil power which in days gone by used to honour religion with the resources of the State, have themselves, in spite of straitened means, of secularism, of unbelief, and of bitter opposition, steadily laboured to keep the Blessed Sacrament upon its lawful throne. You can see this illustrated all over Europe, and that especially in three facts—the increased frequency of Holy Communion; the extraordinary devotion at Mass which has been growing up—I refer especially to the low Mass, the early Mass, the Communion Mass, the Mass for the crowds—and the building of churches. It is this last feature which is most interesting to us to-day, and which is found indeed in the most marked degree in the history, during the past fifty years, of Britain and Ireland. This Church of St. George, built half a century ago, may well stand for the type of the church which our fathers built, in their poverty and their insignificance. They built boldly; they built sumptuously; they built, if I may use the phrase, recklessly. All over this country, from London to Newcastle, yes, and to Glasgow and Dundee, we find the monuments of fifty years ago; monuments great in architecture, solid in construction, ample, nay, too ample for the flock, and heavy, by their cost, on the shoulders of more than one generation. What inspired the men who raised them?

What set these hard-working priests to put their people's pence into brick walls, to importune rich men for lavish gifts, to associate themselves with architects who drew their inspiration from Westminster, and Winchester, and Lincoln ? It was the feeling of the Catholic to whom his church is the house of his God ; it was the zeal of the pastor who longed to make his flock believe in the visible kingdom of Jesus Christ; it was that proud Catholic spirit which recognises the great Catholic inheritance of the Eucharist—that irrepressible Catholic confidence which believes that the community who strenuously honour the Mass will infalliby grow both in numbers and in every spiritual grace. It is said that they were imprudent and contracted debt. I will take it that this is partly true. But insist on what drawbacks you please, there will still remain enough of true inspiration —of holy prudence and enlightened zeal—to deserve all the honour that we can pay them. The church-building and debt-paying priests of these recent generations are the true descendants of the martyrs of an earlier day. They have had to endure toil, poverty, rebuke, contempt, and an anxiety which has generally worn them out in spirit and body, and shortened their lives by years. But when they had built a church, they had built up more than stone walls ; they had strengthened faith, and broadened Catholic spirit, and helped their Redeemer—for in this Christ is in the hands of man—to reach and to attract innumerable hearts of children and of strangers as the years went by. A church like this fulfils that promise of

God when He said of the ancient Temple, " My eyes and My heart shall be there."[1] Of all those who have passed its threshold, trodden its aisles, knelt at its services, the eye of God has not passed over or forgotten a single one. To all those who have visited it to hear Mass, to receive the Sacraments, to pray, to hear God's word—yes, even to those who have stood under its roof with respectful curiosity, dimly desiring they know not what — His Sacred Heart has dispensed its mercies, its gifts, and its calls—a continuous, daily, crowded history of Divine communications. One day, more than five and twenty years ago, it chanced to me to ask a good and clever young man what it was that first urged him to think of becoming a Catholic. He told me that it was a visit to St. George's. He came in at an evening service, and the moment the Blessed Sacrament was exposed upon the altar a wave of tender emotion seemed to sweep over his spirit, as if he felt the presence of the Lord. During all that Benediction, and when he had passed out into the street and was making his way to his home, he found it impossible to restrain his tears ; and he felt that he now could live no longer without inquiring what Catholicism was. How unceasing, how sweet, how powerful, has been the Divine influence which has radiated during all these years from this sanctuary and altar of the Lamb that was slain ? How silently, yet how strongly, has the kingship of the Prince of Peace grown, and spread,

[1] Kings ix. 3.

and conquered, from this holy of holies! May God
be praised for all the blessings and the visitations
of fifty years ; and may He ever remember in His
mercy and fatherhood those who planned and built,
and helped to build St. George's ; and those who, with
much labour and pains, in holy ministration and
loving solicitude, have carried it on even to the
present day ; a day, let us hope, when a new era
dawns upon it, to the greater glory of God and the
good of unnumbered souls, and a second fifty years
begin which God shall bless with even better gifts
and greater mercies than those we humbly thank
Him for to-day.

CHRISTIAN CHARITY.

Preached in the Church of St. Saviour, Dublin, on Sunday, May 14th, 1899.

" Charity covereth a multitude of sins " (1 Peter iv. 8).

CHARITY is one of those great words of human speech which, like " Liberty " and like " Equality," is used and extolled, and is also abused. Men can never cease to use it, for it designates what human intercourse can never be without, unless humanity is to sink into the degradation of the brute. It can never cease to be praised and magnified—unless reason comes to lose its empire, and even instinct becomes perverted and corrupt. And yet, precisely because it is so notable a word, so holy a word, so ineffaceable a word, shallow minds will distort it, the cunning will make play with it, hypocrites will take advantage of it, the sin and evil of the world will assail its truth and try to defile its purity.

Charity springs from human nature, like the water of a well in the gravel. Just as the good and clear water comes up, piercing the sandy soil, impatient of the restraint, of the darkness where it was born, making the grass and the plants live around it, and bringing joy to the living things that discover it—so charity is an elemental force that will not be contained within the breast in which it has its being.

What makes charity? What things mingle, what forces combine, to form it? What processes of reason, what sweet and subtle instincts, what chemistry of the soul and of the emotions, result in that beneficent love which has for its object the men, the women, the little children of our race? You read, in an Epistle of St. Paul, a sustained description of charity—a kind of ode or hymn in prose, in which he dwells upon its loveliness and price. " Charity is patient, is kind ; charity envieth not, dealeth not perversely ; is not puffed up, is not ambitious ; seeketh not her own ; is not provoked to anger, thinketh no evil; rejoiceth not in iniquity, but rejoiceth with the truth ; beareth all things ; believeth all things, hopeth all things, endureth all things."[1] Here we have the elements of charity ; the primitive human impulses which, in their play, shine out on the world as charity. If you sum them up, you find that this rhetorical amplification of one of the greatest of rhetoricians arranges itself under three heads— humility, generosity, sympathy : there you have the well-springs of charity. I am not here searching in the region of the supernatural. I only speak of human nature. If we find a nature which has, first, the lovely gift of self-forgetfulness ; next, the impulse to give, to give up, to give out ; and, finally, the secret of entering into other hearts and feeling what others feel—there we have charity as an endowment of nature ; a gift that seems to be nature's ornament

---

[1] I Cor. xiii. 4, *sqq.*

and crown ; a gift not yet touched with the fire which is in the full sense Divine, yet far removed from those commoner and baser instincts against which even natural reason bids us strive.

It is no wonder, then, that the moralists of every shade of heathenism and every school of naturalism have left on record their praises of charity. For charity is the vital principle of the moral world ; it is the salt of the great sea of humanity. As far as the world without grace can escape corruption and confusion, it is charity which saves and preserves it. Charity neutralises and circumvents the grim and inexorable forces of unkindly nature. Charity wars against hunger and pain. Charity is an eye to the blind and a foot to the lame. Charity levels the unequal lot of men—that inequality which is the creation of their varying powers, strength, and good fortune. But, above all, charity diffuses a precious sunshine even where it cannot dissipate sorrow and suffering, filling hearts with gratitude, joy, and the priceless sense of being loved and cared for. True charity makes genuine brotherhood. For brotherhood is not the result of the mere recognition of equality. A man may be my equal without being my brother. He may have the same origin, the same nature, the same rights, the same destiny. I may acknowledge all that ; and yet, for brotherhood, he may be no nearer to me than one stone of Stonehenge is to another. Only if I feel with him, suppress myself, and give to him—only then is he my brother.

But charity, in the Christian sense, means much

more than all this. Charity was far too intimate an
element of human nature—too essential, too precious
—not to have a share in that plentiful outpouring of
Divine consecration which came to the world through
the blissful coming of Jesus Christ. Humility, generosity, sympathy—how could they find their true perfection without lifting themselves up to that Creator
—that Infinite—Who, far more than any creatures or
interests here below, is the aim of my soul's powers,
the object of my soul's expansion. I will not discuss
how far human charity could have become transformed
into Divine love had there been no Incarnation, no
revelation. It is certain that, as Jesus Christ has
revealed God, and has bestowed upon man that
supernatural grace which lifts him into the supernatural sphere, both in condition and in achievement, so, through Christ, man's native charity has
learnt to look for God first, and all other things
after God.

There may be some who think that the love of
God and the love of one's neighbour are two distinct
and independent virtues. But this is wrong. There
is a brotherly love which leaves out God. True—and
I do not mean to say it is not genuine, as far as it
goes. But it is a meagre, blind, and feeble love. It
is like the blade of the springing wheat which the
bitter East wind has stunted and turned yellow—
which will never be green, and will never grow. It
feels for human beings ; but it does not know what
a human being is. It is ignorant of his destiny ; it
knows not what his true happiness consists in ; it

sees no more than a frail, puzzling, struggling mortal, the sport of fortune, the prey of inevitable death. Among the heathen there were lovers of their fellow-men; but, in their heathen darkness, how futile were their efforts, how slight was their success, how frequent was their despair! And so there are, at this moment, in the world—around us—men who ignore the spiritual and the eternal, and who do splendid things for the physical well-being of the people. Their charity is true —but it is not what it might be. I do not say that one must stop to make an act of faith before one feeds a starving man. That he should be fed is infinitely better than that he should not be fed. But faith in God would, first, bring a precious merit to the kind men who are content with the temporal, and with this narrow earth; next, it would inspire larger ideas, aims more beneficent, work more lasting, alms deeds that not only comforted the mortal man, but helped him to secure immortality of bliss. And, above all, faith would transform philanthropy into a true and genuine Christian virtue. In a virtue the motive is everything. I do not mean that a vice can be changed into a virtue because I aim at what I consider a good result. But human acts take their meaning and their praiseworthiness from *bonâ fide* intention. So human kindness, human charity, is only a true Christian virtue when it loves men for the sake of God. Because to God belongs all our devotedness; and according to right reason, other things may be loved only for Him and in Him. It is

because in my fellow man I see my Creator's will, my
Creator's beneficence, my Creator's grand intentions
for eternity, that I love and help him. My mere impulse may be warm or cold ; my mere nature may be
generous or the reverse : a man is not judged by his
impulses or by his nature, though he may be helped
or hindered by them. He is judged by his intelligent
aims and efforts ; by his active free will which grace
assists. Hence, the true Christian seeks God in his
neighbour. He does not seek the gratification of his
natural benevolence. He does not seek the gratitude
of those he benefits. He does not seek, chiefly or
primarily, the bettering of this world, the decrease
of poverty, the lengthening of life. None of these
things are good in the absolute sense ; they may be
good or they may be the opposite. It is God, and
what he knows of God, that is the test, the touch-
stone, by which he knows what is good for his neighbour and what is hurtful. He knows that when a
man is in grave physical need—when he is starving,
destitute, naked—no questions must be asked ; that
man must be warmed and filled. But in the hundred
questions which arise in the bestowal of charity, it is
the Christian alone who has a rule by which to go.
He must guide himself by the interests of God, or
else his philanthropy will be spurious and pagan.
He must prefer the eternal to the temporal, the soul
to the body, the higher good to the lesser. More
especially if he is in such a position or place as to be
able to influence large movements or to guide men
and nations, must he think rather of the things that

lift men up, than of those that gratify the senses for the hour and the moment.

But if it is the Christian's true rule to prefer God to all lower things in his love, it is his privilege that he has also God's strength to lean upon. He is not obliged to measure the success of his good endeavours by their immediate or visible success. Men may be hard to help, poverty may be overwhelming, degradation may be profound, the sin and folly of each generation as it comes up may seem to grow rather than to diminish. But God need not wait for the operation of physical law. God has a shorter way to hearts and souls than leagues of benevolence, schemes of millionaires, or the busy toil of the philanthropist. The effort of a single man, a man of true devotedness, a man of prayer, a man of saintliness, will often turn the desert places of this world into fairness and fertility, because he puts God first, and God works with him. And if poverty and suffering still go on, still seem to defy the devotion of the saint as they baffle the science of the economist, the Christian will never despair or relax ; for he knows that all these are not absolutely, irretrievably bad : on the contrary, they have promise with them, and hope ; they were the chief elements in the very life of Jesus Himself ; they will be redeemed at a great price in the eternity to come, and the courageous, but seemingly futile and barren strivings of good men for their fellow-men will only add to the joy and glory of that day in which the Lord God Himself will take on Him the office of feeding the hungry and of wiping away the tears of the afflicted.

True Christian charity, then, is first and foremost the love of God above all things, and only secondarily the love of our neighbour. So reason teaches. So God's revelation enforces. So must we read those noble passages of the New Testament which enshrine the ideas of a St. Peter, a St. Paul, and a St. John.

Does any one dispute this? Does any one object that, in saying this, the Christian preacher extinguishes the fire of brotherly love, dries up the wells of kindness, makes human love a mere transaction between God and those who wish to save their souls? Ah! if such objectors only understood what those last words mean; understood how no soul can have any transaction with the God of love unless it brings all its good and holy impulses to be blessed and consecrated by Him! Extinguished! Dried up! Divine grace extinguishes nothing but what is hurtful; dries up nothing but what is bad. Divine faith urges me to save my soul, it is true; it shows me that the great commandment is to love God with all my heart; but it also shows me how, to a child of earth, there is no safer path to heavenly happiness, no more efficacious means of loving God in all truth and sincerity than loving one's neighbour as one's self.

And this, I take it, is the meaning of those words of St. Peter, "Charity covereth a multitude of sins."

There can be no reasonable doubt that, in this passage, the Apostle is speaking of charity to our neighbour. He says: "Above all things have a constant mutual charity among yourselves." And the passage of the Book of Proverbs,[1] to which he is certainly referring, runs thus : " Hatred stirreth up strife ; and charity covereth all sins."

But how does charity cover the sins of the charitable ? How can sins be covered ?

I might reply, without being in any way irreverent, that the sins of men are never " covered," that is never merely "covered" or hidden from the sight of the great Judge ; they are either open and bare to His eye, or else they are completely washed away.

It cannot be denied that the word " covered " is often used in the Bible of sins that are forgiven ; for example, it is said in the Book of Psalms, " Thou hast pardoned the iniquity of Thy people ; Thou hast covered all their sins."[2] This suggests to us the true meaning of " covered." It really means " made to disappear." There is a terrible passage in Ezechiel,[3] in which the Lord threatens that the guilt of Jerusalem shall be as blood upon the smooth rock . . . blood that cannot sink into the charitable earth and be " covered." In this passage the word means " utterly disappear."

St. Peter means, then, that charity causes sin to disappear, as blood shed upon the sand is mercifully absorbed and obliterated. But how is this ?

There is, and there can be, only one way to wipe out personal sin. That is—the conversion of the heart to God, with love, repentance, and the resolution to amend. This is the very process, the very

[1] x. 12.   [2] Ps. lxxxiv. 3.   [3] xxiv. 6.

stirring of our spiritual being which, by His grace and the Sacrament's help, washes sin away. But observe, it is a common usage in speech to indicate a principal instrument as if it were the process or act itself. Thus, when the fields are parched, the farmer prays for the south-west wind. Will the wind refresh his hard and thirsty furrows? Will the wind fill the springs and the water-courses? No. But it will bring on its wings the life-giving rain. And, therefore, God grant that it may blow!

There is no means, among all the acts, pursuits, and operations of men, outside of sacramental power, which has so strong, so full, and so immediate an effect on the forgiveness of sin as the love of one's neighbour. Charity is the grand effacer of sin. For charity brings those graces and dispositions which most of all tend to bring about true contrition, true conversion, persevering love, and immunity from the judgment to come.

Consider how brotherly charity brings about that turning of the heart to God, which we call "conversion." I do not speak of any one sort or species of conversion. There is conversion from mortal sin, conversion from venial sin, conversion from tepidity, conversion from worldliness. The element in these various kinds of conversion of which I here speak is one and the same. It is a certain turning of the heart and soul to God. It is a certain awakening to one's Maker, a realising of one's Last End, a re-settlement of our spiritual point of view, tending to make God what He ought to be, first in all our thought and activity, the only aim and love of these hearts that He has made. I say that nothing tends to set up and to preserve this condition of soul like kindness to others. A man cannot be genuinely kind without going outside of himself ; and no man if he is a believer, can go outside of himself without finding God very near him. A man's heart cannot soften to distress or poverty without becoming sensitive to the Divine influence ; for there is no force which melts human hardness, and disposes man to throw himself at his Creator's feet, like pity, compassion, mercy. Because my heart is moved to my neighbour, I feel the need of One Who will be moved to me. Because I pour myself out over other's sorrows, I realise how my own sorrows want a friend. Because I cease to shut myself up in my selfishness, I cannot stop till I surrender myself to my only Father. Because I bestir myself to render help to others, I feel my latent love of God begin to glow. Because I take up the battle with evil, with trouble, with hardship, I become encouraged with the thought that I am on the side of the Lord of Hosts, and my soul is lifted up to cling to Him the more. " A merciful man doth good to his own soul," saith the Holy Spirit.[1] It is a fulfilment of that promise of God in Ezechiel,[2] " I will open your graves and will bring you out of your sepulchres, O my people . . . and you shall know that I am the Lord." Have we not seen it ? Have we not known it ? A man, baptised a Christian, has sunk into unbelief ; God gives him the

[1] Prov. xi. 17.   [2] xxxvii. 12.

grace to interest himself in the poor—and behold the awful realities of life and of death awaken his conscience and his faith in God comes back. A man is dead in mortal sin, callous to conscience, regardless of the judgment. Pity finds her way into his heart —pity for the orphan or the suffering—and it comes about that his frozen heart is thawed and the great truths of eternity sound as they never did before. The worldly, the indifferent, have the grace to be touched by the privations, the wretchedness, the misery of our great cities; and that grace does not stop till it has forced them to feel the spiritual barrenness and degradation of their own lives and brought them to turn to Jesus. For in that softening of the heart to the poor and the needy there is a preparation of the spirit for all high and heavenly things, so that the Holy Spirit, coming down like a dove as of old, finds ground on which to rest His feet, and abides there to efface all sin, and to make such hearts His own.

But if mercy prepares the way for the spirit, it is even more strikingly true that it keeps the soul strong and firm in the grace of the spirit. What is mercy, or charity, besides being an impulse or an emotion? It is a strenuous business and work. And what is that work, as far as I myself am concerned? It is giving out—giving up—sacrificing. And it means a genuine detachment of the heart from the things, which most of all fetter the heart and tend to withdraw it from its God—that is, the riches, the good things, and the enjoyments of this world below. A man, to exercise charity, must give ; he must take from himself and hand over to another ; whether he is well off himself, or whether his means are small, whether he gives much or little, he is sure to feel that giving. Is there any propensity of nature which, on the whole, is more universal in men than attachment to what one possesses ? Is there any part of nature's sensitive surface that is more easily pricked, more quickly responsive, more deeply resentful than the feeling of possession ? There is nothing more healthful than to mortify and kill this innate grasping, this lust of having and holding, with which man is born. It is a life's work—and it is well worth all the time and all the effort. For a truly detached heart is a heart that is absolutely prepared to love God wholly and completely. What do we see in the lives of the Saints ? We see men who strip themselves of all they have—who flee— who live far from money and pleasure—who reject with the passion of holiness any speck of the dross of earth which might defile a heart all dedicated to God. This is surely a lesson. Why can I not love God more purely, more securely, more continuously ? Is it not because I am bound and stifled by the things I have? It may be little that I have, little that I can give up at the utmost. But it chokes and gags me, because I have never shaken myself free from my attachment to it. Let me think of my fellow man ! Let me seek out the hiding-place of poverty ! Let me search for the starving and the suffering ! Let me remember the orphan and the child that has no home! Let me give something, do something, suffer something for those on whom misfortune lies heavy and dark, and it is God's promise that I shall put myself in the way of being a free and single-hearted creature.

This is the ground of the Scripture doctrine that kindness to our neighbour is a test and measure of our love for God. You remember the immortal passage of St. John : " He that shall see his brother in need, and shall put up his bowels from him, how doth the charity of God abide in Him ? "[1] The opposite may seem to be possible. It is true a man will never say explicitly, " I love God ; but my neighbours I do not trouble myself about." The most elementary Christianity will not suffer him to say this. But it happens—not rarely, but continually and everywhere —that men and women do neglect their neighbour's needs and yet seem to themselves to love God. In other words, there are decent, pious, church-going, sacrament-frequenting people in scores and hundreds, who neither know the poor nor care for the poor. There is nothing more dangerous than the so-called " piety " of those who thus neglect God's will and commandment. Their piety is mere sentiment ; their peace of soul is a hollow and an evil peace ; they honour God with the lips alone. Test them. Try them with a plain and easy case of charity. Such people turn coldly away. Or perhaps, with God's help, they enter into themselves—they recognise the falsehood of their life—and they resolve to do more

[1] 1 John iii. 17.

for the poor.   But, if this test of a neighbour's need
had not been offered them, they might have gone
on even to the judgment in the false security that
they loved God, when, in reality, their love was only
the lethargy that ends in death.

But not only is the love of one's neighbour the
test of one's love of God, it is also the intensifying of
that love.   We are made that way.   An emotion,
even if it is faith, or hope, or charity, languishes if it
is shut up in the heart.   You must express it, or it
dies—sooner or later.   To put it into words, or sighs,
or tears, is profitable, and it wakes into flame.
But to put it into action—to stir up mind and will,
imagination and physical faculties, in the effort and
strain of putting it into external execution—this is to
feed it with fuel as one feeds a fire, to nourish it, to
give it growth, and strength, and endurance.   Thus
a man who exercises charity intensifies his love of
God.   The effort, the sacrifice, the self-mortification,
are like the blast of the north wind that blows
up the beacon on the mountain-top.   The great
Apostle, when he thinks of the needs of his
brethren, cries out that his heart is " enlarged."
It is the word of the Psalmist, " Thou hast enlarged
my heart."   This is what Christian charity does.   It
is thus we read that in the times of the persecution,
the zealous servants of God made their way into the
dark prisons, and seemed to see Christ Himself in
those beaten and tortured confessors lying there.
The history of missions gives us similar pictures ;
the priest, the monk, the Bishop, who had learned

to love God in their secret prayers, found that they seemed to see Him and feel Him when they stood face to face with the heathen waiting to be saved. A St. Hugh of Lincoln kissed the feet of the leper, as he would have kissed those of Christ on the Cross. A St. Louis Bertrand embraced the poor dying slave, as if it was his Lord and Master. A St. Charles gathered up the orphans of the great Milanese plague as if each of them was the Infant Jesus. A St. Vincent exercised for half a century his miraculous ministry, relieving, consoling, sheltering, saving, as though the Divine Shepherd had given him His own heart. And never has it yet happened that a Christian, in a Christian spirit, has given to the poor, comforted the suffering, or ministered to the children of the poor, without his love of his God growing warmer, more real, and more robust.

Is this what is meant by that comforting assurance that " Charity covereth a multitude of sins " ? That is the way I interpret it. Charity, real brotherly charity, maketh all sin to disappear. Sin and charity cannot live together. Try it. Nay, you have tried and experienced it. A man's soul has been in a bad unhealthy state—like some old house that has been shut up for years ; sound enough and dry enough, but close, unwholesome, evil-smelling. The owner comes back, and the doors and windows are opened ; and then the air and the blessed sun pour in and that house is sweet and habitable again. A man opens his doors and his windows by kindness and charity. My brethren, open yours. Let in God's grace and light. You know not what He has to give you, if you only open out your hearts to do good generously to the creatures whom God loves. And I will go further.

No Catholic can think that if he is charitable his sins may be covered over even if he does not repent. No Catholic can think so. To love one's fellow man without being sorry for having offended God, and to think that there will be mercy and forgiveness in the judgment, is only to mock God. And yet there is in every heart a deep conviction that on him who is merciful God has mercy. And it is a true conviction—a salutary conviction. For such a man there is mercy, and always mercy. Mercy follows him and watches him like a guardian angel. Mercy calls him, whispering conversion to his heart. Mercy guards him in temptation, keeps him near his Church and his altar, gives him strength to persevere. Mercy pours out over his life a kind of fertility, a kind of abundance, which overflows even upon his temporal concerns— multiplying his possessions in proportion as he gives, keeping off suffering because he ministers to those who suffer, blessing his children because he is pitiful to the orphan. Mercy is at his death-bed, keeping the enemy away, lighting the gloom of the hour of fate, filling the air with celestial influence. And mercy awaits him at the judgment—for if there is debt to be paid that supernatural fires should exact, charity to the poor will pay it all; and Christ will say, " Enter the joy that is prepared for you, for when you ministered to My little ones you did it to Me."

You are aware what it is—who it is—that I plead for to-day. The North William Street Orphanage for Girls, under the loving care of St. Vincent's daughters, the Sisters of Charity, is one of those enterprises of Catholic charity which make us thank God for our Catholic faith and spirit. One hundred and eighty orphans, gathered in by the Sisters, are saved, taught to know their Heavenly Father, educated, and prepared for their life. The work is a good and strenuous bit of Christian apostleship. This city, in which there is so much of which a Catholic may be justly proud, shows few sights more blessed and consoling than this community of Sisters and their family. But no one here present—no one who feels his heart warm to this work of God—must be content with barren sentiment. The work depends on alms. The work largely depends on the results of this very day. I ask you to make each of you a sacrifice for charity—for the orphan—for the poor. I ask you to be generous. May God illuminate all here, and soften every heart, that some little good may be done, some tears wiped away, some heavenly sunshine brought into pitiful lives, in the name of the Heavenly Father of us all. Amen.

OUR APOSTLES.

*Preached in the Church of St. Augustine, Preston,
on Sunday, September 5th, 1898.*

"As the Father hath sent Me, I also send you" (John xx. 21).

SPEAKING to-day in a church dedicated to St. Augustine of England, in this year which begins the fourteenth century of his work and his renown, I would ask you to lift your hearts above controversy, above the annoyance, inevitable as it is, which springs from strife and contradiction, even above the details of dates, places, and authorities, and to dwell upon the mystery and the spiritual significance of his Apostleship.

Some thirteen centuries ago, the mercies of God came down like rain from the sweet heavens upon this island that we call Britain, and this race that we call English. For many years, even after the days of Bethlehem, of Calvary, of Pentecost, the skies had been of brass above this land. Set in the seas, its temperate summers and genial winters had followed one another; and the westerly gales, year after year, had brought as in battalions the clouds and mists which nurse it, wrap it round, and keep it green and fertile. But the dew of Christ's Cross it had not known. Our chronicles speak hesitatingly of St. Joseph of Arimathea, and even of St. Paul. They tell, with greater certainty, of Lucius and Eleutherius; and it is certain that, in the West at least, a noble Christianity flourished a century before St. Gregory; whilst even in Roman days, two centuries earlier again, there had been churches, confessors, and martyrs. But, speaking broadly, there was here, in the sixth century, a pagan race and a heathen land. In those days mercy came. It came like the storms of the autumn, abundant, masterful, bringing life and fruitfulness. There was to be no return of the dryness or the dearth.

The Christian history which began in the closing years of the sixth century was to be continued on without a break for a thousand years—a history which fills us with thankfulness as we look back over its long courses; a history which, although marred and interrupted at the time of the revolt from faith and unity, in one sense is not yet cut short, but belongs to us—even to us who meet here this day to remember and celebrate St. Augustine.

And in thinking of him, we may think also of those other men who were with him, in spirit or in the flesh. It is impossible, in this year, not to remember Gregory the Great. It is impossible not to recall Laurence, Mellitus, Justus, and Paulinus. Nay, I would go further, and say that we ought not, in numbering our Apostles, to omit the names of Columba and of Aidan. " What are these, my Lord ? " said the Prophet to the Angel, when he was shown in the night the vision of the horsemen gathered among the myrtle bushes down in the

hollow—" What are these ? " And the answer was :
" These are they whom the Lord hath sent to walk
through the earth."[1]

We shall never fully understand this mystery, of
the " sending " of men to men, on the part of the God
Who made men. There are in it so many elements
which call upon us for our adoration, for our praise,
for our love, for our responsive self-oblation. God
need not have created ; and if He had not created
beings with intelligence, there would have been no
call for that outward rushing energy, as of a mighty
fire, by which, as it is, we principally know Him.
Yet within the very Godhead, purely spiritual, purely
simple, as it is, it is revealed that there is the pro-
cession of the Holy Spirit. This, among other
things, means the Godhead as a source, a spring, a
fountain. I do not dwell upon the personality of
God the Holy Ghost ; I only adore it. But, whilst
it means more than all the seraphim and cherubim
can ever know, it also means this—that the Infinite
contains within itself, as in their native source and
sphere, all the conditions and elements that we know
by the names of energy, force, power, and activity.
Thence came creation. With creation, still from that
abyss, came light, strength, guidance, and fatherly
solicitude for the immortal souls which creation had
brought into being. Thence came the Incarnation—
the crowning work of God's mysterious " sending "
—wherein He Who was sent was the true and adequate Messias, in Whose sending were all other

[1] Zacharias i. 8.

sendings to be contained. Man might have expected God not to forget him ; not to let him go ; not to leave him without a message. But it was this " sending " of the Son Incarnate which our Heavenly Father imagined and carried out—this, and none other. It was this that the ancient Prophets and kings endeavoured to find a name for. It was this that they called the " rending of the heavens,"[1] because it was no ordinary communication from above, but indicated a sweet violence, a loving high-handedness, such as God permits Himself when He would show His love for men. It was this that seemed to them to be a melting of the very hills, a setting on fire of the very rivers.[2] It was this which appeared to them to be written in the very first line of the first chapter of the great book of God's dealings with His creatures—" Behold I come."[3] It was for the Incarnation they sought out (without finding it, for it was invented by God Himself) a new name for the city of God on earth.[4] That great coming of Him Whom God sent was to be as if one came bounding and leaping over the mountains and high places of the earth—over all the pride and might and achievement of humanity.[5] He was to be a Lion of Juda ;[6] and yet a Lamb—" send the Lamb " was their prayer, the Lamb that was " to rule the earth."[7] Their visions showed Him as the oncoming storm, which was to demolish the forest and lash the seas into fury ; yet as the One Who was to bring what it seemed the

[1] Isaias lxiv. 1.　　[2] *Ib.*　　[3] *Ib.* xxix. 8.　　[4] *Ib.* lxii. 2.
[5] Canticles ii. 8.　　[6] Apoc. v. 5.　　[7] Isaias xvi. 1.

warring and agitated earth could never have—Who was to bring rest and tranquillity, and to be called the Prince of Peace.

In this Old Testament description of Him Who was to be "sent," we have a picture of all the Apostles that the world has known. For as the Father sent Jesus Christ, so Jesus sent the rest. In their careers there was to be similar power, similar proof of never failing solicitude, similar personal characteristics. First the great Apostles (as St. Paul calls them) ;[1] then those whom they trained, and who carried the Faith to Asia, to the cities of Greek civilisation, to Roman Gaul and Spain ; then those whom the monasteries of the fifth, sixth, and seventh centuries sent out, to Ireland, to England, to Germany and the North ; then, later on, the apostolic men who went over in the ships of the Western pioneers to America, North and South, the Apostles of the Indians, of the Chinese, of the Negroes ; all those who, even to our own day, are advancing the banner of the Cross on the outskirts of civilisation, spending their strength and often laying down their lives in the far East, in the ten thousand islands of the Indian seas, in the swamps and Saharas of the African continent. All these, if they are true Apostles—and who can doubt it in the face of their deeds—are sent of Christ ; and they are like Him : or, it may be said, they carry Him to the nations and represent Him, and that chiefly in three senses :

1. First, like Jesus Christ, they are the true and

[1] 2 Cor. xi. 5.

powerful makers of the world's history. Since
Christ came, it is not Oriental philosophies, or Greek
culture, or Roman law, or the prowess of the Frank
or the Teuton, that has directed man's destiny; but
Christianity. All these elements have had their
weight and their influence; all these, even at this
day, have their followers and their votaries, ready to
extol one or other of them, and to preach it as a
sovereign remedy for the world's needs. But it is
the Apostles who have effected most. It is the
Apostles who have changed barbarians into civilised
beings, who have brought races together, formed
kingdoms, transformed the face of the land, taken
possession of literature, and fashioned the institutions
of the modern world. This has been so in the past.
It is so in the present. As to the future—here is a
matter on which prophecy is safe. If Christ is to be
" with " His Apostles all days, even to the consummation of the world, there can be no doubt about the
future. And let us not be deceived by the signs
and portents of a generation which seems to be
occupied in effacing the work of past Apostles,
and slipping off the yoke of Jesus Christ. God
will always have His Apostles. If we look back a
little, to where the dust of actual life has somewhat
died down, we can see, even within our own days,
how the Cross has not only been advancing in Africa
or China, but has held its own in Europe. And let
us be sure of this—that it is a large part of the
Christian duty of every man to recognise the Apostles
of the age ; to recognise the men and to recognise

the principles. The principles are the undying truths of the Faith—the principles of grace, of morality, of immortality, of sacramental dispensation and Church unity ; the men are those who are endowed with true and genuine mission, and who show in their lives the Gospel and the Cross. It is not difficult to miss these men and their principles. True, the Church herself is visible enough. That is our great safeguard. But even whilst adhering to the faith and practice of the Church, there are many weighty and serious questions—questions relating to what are called politics, to literature, to the poor, and to labour —in which a man may go wrong unless he can re- cognise the Apostles of the age. And not to recognise them is to throw one's weight against the working of God.

2. Next, the world's Apostles resemble Jesus Christ in this—that they wield the power of the Cross. They bring into this lower world that influence, those blasts and currents from a higher sphere, which were earned for the world by Calvary. They bring the reign of Divine grace. They carry the Ark of God, before which the devils tremble and the walls of strong places fall down. They bring God's most powerful word, which is creative, life-giving, healing, inevitable. They bring the perpetual Sacrifice, and set up the altars around which angels and men unite in worship. They scatter as they go the unction and the fragrance of the sacramental gift, more precious than all the gold of kings. They draw men to God, through Bethlehem, Nazareth, and the Cross. They convince the world

of sin—the hurrying, unreflecting world, which would fain go on as if everything pleasant was also right and just. They strengthen, beautify, and sanctify all the good which has survived the primeval fall—sanctioning with a more awful sanction those bonds and relations of the family and the state on which civilised life depends. They bring an answer to man's unceasing questions, and push out the walls of time and space till the eye of mortals can make out, dimly but solidly, the realms and durations of immortality. The Apostles are always strangers on the earth, whatever century they arrive in. They are the ambassadors of a Power which must always be foreign—Lord and God as He is, and loving Father —for His work is always to change and save the world. Therefore those whom He sends seem so often to neglect, to trample upon, to despise, the influences which men consider so potent and so indispensable—and to prefer to be poor, lowly, and unregarded rather than to have money at their command or to sit in the councils of the great. And by this shall men know them when they come.

3. And, finally, the Apostles whom God sends are the heralds of the ever-living, ever-burning, everflowing love and solicitude of God for men. As Jesus Christ, by His coming, His life and His death, has made it now impossible for the world either to forget God or to doubt about His love, so the glorious choir of the Apostles, led by St. Peter and the Eleven, pass on from century to century a loud unending canticle of good tidings, which leaves no

generation without knowledge. "Day unto day uttereth speech, and night unto night showeth knowledge. There are no speeches nor languages where their voices are not heard. Their sound hath gone forth into all the earth, and their words unto the ends of the world."[1] How interesting and awe-inspiring it is, in all ages, to study the Divine Love, choosing and sending out His Apostles! He picks them out, as it would seem to men, at hazard and by chance ; but it is in accordance with one of those wondrous laws which, like those which control the stars, are hidden from the eye of man. They come from cities and from the desert, from the army and from the cloister, from the market-place and from the schools, from palaces and from the poorest cabins. They may be strong or weakly, cultured or rude, the fisherman or the publican, the believer or the persecutor, the king with his armies, or the bare-footed friar. The Divine Solicitude calls them, and you hear them, if you study their lives, answering, articulately or not, as their Leader answered, " Behold, here I am ! " But as they are called they are transformed. From childhood, perhaps, or from the day of their call, they begin to glow, as the fire glows when it is caught by the breath of the wind, with that strange, unique, Divine ardour which is called zeal for souls. In their prayer the sense, the very vision, of immortal souls crying and perishing, importunes their whole being ; like their great example, Paul of Tarsus, they see in the night the Macedonian

[1] Ps. xviii. 3, 4, 5.

standing and beseeching, and saying, " Pass over and
help us.' "[1]   Their homes, their country, their father
and mother and brothers and sisters, have no hold
on their hearts like that which is exercised by the
thought of tribes and nations still sitting in the
shadow of death.   The Divine Solicitude, in forming them for His Apostolate, takes from them the
love of the earth and the fear of pains and suffering.
They start without scrip or staff; they face long
journeys ; they embark on stormy oceans ; they land
amid the heathen and the savage ; they live without
roof to their head, in hunger and thirst ; they are prepared for any kind of death ; and often they do die,
and die, sometimes in torture, sometimes, like St.
Francis Xavier, alone and desolate, far from the very
Sacraments, committing their worn bodies to the providence of God.   But, meanwhile, the souls for whom
the unforgetting solicitude of God is thus working,
are found, gathered in, saved ; the light of Christ
rises like the dawn of day, the regenerating waters
spread, the altar is set up, the Church and the school
mark the reclaimed regions, and new generations are
born into a consecrated and Christian land.   God has
shown the might of His arm.   Those humble, zealous
men have commanded the earth, the sea, and the sky,
and they have obeyed ; they have ruled the savage
beast, defied the deadly poison ; they have spoken
with strange tongues, healed the ills of men, and
raised the very dead to life.   Thus has the love of
God endowed those whom He has sent to win souls

[1] Acts xvi. 9.

to the Blood of Jesus. Within and without they are transformed — transformed by a power that knows not how to restrain the lavishness of its manifestation wherever it is a question of saving the souls of men.

The Apostles of England, like the great Apostles, and the Apostles of every other country, have exhibited in their lives, and in their persons, these notes of the Divine sending. But as to England, and as to that epoch, thirteen hundred years ago, when her grand and principal conversion took place, her Apostles were many, and the influences set in motion by our Heavenly Father's love, although in a sense they may be summed up in the man who spoke to Ethelbert at the oak on the shore of Thanet, yet are manifold and interesting.

The first, and the greatest name among the Apostles of England is that of St. Gregory the Great. Gregory never saw England. Held in captivity by his supreme office amid the stupendous ruins of the city of Rome, he could only dream in his holy contemplation of the race whose fair children had appealed to his heart in the Roman slave-market. But he never lost sight of the design which then took hold of his spirit. Sending his pastoral epistles to the bishops of the Gauls, he could not refrain from speaking of the people beyond, in that " little corner," as he termed it, of the earth. Thinking that the hour has at last come, he picks out St. Augustine and his fellow monk—" out of my own monastery," as he says. Following them in spirit, sending them on when they

faltered, stirring up kings, queens, and bishops to
help them on their way, he sits, himself anxious,
stirred to the depths of his being, in his Apostolic
See, filled with the spirit of an Apostle. For every
Pope is an Apostle. More than other pastors,
is the Supreme Pastor sent — and there is no
point of the horizon which the Pontiff's eye does
not scan to see what race or nationality is in need
of the heralds of Jesus Christ. But the Roman
Gregory would have journeyed to Britain himself if
he could. " I am denied a part in your labours—but
had I my wish, I would be with you."[1] Not being
able to go, he did his part at home. It was not only
that he gave the word and the " mission "—or that he
spent himself in active and effective assistance. His
accents ring with the true Apostolic spirit—that the
work is the work of God ; that all His instruments
are weak and feeble ; that amidst signs and success
there should be fear and humility ; and that the
prayers lifted up in the city of Rome are more effective in converting the English than the labours of the
men who sought their shores. And with the most
literal truth may it be said, as our own Venerable
Bede has said, that Gregory was the Apostle of the
English race. It was to him the mission came from
above ; it was he who, in the long hours of his contemplation, in the fervent acts of his prayer, under
the heavy pressure of his work, amid the anguish
of his many solicitudes and the sharp suffering of his
martyred body, lifted up to that God from Whom

[1] Ep. vi. 51.

all conversion comes the prayer and the longing which drew down such mercy on Kent—such mercy on the races of the English.

Leaving the embassy of St. Gregory to make its way across the seas and the land, from king to king, from one Franco-Roman city to another, from monastery to monastery, till they came in sight of Thanet, let us turn for a moment to two islands in the far North which are to be as momentous to the English race even as Thanet itself. Away in the West is Iona ; nestling close to the shore of Northumberland in the East is Lindisfarne. Iona was the spiritual mother of Lindisfarne ; and from Lindisfarne went out the light of the Gospel which met the banners of the Roman monks on the banks of the Yorkshire Ouse. There were some differences between the two Apostolic bands. They both brought Christ ; they both brought the transforming power of Christianity ; they were equally filled with zeal, endowed with miraculous powers, and rewarded with success. But the Irish monk had hardly that large belief in the things about to be, that sense of the coming on of a great Christian era, which marked the Romans. Columba was a great founder and missionary ; Aidan was a Bishop who laid the sweet yoke of Christ on chiefs and races. But their fellow-workers hardly trusted themselves out of sight of their island-monasteries, as if at any moment they might have to take to their boats and abandon their labours on the mainland. But the Roman, reinforced later by the English whom he had trained, not only preached but settled down. He through up his oratory of wattles, he ran up a shelter on the ruins of abandoned towns, he cleared out heathen temples, he pitched on sites which we know were good, because they still serve our fairest towns—and he let the people see that he was to be their teacher, their pastor, and their friend. Hence, in Northumbria, the tide coming from the South was too strong for the waters from the North ; and by degrees the Kentish Apostolate swallowed up the labours of the Celtic monks. Yet everywhere in Northumbria—beneath the stones of Holy Island and of Bamborough, of Hexham, of Jarrow, and of Whitby, there lie the traces and the remains of the Irish and Scottish Gospel-labourers who overran it in their zeal, and prepared the harvest for St. Paulinus, St. Oswald, St. Chad, and St. Theodore.

St. Augustine himself is a figure who is very human, yet not without the halo of mystery. It is not difficult to picture the monk of the Roman monastery—the leader of the band which made its painful way from Rome to the sea, from Ostia to Lerins, from Lerins to Marseilles, Arles, Aix, up the Rhone, and then down the Loire, till they paused, perhaps at Rouen, to make their final preparation for the crossing of the Channel. What we know of him is, that he was chosen, and twice chosen, by Gregory himself, and that his life, till he had reached middle age, was hidden from the world. Of him St. Gregory says that he was "well versed in the monastic rule, filled with the knowledge of Holy Scripture, and endowed, by God's grace, with all good works " :

that is, to express it in words better understood by
ourselves, he was an ascetic, a theologian, and a holy
man. The great Pope seems to have had a special
friendship for him, for in more than one of the com-
mendatory letters in which St. Gregory asked kings
and prelates to help him on his way, he speaks of
the " singular affection " borne to him by Augustine.
He speaks also of his spirit of zeal for souls. We
know—and know by heart—the incidents of the first
landing ; the band of forty, the cross and banner, the
interview under the oak, the settlement at Canterbury, the miracles and the conversions which followed.
It is Gocelinus, a monk of St. Augustine's, Canterbury,
of the thirteenth century, who tells us that the Apostle
of the English had a noble face and a commanding
figure, and that he towered head and shoulders above
all his companions. But Augustine has not left us a
biography of his mind and soul, as Gregory has.
From him we have no luminous letters, no ex-
pansive commentaries containing digressions, pre-
faces, and outbursts, which read like the confessions
of a more celebrated St. Augustine. His monastic
spirit we can only imagine ; but considering that St.
Gregory trained him, can we doubt that St. Gregory's
quies—St. Gregory's spirit of the hidden life—was to
him among the familiar conceptions of his mind ?
Can we doubt that when Gregory, in the hour of
Augustine's success, reminded him how he ought to
recollect his own nothingness, and " judge himself
discreetly within," the disciple recalled the days when
such admonitions to interior recollection as fill the

pages of the *Regula Pastoralis* were the education of his soul in Rome? We have no record of his sermons—those wonderful discourses which moved the heart of Ethelbert and his Angles, and brought thousands to holy Baptism. The thirteenth century chronicles set forth the words spoken at Ebbsfleet. They may, and most probably do, represent the spirit of that appeal, and there is one sentence which seems to come from an Apostolic heart : " Be assured, most loving King, that to this purpose and enterprise we have been constrained by the necessity of great love." Yes, that mysterious and heroic figure journeyed, preached, and laboured during those seven years of his Apostolate with the fire of love and zeal burning in his breast, given up to his mission, God's instrument of mercy, a man and a Saint in whose hands God had placed the destinies of a people. It was his prayer, his austerity, his word, and his example which, under God, converted our fathers, and it is this which we must never forget.

We must never forget him—nor the great Pope St. Gregory, nor Columba and Aidan, nor Laurence and Mellitus, Justus and Paulinus. Their work seems to have been done thirteen hundred years ago, when, by their prayer and toil, the sweet Gospel of Jesus Christ brought life and liberty to this island. But, in reality, it is not done to this very day in which we live. The Apostles do not die. England awaits another conversion. In good time, and as God wills, Apostles will arise, and the zeal of the undying Roman See will send them ; nay, do we not feel that

Apostles have never been wanting, and that there are Apostles labouring, with that Roman See's anxious blessing, even at this very moment. But when the great increase may be given—when the great harvest may be reaped—this we do not know. We only know that if St. Augustine was our Apostle once, he is our Apostle still. His intercession can do more than his words and suffering on earth. The land to which Gregory sent him—or, rather, to which Jesus sent him—must be as dear and close to his heart as ever. His body, which reposed for a thousand years under his splendid tomb in St. Augustine's Abbey at Canterbury—his body that slept there so long, in the earth which he had sanctified, surrounded by the tombs of his companions—is now lost to his country and his race, till the resurrection. But his spirit lives and is mighty, with the might of the princes of God. Let not his clients, here and everywhere, forget. If they love their country—if they have the interests of Jesus at heart—let them never forget St. Augustine, but day by day, festival by festival, weary him with prayers that he would intercede for England, and do over again from heaven, in this century, the work which he did on earth thirteen hundred years ago.

THE ARK OF THE COVENANT.

*Preached at Oscott, on occasion of the inaugura-
tion of the Central Seminary, September 8th,
1897.*

THE Ark of the Covenant was the symbol of the
presence of God ; almost the vehicle of God : to the
Hebrews it meant God's nearness, God's favour, and
God's protection.   The Blessed Mother of God is
called the Ark of the Covenant.   The singular apt-
ness and appropriateness of this among her other
august titles has, perhaps, not hitherto struck us.
Yet it is she, above all the things that God has
created—putting outside of the comparison the
Sacred Humanity—who, in this dispensation of the
New Testament and of the grace of Jesus Christ,
brings God near to us, and unites our searching,
struggling, and failing souls with the Creator Who
made them for Himself.

We must remember that we have drawn near to
God by means of the Incarnation.   God is no longer
only in the distant heavens ; He is no longer hidden
behind the clouds ; He is no longer invisible, silent,
unimaginable.   In the supreme spirituality of His
divinity He is still, it is true, incomprehensible and
inconceivable.   We have still to prove His existence
by abstract thought, to feel after His attributes as

one feels for ways and steps in the dark, to labour in forming mental images of His goodness, justice, and truth, and then to condemn them one after another as hopelessly inadequate. But as He has, in these final times of His love for man, taken to His Divine Personality the nature of a man, He is now within the grasp of those busy and powerful human faculties which deal with the forms and shapes of the world below, which take in and reply to the warmth of affection, the joys and tears of humanity, and the fragrance of histories that have long been past. " Thou art beautiful above the sons of men ; grace is poured abroad in thy lips, therefore hath God blessed thee for ever. Gird Thy sword upon Thy thigh, O Thou most mighty. With Thy comeliness and with Thy beauty set out, proceed prosperously, and reign. Because of truth, meekness, and justice ; and Thy right hand shall conduct Thee wonderfully."[1] This picture of the Incarnate God, which is paralleled by others in the Old Testament, as, for example, in the eleventh chapter of Isaias, sets forth in brief fashion, with far-reaching words, what the heart and imagination find in the Incarnation—the beauty, the wise and gracious speech, the triumphant might, the wisdom, the kindness, the Divine teaching, and the glorious success of Him Whom we have learnt to call by the pregnant name of Jesus. And these traits are nothing less than the features of God Himself, as we find Him at Bethlehem, at Nazareth, in Jerusalem, in Galilee, and on the hill of Calvary.

[1] Ps. xliv.

It is hardly necessary to point out that Jesus would
not have been the Jesus we know unless there had
been also Mary His Mother. He might have saved
us in many ways ; but the way which He has actually
chosen involves the most Blessed Virgin. For it may
be truly said that the Incarnation itself, and that
special feature of Our Lord's coming, which brings
God near to man, is best seen and most emphatically
displayed in the mysteries of His birth, His childhood, and His hidden life. That He is human—
that He is meek and gentle—that He chooses poverty
and obedience, that He has annihilated Himself to
prove His love for each of us, and the value of every
single soul, these things would have revealed God
and drawn us to God had He never uttered a single
teaching, or worked a miracle, or become obedient
to the death of the Cross. His public life is a part
also of His gracious mercy ; Calvary, besides paying
the price of our redemption, leads the Christian soul
to secrets which are not read in any other page of
God's dealings with His creation. But the Em-
manuel—God with us—stands forth, in His beauty,
His sweetness, and His power, long before the mysteries of the last three years begin. But what do we
find ? He is human, with a depth and truth which
take us captive. There is an announcement made to
a daughter of Juda ; there is the mystery of virginal
conception ; there are the troubles of husband and
wife ; there is the journey of Mary and Joseph ;
there is a birth at Bethlehem ; there is the stable
and the crib ; there is the flight to Egypt ; there is

a visit to the Temple, a loss, and a finding ; and there are then the eighteen years of subjection and obscure labour at Nazareth. If this is what you call Jesus—this series of ineffable and sweet pictures— who is it that is an essential element in them all ? Who is it that by her very intervention in the mystery of His coming proclaims His gracious humanity? Who is it whose absence or non-existence would make this touching and attractive history impossible ?

And it was for this purpose He created her. As the heavens show forth His greatness and the earth His power, so Most Holy Mary, a greater creation than the heavens, a more beautiful universe than the earth and the seas, proclaims to angels and to men, silently, by her very being, the depth and truth of God's pity and mercy to the creatures whom He has destined for Himself. You remember St. Paul : " For the invisible things of Him from the creation of the world are clearly seen, being understood by the things that are made."[1] With equal force and truth may we say that the " visible things " of Him—the great plan or counsel[2]—the dispensation of the Word made flesh, are made clear and convincing and indisputable by her who has been made His Mother. The intelligence and the heart of men and women can never make a mistake or harbour a doubt if they cling to the solid fact of the Virgin Mother. And the enemy of all good, whether he has desired to obscure the divinity of Jesus or His humanity, has always tried to push His Mother from her place ; whilst the

[1] Rom. i. 20. [2] Isaias ix. 6.

Catholic Church, holding fast to the traditional truth, has in every age made herself the herald of her great office, speaking out with clearer insight as errors have required her to speak, and dispersing all the great heresies before the waxing splendour of her prerogative.

It is, therefore, an essential point in the spirituality of a priest that he should look upon Our Lady as, to him, the Ark of the Covenant—that is, the expression, the symbol, the instrument of Jesus in His dealings with the soul.

First, let us understand how much need there is for a priest to study well the Incarnation.

In the priestly office, to which those here present are called, there are two lessons, above all others, which have to be learnt, and to be learnt from the Incarnation. A priest is not first an evangelist, and then a friend of God, but first a friend of God, and then an evangelist of God's good tidings. For if he proclaim God's Gospel ever so loudly, he will gather no souls to the harvest unless he is already a man of God, overflowed with the grace of Christ, steadily fixed in supernatural principles, and habitually dwelling very close to his Heavenly Father. Thus, a priest is bound, by his office, to study Almighty God. Let the expression be pardoned. It means, evidently, that as God is the only sanctifier and the only shepherd of souls, no priest can be holy and no priest can help his flock or his fellow men, unless he understands the designs and the ways of God. This knowledge can only be gained in the study of the

Incarnation ; because it is only as man that the Divine Creator can exhibit any attribute which men can imitate, or make choice of any means which fall within the scope of human action.

But what do we find in the Incarnation? That God is prepared to stoop to the lowest, and to adopt the last extremes, in order to save souls ; and that God thinks it wiser to work without earthly resources, and rather by means of obedience, poverty, obscurity, and suffering. This solicitude of God—His friendly and fatherly anxiousness—is the first lesson. This astounding choice of detachment, rather than of ample means, is the second. These lessons, priests, above all, have to learn. It is not enough to say that a priest must himself be zealous for souls, and himself detached from earthly things. To say that is to read a priest a chapter of spiritual reading, which he will perhaps dutifully listen to and will reverently accept for instruction and edification. But the true source of that chapter of spirituality will probably escape him. He will attribute it to the retreat-giver or the spiritual writer—to this or that Father of the Church —to this or that Saint or solitary. The school in which the Saint or the Father first heard that lesson he perhaps will not realise. And indeed this some-times happens by the fault or omission of the writer or the preacher himself. It is not every spiritual book which translates Jesus and transcribes Jesus. Some, like children who bring home water from a well, spill much by the way, and in offering what is saved make too much of their own small vessels.

That a priest should learn a lesson from among the
many lessons to be found in spiritual treatises is a
matter not to be despised ; but it is not enough.   He
must study God in the Incarnation.   For until he
studies Him, and studies Him thus, he does not really
believe that God's solicitous love is what it is, or God's
deliberate choice what it is.   Until he studies the Incarnation there is always the lurking feeling that zeal
for souls is only a duty, and detachment only a pre-
cept of propriety, which circumstances may often
supersede.   When he studies God he soon perceives
that the Divine Solicitude is one of those laws of
Divine Being which, if a priest do not take in and
assimilate himself to, he is out of the sun's rays,
out of the sweep of the rushing stream, out of the
path of the mighty winds of Heaven ; and that the
Divine detachment, so far from success coming in
spite of it, is the very means without which success
is impossible.   He is like the savage who finds a
magnetic compass, and at first admires its divisions,
its letters, and the grace of its quivering needle, but
afterwards learns with awe to mark how the tiny
point is never anything but steadfast to the pole.
" For ever, O God, Thy word standeth firm in
Heaven. . . . Thy justice is justice for ever,
and Thy word is truth."[1]

To learn Divine lessons from Jesus is a different
process from learning from the lips of teachers or the
pages of books.   Learning from Bethlehem or from
Nazareth requires preparation of the powers, spiritual

[1] Ps. cxviii. 89, 142.

journeyings, a clearing away of darkness, silences, and intensity of the listening heart. Often, when a man stands before the stable, he does not know it. Often when the Child Jesus is before his eyes, he does not recognise Him. Often he calls Him by His name, and does not apprehend what that Name is meant to reveal. We are baptised into His fold, yet live many a year and hardly know Him as our Shepherd. We eat His flesh and drink His blood, and yet do not turn our attention from worldly vanity. We sit in His school sometimes for long years, and there is no deep conversion, no real insight, no convinced following of Him Who alone can save us. What is more, we stand on the steps of His altar and serve even Himself in the dispensation of His most striking love, and yet we only dimly see His heart, His ways, His choice, His inward mind.

If such are a priest's difficulties, and such his needs, it is easy to see how Our Lady must help him. It may not be true always, and of every one—but it generally happens—that the heart awakes to such views of Jesus through the thought of His Mother. We are apt to grow up with a very abstract and, if I may call it so, academic, idea of our Blessed Lord. We are taught that He is God—as He is—and the opening mind grows accustomed to look upon Him as on some far off summit that we can always see from the home where we live. He is Divine, He is adorable, He is the Lord and Saviour. He is humble, obedient, overwhelmed with suffering. All this we know, and all this we dwell upon—from a distance.

We adore, we thank Him, we love Him. But something more is needed. We must come to see and
feel that His personality (speaking humanly) is our
healing ; that all His virtues are, as it were, a fulness meant to pour out upon ourselves ; that His
Heart, the Heart of the God-Man, is intended to
find its way, with all its humility and generosity, into
our bosoms, altering our poor hearts to its likeness.
But it is the thought of Mary that brings us to see
this.   Mary is kind, gentle, pure, perfect ; from
earliest years we find ourselves trying afar off to
imitate her, to express her, to form ourselves upon
her.   One day we open our eyes and realise that we
should also imitate Jesus, from Whom Mary's perfection comes ; imitate Him, that is to say, not only
because He is our pattern—for that idea we may
already have had, although it is often very abstract
with most of us—but imitate Him as one Who is
clothed with all that is perfect, for the express purpose of penetrating our souls through and through
with His perfections.   He, Who has so wrought upon
His Blessed Mother as to make her soul so beautiful
and so grand, is one who must also work upon my
soul and yours.   To find this out is to take a great
step.   Mary leads most of us to it.

As for Mary's intercession, I need not dwell upon
it in detail to-day.   If the blessed and immaculate
Mother of God loved that Son, to cherish Whom she
was created, can it be conceivable that she would not
love and cherish those servants of Jesus, who above
all others have to fill the world with His presence

now that He sitteth on the right hand of God ?   But
if she loves and cherishes the priesthood, it is by
drawing the priests of God nearer and nearer to
Bethlehem and Nazareth.   For this she evermore
intercedes ; pleading with the sweetness and power
of her office.   But she does more than intercede.
Or rather, her intercession is not that of one asking
for fragmentary graces, and for favours that are
handed to the receiver by another hand.   All her
power comes from her Son.   But the firm Catholic
tradition is that, as regards the immediate distribution of grace, it is she who is the agent.   As the
sweet waters of a land of hills and streams are
gathered first into some stupendous, peaceful expanse,
held up by walls and barriers of man's art, and then
directed in unfailing streams of refreshment to the
cities of the plains and the homes of rich and poor,
so the Lord and Creator of all things has fashioned
Mary to hold, as by her prerogative, all the mercies
of His Precious Blood, and to pour them out to
immortal souls.   And as she pours them out each
grace, and each stream of graces, carries with it something that is peculiar to Mary.   As the Incarnation
is the Incarnation such as we know it, principally
because she is in it, so grace, as we have it, has its
colour, and its distinct or specific effect which it would
not otherwise have had. from its coming through the
hands of Mary.   Now grace is of many kinds.   But
so far as it is active, it is always a quickening of
the powers of the human soul—first of its spiritual
powers, and, secondarily, of the imagination and the

other faculties that dwell in the flesh yet share in the spirit. Therefore the illumination, the inspiration, the heart, the good purpose, the love, the loyalty, and the clinging to God, which, in man's frail nature, are the effects of Divine grace—all these, although most truly the gift of God, and God alone, have in them some element which they derive from having passed through the ministering hands of her who brought forth Jesus at Bethlehem. If a heart, in the morning silence, is lifted up to adore and praise its Creator, that grace comes now with an added softness and human feeling, which sweetly enfold in their sweep not the intelligence only, but all the human powers. It carries the tender touch of Mary's hands. If the devout soul is moved to offer all its powers and self to God, that grace, coming through Mary, bears along with it to the creature, always in awe of its judge, some sense of that infinite stooping down of the Most High, which it is Mary's perpetual office to proclaim, and which has made the creature's oblation so full of trustful joy. When we have the grace of thanksgiving, we cannot doubt that that grace comes to us fragrant with that unspeakable association of frank recognition of God's favours with truest humility, which is expressed in the *Magnificat.* If we ask and offer our petitions, Mary puts into this grace of her Son that recognition of the nearness of God's merciful eyes and ears which can never be sufficiently vivid. The great grace of self-effacement and humility, carries with it, from Mary, a sense of fellowship with the lowliness of the greatest of all created beings. And when we bewail ourselves for sin, and think of the anguish of the Cross, that supreme grace of contrition has in it, from Mary, the savour of her own compassion, which opens new fountains of our own grief, and helps to melt that hardness of nature which stands in the way of supernatural sorrow. But it is especially what I have called the lesson of the Incarnation itself which Most Holy Mary teaches the soul to read. To study the Divine Solicitude with her as mistress, is to behold with our eyes the Sacred Heart white with the fire of super-abounding and irresistible grace—the grace which made her what she is, in order to demonstrate what God would do for human souls. To study the world's Saviour, choosing as His means of conquest the lowliness of Bethlehem, the obedience of Nazareth, the poverty, obscurity, and continuous suffering of His human career, and to study this with Mary standing by, is to hear her low, sweet mother's voice patiently striving to make her child understand, and pleading with it to look, and look, and look again.

These things we do not always recognise or know. But even when we are not absolutely thinking of Mary, her benign influence is raining down upon us, accompanying the graces of Jesus. Or, to put it more exactly—since all comes from Jesus—the graces that He gives, He gives with a particular stamp upon them, representing the effect of Mary's position and office. So that, on the one hand, He never touches us save with a touch which has Mary's touch on it, and on the other, in every act or inspiration by which we turn ourselves or lift ourselves to Him, through grace, there is always present some subtle vibration at least of that all-pervading ministry which is given to Mary in the kingdom of her Son.

It follows, then, that a Christian heart should never separate Mary from Jesus, as it never separates the Incarnation from the Deity. Not that there is here advocated any forced or mechanical effort to pray to Mary whenever we pray to Jesus. Devotion should be free ; and the human heart cannot, like an angel, breathe a whole spiritual system in one intellectual act. But it is good to recognise what Mary is to us, and to adjust our spiritual life to such a true and fertile recognition.

And it is true that this recognition of Mary's place and office is one of the most striking notes of the Holy Catholic faith. It is no matter whether we look at the lives of the Saints or at the living practice of every-day Catholicism — we learn the same lesson from both. The Catholic mother consecrates her infant to Mary, as we read that St. Felix of Valois, when a child, was dedicated to her by St. Bernard himself. Catholic youth, in their homes and colleges, are taught, as St. Francis da Girolamo taught his young hearers, that "it is difficult to save one's soul if we have no devotion to Mary"; and as indeed St. Bernard and St. Bonaventure had reiterated long before him in every form of ardent phrase. Every kind of memorial, of commemorative practice, of pious homage, such as is adapted to keep her cherished memory always before the heart, is familiar in the ordinary course of Catholic life. We venerate her image in our churches and our homes—and perhaps we remember with emotion how her saintly servants did the same : as St. Anselm, spending long hours of the day and night before that image in the church at Bec ; St. Hyacinth, carrying away her image in his arms ; St. Raymond, always praying prostrate before it ; St. Peter Claver, solacing his hard apostleship with the book of prayers and engravings of her which he carried in his bosom ; St. Francis Borgia, distributing everywhere copies of her well-known picture in S. Maria Maggiore; St. Francis Caracciolo, saying an *Ave Maria* whenever he passed an image of her ; and our own St. Edmund, with his little statue of his Queen before him on his desk in his student's cell at Oxford. We wear her scapular of Mount Carmel, recalling those words she spoke to the English St. Simon : *Ecce signum salutis, salus in periculis.* We love to carry her medal—a devotion dear to that Apostle of the Catechism, lately canonised, St. Peter Fourier. The Litany of Loreto is familiar in public acts and in our private prayers—even as St. Jerome Emiliani used to draw the people from far and near to hear his orphans and himself recite it—even as St. Vincent Ferrer used to repeat it over and over again in his journeying from one mission to another. The *Salve Regina* has been marked by the present Pope as the common and universal invocation of Christendom, in the Church's pressing needs. But our fathers were never weary of it : and it is touching to recall how St. Vincent de Paul, in his Tunisian captivity, converted his Arab captors by it ; how the martyrs of Gorkum chanted it as they were driven by the pikes of their persecutors to their glorious death ; how often the servants of God have owed to it their conversion, as the Venerable Vincent Caraffa. Of the Rosary we can only say, with St. Alphonsus, that no one knows how many by its means have been delivered from sin, led to a holy life, to a good death, and to salvation.[1]

There is no one here present, then, whose heart is not impregnated with this Catholic spirit—this spirit of the Saints—this conviction that, as Mary is the Mother of Jesus, so Mary is the Mother of Grace. But to-day we are met to perform an act of dedication and consecration which should both renew our devotion and perhaps, also, lift it up to a higher sphere. We are assembled to renew the consecration of this house and seminary to the Immaculate Mother of God. Such consecrations are solemn acts of life, and may be far-reaching in their effects upon the soul. There is a consecration which is God's greatest and first commandment—the consecration of our love, heart, mind, strength, and all we are, to the God Who made us. Every other consecration is only a means to keep this one fresh, to keep this one true. Thus we consecrate ourselves to the Infant Jesus, to the Sacred Heart, to Jesus Crucified. The consecration to Mary, which is so common in the Church, rests on a solid and deep theological doctrine—her

[1] *Glories of Mary*, ii. 148.

unique intercessory position and office. Since Mary
is what she is, we can best love and serve God through
Mary and in Mary ; just as we can breathe best in
the purest air. Therefore, not only can we never be
wrong in putting our powers, our work, our aspirations, our very merits and salvation into her hands ;
but the more we do so, the more effectively do we
give ourselves to the God Who has created her for
this very purpose. Hence the great Saints who have
altered the face of the earth have not only dedicated
themselves to the Blessed Mother, over and over
again, but have laid all their work at her feet—the
orders they have founded, the monasteries and
churches they have built, the institutes of charity
and compassion which they have spent themselves
to set on foot. Thus the great promoter of the
sanctification of the clergy, St. Charles Borromeo,
placed every one of his colleges under her special
patronage.

For many a long year has the venerable name of
Mary been invoked over this house of Oscott. Our
fathers, when they adopted the name, knew what they
meant—and we also know. For long years have her
festivals been kept here with love and splendour, and
her children have felt themselves to belong to her in
special and comfortable patronage. Now, when a
new chapter is opened in the history of a great
College, what can we do that is more just, more
pleasant, or more consoling, than dedicate afresh the
house and all it contains to her who has so long
watched over it with a mother's love ? For ourselves,

individually, we know and feel that our vocation to the
priesthood, and our fidelity to that vocation, are most
undoubtedly a part of that dispensation which the
Incarnation places in her hands. Arise, O God, let
Thine enemies be scattered! With her help we are
safe. Therefore, continually from the time the call
seems to have come, we have turned and we do turn
to Mary. Perhaps this new and solemn consecration
may show us new light in spiritual things, and draw
us to Jesus in things we have not yet imagined. And
looking beyond ourselves, to the whole priesthood of
this country, to the Church throughout the land, to
the body of professors and students in this central
seminary of Southern England, to the future interests
of Jesus Christ for many generations to come, we
may well unite with loyal hearts and fervent aspirations in the act of loving homage by which we are
about to profess anew our trust in the Mother of grace
and mercy—the Mother of God made man.

THE SPIRIT OF ST. EDMUND.

Spoken at St. Edmund's College, Old Hall, November 16th, 1893.

Sic rerum summa novatur,
Inque brevi spatio mutantur sæcla animantum,
Et, quasi cursores, vitai lampada tradunt.

"The Lord is good, His mercy endureth for ever ; for I will bring back the captivity of the land as at the first, saith the Lord" (Jer. xxxiii. 11).

THE celebration of the hundredth anniversary of the foundation of this house, which falls upon this very 16th of November, is an occasion of thanksgiving and of joy. When the Bishop and his little flock gathered around our Blessed Lord here, on this day, one hundred years ago, there was to all appearance more reason for mourning and apprehension than for bright auguries or confident hopefulness. Yet, on the whole, this century of years now closed has been a bringing back of Juda and Jerusalem, a bringing back of the captivity. That is what we can see now. This house of St. Edmund is a representative part of our English Catholicism. It has stood with stability for a century, and it has progressed and thriven. This means that strong roots have been fixed in the soil of this country, and that a vigorous and fruitful tree may be reckoned upon. I do not inquire how much of that vigour and that fruitfulness are evident even at this moment. If we look upon this past century as no more than a century of beginnings, we may well praise and bless Almighty God for the stability and the steady growth of a college like this. There is no phenomenon in our present condition which is more prophetic of substantial success than the stability of our Catholic institutions. During the storms of the great Revolution the wreckage of our seminaries, our monasteries, and our houses of religious women, was thrown up on the shores of this country—a country strange, inhospitable, and unknown. The servants of God landed in England destitute and discouraged. They found toleration, and even charity, and by degrees they settled in the South and in the North, in ancient manor-houses, on bare hillsides, or in the suburbs of great cities. They set up their roof-tree, and built their altar once more to the Most High God ; and they began the struggle for existence. They were threatened by many dangers ; by poverty, by the falling off of their numbers, by the lack of things academic and things religious, and even by persecution. But the remarkable thing is, that few, or next to none, of those communities which came over about 1793 have disappeared. We have them amongst us still. They have lived ; they have kept up their numbers ; they have contributed to the Catholic life of the country, and taken their share, each in its own way, of the labour and the sacrifice which God has inspired, and which God will also infallibly bless. Our colleges and religious houses are almost all a century old. Such stability indicates the special Providence of God. Of them we may say, as the Psalmist says of the Jewish people, " Thou hast planted their roots, and they have filled all the land."[1] If the Lord our God has guarded them and watched over them during so many years of peril, what can be His purpose, except that they shall still further develop, and with them the whole kingdom of God in this country?

That this merciful design may suffer no hindrance from ourselves—that we may enter into His counsels with all the powers of our soul—this is the reason that we celebrate a day like this with the prayer of thanksgiving, and that we venerate the name of the heavenly patron who has been to us for all the century the pledge of Divine guardianship. Even if St. Edmund of Canterbury were not your titular Saint, I should find in his life a most striking religious lesson, such as may, with the greatest profit, be brought before a community which is dedicated to the building up of the kingdom of God. In the life of St. Edmund there is certainly little repose or stability, and apparently little success. But foundations such as God lays may be laid in storm as well as in sunshine ; better, indeed, in martyrdom than in peace. The only condition is that those foundations be Christ's own and not another's. St. Edmund died in 1240. The national apostasy may be said to date from 1536. During that long three hundred years religious calm prevailed in England. Her churches multiplied, her liturgical service grew richer and

[1] Ps. lxxix. 10.

richer, and her simple people served God under the
wings of the Church.   Undisturbed stability is best
shown by material evidences.   At the end of this
period of three hundred years there was not a Church
in all Christendom whose temples, shrines, foundations, and institutions were so rich in accumulated
treasures and works of art as our own.   This points
to a period of peace ; of continuous Masses, Sacraments, and preaching ; of faith and simplicity ; of
Catholic living and Catholic dying.   It was the
English Saints who purchased this inestimable peace.
Among them all there is no one, after Thomas or
Anselm, who poured himself out more generously
than St. Edmund.   His life culminated in the seven
years of his episcopate, for which he had been prepared from his earliest youth by the Holy Spirit.
Those seven years were years of martyrdom, opposition, trouble, and hardship—every one against him,
the king, the bishops, and his very household ; the
desolation of the Church without remedy ; even the
Holy Father mis-informed and hostile.   And under
all this his spirit was oppressed with a bitterness the
like of which perhaps no other English Saint seems
to have experienced.   His life was the fulfilment of
the remarkable vision of his mother, who saw his
head crowned with thorns all on fire.

I may, perhaps, take for granted that the outlines, and even the details, of that heroic and crucified life are known to you.   Let me, therefore,
ask you to follow me in reading the lesson which it
teaches.

I find in St. Edmund three *charismata* or gifts : learning, innocence, and austerity.

" Learning" is a very inadequate word to describe that devotion to sacred studies which, had he not been raised to the episcopate, might have been named as the very characteristic of his spirit and the purpose of his life. In his early childhood we find him at Oxford, beginning the career of his studies—where so many in that age began them— in the very porch of the church itself. We see him advancing in knowledge with the quickness of natural talent and of purity of heart. The Child Jesus sits unseen at his side in school, and appears to him visibly in the playing fields. He throws himself into the intellectual life of Paris, where Alexander of Hales was teaching, and where Albert and Thomas of Aquin were shortly to appear. He lectures amid the unorganised beginnings of Oxford. He leaves the fascination of secular studies for Divine theology, and at Oxford his disputations and discussions draw his hearers by that combined depth, fluency, and devotional feeling which mark the intellectual man who is also a Saint. In the writings which remain to us we have the scholastic form of the *Sentences* and the *Summa*. He may indeed be justly styled the first pioneer of scholasticism in this country ; and, although there is no record of the fact, he must have been a chief instrument in bringing to Oxford that Dominican Order to which all his life he was so devotedly attached ; for the first two Dominican teachers had been his own disciples. St. Edmund is the intellectual founder of mediæval Oxford. He is, therefore, one of the pillars of that great edifice of scholastic theology which is with difficulty distinguished from the temple of Catholic doctrine itself.

The gift of innocence is a special characteristic of St. Edmund. It is a peculiarly interesting feature when taken in connection with his busy uncloistered life, and his wide sympathy with every form of intellectual excellence. Next to the grace of God, it seems to have come from his mother. Indeed, the very combination of which we speak—of study and innocence—was a part of her fostering system in his infancy ; and there is a remarkable vision which represents her in after years as the cause of his giving up "arts" for theology. In the whole of the lives of the Saints there is no story which carries with it such an aroma—such a conviction—such an evidence—of innocence as that of the apparition of the Child Jesus, when Edmund was fourteen years old. The same impression is confirmed by the incident of his dedicating himself to Our Lady by placing a ring upon her finger in the Church of St. Mary at Oxford, pledging himself to her as the Queen of Virgins and the patroness of holy purity. We have similar evidence in his great devotion to St. John the Evangelist ; in his habitual visits to the image of St. Frideswide, the virgin patroness of Oxford, in the little church of Binsey, and to the Ladye Chapel of St. Merri, at Paris. Those who knew him from his infancy were able to affirm that he was never stained by deadly sin. It is certain that he was keenly alive to the connection between innocence and true theologica science, as taught in Holy Scripture. His studies never made him miss daily Mass or the Divine Office. He assiduously practised the Sacrament of Penance. He sat at study with an image of Our Lady on the table before him. He went from prayer to lecture, and from lecture to prayer. His saying of Mass inflamed every beholder with devotion. He watched night after night in the churches. Over and over again he broke off his courses of teaching, because he was afraid of vanity, and wished to flee into the solitude of religious houses and to exercise himself in offices of charity and religion. His whole life, given up as it was in great measure to study, to preaching, and finally to pastoral solicitude, is truly and touchingly described in that outburst of devotion with which he welcomed the holy Viaticum : " Thou, O Lord, art He in Whom I have believed, Whom I have chosen for my portion, Whom I have loved, Whom I have preached and taught ; Thou art my witness that I have sought nothing on earth but Thee alone ! " The fruit of innocence is detachment. The innocence of the child, of the youth, of the man, ripens at last into that perfect purity of heart to which is given the sight of God in this world and in the world to come.

The austerity which marked the whole career of St. Edmund might seem surprising when we remember his innocence. To Catholics who are acquainted with the principles of the spiritual life, and who read the lives of the Saints, it is no surprise, but merely natural. As he owed to his mother his innocence, so to her he was indebted for his early initiation into the mysteries of the Cross. It was her spiritual discernment and Catholic instinct which made him grasp from his earliest years the great spiritual truth that there is no advance either in holiness, or in Christian intelligence, except by the Cross. Under her direction he fasts and uses the hair-shirt in his first boyhood : she promises him that these practices will secure for him the tender solicitude of God ; and we are assured by a biographer, who probably uses the Saint's own words, that when he and his young brother first went to Paris, it was in answer to this youthful austerity that their Heavenly Father both kept them from bodily want and opened their minds to understand. Throughout his whole life the Saint's mortification in regard to food was so great that he was constantly emaciated and pallid ; he never seems to have lain down in bed or had a real night's rest for six-and-thirty years ; and he wore during most of his life a hair-shirt, which, as described by his biographers, recalls St. Rose of Lima or St. Peter of Alcantara. These things it would be imprudent in most of his clients to imitate, or to attempt without advice ; but the spiritual lesson is for every one of us—that no man can learn Catholic truth, teach Catholic learning, preach the word of God successfully, or labour for souls with fruit, who does not live a mortified and austere life. The mystery of the Cross is this, that without the smart and the anguish of pain, willingly accepted, the best acts of love and union must be wanting in a certain intensity and efficacy. Austerity is the reparation of the sinner, the medicine of a life misspent, the healing of a nature depraved by guilt; but it is also the pure cold air which fans the innocent heart's aspirations to its God, and which draws God to speak to mind and spirit, to communicate His wisdom and to stir up His mighty power.

This College is a house for the training of those who are to labour in spreading the kingdom of God. In the past, how many priests have left this roof to work in England! Even now, when its schools of philosophy and of divinity have been removed, there are, and there will always be, many who will one day stand at the altar. And even if many of its students never enter sacred orders, yet they have a large share in that responsibility for the well-being of Catholicism and for the conversion of the country of which none of us can divest ourselves. Nay, what is more, they are trained, and they will be trained, as if they were to be priests; for one characteristic of our colleges from the beginning has been that, in educating lay students and Church students together, we have not lowered the standards of piety and discipline to suit the world, but have lifted it up to what is required for the child of the temple.

Standing at the close of one century and the beginning of another—with the memories of all that has gone on within these walls present to the spirit, and anxiously looking towards the future, it seems to

me that we may draw inspiration and encouragement
from the thought of St. Edmund, and from this day
itself.

St. Edmund reminds us, first of all, that to build
up the temple of God there must be learning. There
is no need to disguise from ourselves the fact that
the English Church, during the last hundred years,
has not been a learned Church. How could she be?
She has had to find bread to eat and a roof to
shelter her. She has had to struggle against
extermination. She had to put up her altars and
her elementary schools. She has had to impose
hands on her priests with the least possible
delay, in order to save the remnant of believers,
or to cope with the numbers that asked her for
Sacraments. Her missions have emptied and drained
her schools, as missions always do. She had no
lack of great names when her camps were beyond
the seas. Means, leisure, universities, and the
contagion of intellectual life bred men of splendid
achievements—a Stapleton, a Harding, a Bridgwater,
a Bristowe, a Cressy, a Hook, and an Alban Butler.
Neither have learned men failed her even in her
beginnings in this country. But learning, it seems
to me, should be among our chief petitions and
aspirations on this centennial day of St. Edmund.
For, in the Catholic Church learning is not an
ornament, or an amusement, or a luxury, but it is a
necessity. Speaking of the Church at large and of
the well-being of each part of the Church, we must
unhesitatingly say that it is a necessity. For learning

is the fuel of the Faith. It is true that learning sometimes leads to doubt or to rashness ; but that is accidental. What learning really does is to widen the field on which faith shines, and to gather together and heap up, as the priests in the Temple heaped up the victims, material of every kind for the action of faith thereon. Faith may, and often does, burn with very little knowledge ; but for a blazing holocaust of faith there must be the treasures of the student's labour, or the infused knowledge of the Saint. Moreover, without learning the Church herself does not grow. There are men who sit at home and whose ideas circle round the fence that divides them from the outside world ; and there are men who travel over oceans and continents and bring home stories of a vast and beautiful universe. The kingdom of the Precious Blood is a limitless inheritance ; but it is an inheritance to be won by the work of human faculties. Growth and development mean the co-ordination of truth, the comparison of truth with truth, the setting out of consequences, the unfolding of meanings, and the slaying of pernicious error. And finally, learning is required to meet learning—Catholic learning to oppose heterodox learning ; or else the Church of God will be despised, and the progress of God's kingdom prevented. In all these different fields of learning this College and other Catholic colleges, and the Catholic body at large, have done by no means despicable things with the means at their disposal. Think of what has gone on within these walls during the century of

years which has just closed.   Men have studied and
men have taught.   For the sake of Christ's kingdom
they have spent themselves and been spent.   No rich
endowments, no ample scholarships have stimulated
them.   No crowds have come   with fees in their
hands for degrees and for fame.   Yet they have
carried high, and handed on, the   torch of sacred
learning.   They have sent men out with classics, and
with divinity, with the subtleties of Church law and
the broad views of the Fathers.   They   have   risen
early and lain down late, they have sat in solitary
cells, they have worked in their library, they have
gathered classes around them, and the men they have
sent out have taught the faithful of this country to
know their religion, and to appreciate it.   From the
pulpit of many a church in London and elsewhere,
and sometimes in books and writings, they have set
forth the Church Catholic, with her history and her
prerogatives, and the kingdom of Christ's redeeming
love in its vastness, its divinity, and its magnificence.
They have preached the Sacred   Heart,   and the
Immaculate Mother, and the " privilege " of Peter.
We reverence these men who have held fast to study
and have carried on the traditions of Christian schools.
Let our younger men imitate them.   Let the century
that is to come seize the sacred torch and bear it on
yet more boldly, yet more swiftly.   Let us all understand that learning is absolutely essential.   May
St. Edmund foster that thought, and inspire the
sacrifices necessary in order to carry it out !   There
is no need to be discouraged at the vast development

of non-Catholic learning which has marked the last fifty years. What do we see in the labours of non-Catholics? Magazines of facts, views beyond number, historical research, and a leaven of religious error. I do not say that we are excused from meeting them on their own ground. We must meet them. We must know all their facts, weigh all their opinions, follow them into every cave and *archivum* of the past, and expose all their errors. But our own learning is really of another kind. We start from assured premises. We have the once-delivered Faith. To open out that Faith—that is our learning. To follow the Fathers, the Councils, and the Saints ; to have all that has been said at our finger tips, and to add our own contribution, small or large, to the vast and glorious system—this is our learning. This we must have first. It calls for no slight labour. It requires philosophy, science, and art ; history, ethics, and the science of man. When we have it, and our schools have produced a new Albertus Magnus, or a nineteenth century *Summa*, then the very weight and light of that achievement will do more for the kingdom of God than a hundred volumes of polemics and of refutations. Nevertheless, these latter we must also have, and the Divine help which gives us the one will also give us the other. May St. Edmund intercede for us all, that there may come down on the schools of this country, during the coming century, the spirit of wisdom, of understanding, and of knowledge !

But we require his holy prayers, not only that

learning may grow and flourish, but that it may be learning of the real Catholic kind. There cannot be such learning without innocence. There may be research, discovery, philosophical treatment, Scripture criticism, and many other things; but not the building up of the Faith. For this must come from the Holy Spirit; and that Spirit will not enter into a nature that is "subject to sin."[1] The traditions of the Catholic schools are, that the young must be kept innocent, and that the mature must live in dread of .sin, or there will be little progress in learning. Catholic schools have been always under the shadow of the Church. When we look back on the solemn and God-fearing Catholic customs of the early years of this past century, may we not fear that in the coming century the good old traditions of Catholic unworldli- ness will have to fight with the spirit of the age? What is it that we see? Are not our young people beginning to imbibe those hard and selfish principles which are now so common? The innocent heart expands like a blossom to its God, to Jesus Christ, and to all that belongs to the world of grace. There is no possibility of this to a heart which is shut up in self, and which is only interested in the chances of the present life. Yet we expose Catholic boys to this danger more freely every day. It may be impossible to help it; but the seclusion, the carefully guarded "ignorance," of our Catholic students is disappearing. Their scholastic year is far shorter than it was; they live as much in the world as at school; in the world

[1] Wisdom i. 4.

—because strict and edifying homes are also becoming more difficult to find. They mix with non-Catholic boys, who are prematurely knowing and cynical, who speak with easy toleration of religion, and who cannot even conceive what Catholic piety is. Their impressionable minds are thrown into the midst of a world in which supernatural principles, Sacraments, and childlike prayer are virtually unknown. They run the risk, not only of falling into sin earlier than they might, but of suffering the destruction of that simplicity, that respect, and that strictness of ideal, which should characterise every Catholic student. Perhaps these dangers exist, without any real check, even with our more mature students who are actually studying divinity. College rules may be unexceptionable; but long vacations, the diffusion of print, and the easiness of travelling have broken down the gates of the seminary, and even the young levite is a man of the world, in whose intellect sacred learning has to struggle with mental difficulties which no immature mind should even know of; in whose spirit there is working the sour leaven of independence and criticism, and in whose heart there are too often the images of things which soil it beyond the ordinary power even of grace to purify. Our forefathers strove to keep boys innocent; "ignorant," if you please, as far as innocence implies ignorance; and such ignorance might be calculated in some degree to check maturity of character, or to interfere with prospects in life. But innocence has its reward. It is only the pure of heart that see God and the things of

God. It is the child of the temple to whom God's revelation is made. And if we wish to see the glory of a great revival of Catholic theology, we must have the self-restraint and the fortitude to resist worldliness, and to keep up the old Catholic strictness.

St. Edmund teaches yet a further lesson. The hope of the future, the hope of learning and the hope of the progress of God's kingdom, lie in the Catholic tradition of austerity. It may well be doubted whether on this head we have not departed from the practice of the men who brought back the Captivity. The records of those days tell us how they suffered and endured. They tell us of the narrow walls, the hard fare, the early hours : they tell us of economy, simplicity, and mortification. Men venerable in years and services shared alike with the latest comer. There was a tradition of silence, of repression, of severity. The cold winter's morning found the community on their knees in the chapel. The recreation was carefully measured ; study and labour filled the day ; and in the refectory they read the stern yet glowing chapters of the *Imitation of Christ*. These good traditions have remained with us. But have we carried them on in their full vigour ? One thing at least must never pass and be lost : whatever rules are altered, and however fashions and customs change, we must hold fast to the Christian principle that it is the Cross alone which can lead us to victory. One generation may find the Cross where another may not look for it. We live in our own times, and the details of our life are not those which prevailed in the lives of our fathers. But it is certain that our religion is the religion of the Saints ; and that no college, or Church, or people, which repudiates the Cross, can have a future. The life of the glorious St. Edmund is not out of date ; it was never less so. If the ease of life and the luxury of living have increased and are increasing, they form no rule, no example for us. We are to use the world's appliances, perhaps—but not to let it sap our Christian sobriety. We are still to be austere ; to profess austerity, to uphold austerity, to understand the reason of austerity. We are to be austere, not because a simple life is a noble life, or because self-indulgence is unmanly, or because we have not the means to provide ourselves with luxuries ; but because the gifts of the Holy Spirit do not operate except where they find the severity of the Cross. Nay, the very life of affected simplicity and ostentatious modesty which in these days is so commonly seen at non-Catholic schools and universities— what is it too often except the absolute antithesis to the spirit of Christ Jesus ? Its motive and purpose is that very self-indulgence—the more subtly dangerous in proportion as it is less gross—which the mystery of the Cross was intended to kill.

These thoughts are suggested by the name of St. Edmund of Canterbury. These thoughts derive their appropriateness, and I will say their solemnity, from the venerable anniversary which we celebrate to-day. That these stones, and the roofs which cover this spot of ground, have arisen and have multiplied, we

have to thank God with our fervent prayers. That
there has passed here so long a history of human
lives, of Christian achievement, of study, of innocence and of the imitation of Jesus Christ—for this
we must go still deeper into our hearts to find an expression of our gratitude to God. For it is not only
that this has come to pass, and that its story is written
in the records of the heavenly Sion and in those of our
Church and country ; but that this departed century
is our own inheritance. Because this century has
been, we are here to-day. Because these years appeal to us, we are stirred with aspirations to all that
is holy and noble. These stones mark the spot ; but
we venerate them because they cry out, every one of
them, of prayers and labours and sacrifices. The
spirits of the departed fill these halls and cloisters.
This church is fragrant with the incense of how many
hearts, that have lifted up their adoration and their
love ! These precincts and all this hallowed enclo-
sure are like the threshing-floor of the favoured
Israelite on which was placed the Ark of the Lord
of Hosts. This house, where our Blessed Lord has
dwelt since that first Mass and first Exposition, is
more truly the House of the Lord than that to which
the promise was made of old : " I have chosen and
have sanctified this place, that My Name may be
there for ever, and My eyes and My heart may
remain there perpetually."[1] Our fathers could tell
us, if their voice could be heard on earth now, that
the choice of God, and God's sanctifying power,

[1] 2 Par. vii. 16.

have indeed brooded over this sanctuary from decade to decade ; they could tell us how truly and absolutely it has been His most Holy Name, and no other, that has been its owner and its Master ; how His eyes have watched over it, and how His Sacred Heart has blessed it and built it up. They are not here to speak for themselves : they are with God, as we hope ; and their bodies are buried in peace, some on the spot of the wide battlefield where they fell in the service of their King, some near us, in your vaults, guarded by your suffrages, as if you were still one community. As the years and days go on, we shall join the bands of those who are departed. But whoever shall come and whoever shall go, it is the same God—the God Who is good, and Whose mercy endureth for ever ; and may it be in every sense the same house, for no house can perish which the Lord shall build up.

THE APOSTLE OF ENGLAND.

*Preached at the Centenary Celebration, Ebbsfleet,
September 14th, 1897.*

" My Father worketh until now, and I work " (John v. 17).

MOST EMINENT CARDINAL,[1]—These were the words
which, nearly thirteen hundred years ago, Gregory
the Great wrote to St. Augustine in England.   The
letter—the long, paternal, joyful letter—may still be
read, in which he gives " glory to God in the highest "
for the beginning of the conversion of the English.
" Whose work," he said, " is this but His Who said,
' My Father worketh until now, and I work ' ? "
Standing now on or near a spot which St. Augustine's feet once trod, where his voice was first lifted
up, where his band of monks chanted, and where the
English King met him, we can measure that work
with greater knowledge than St. Gregory had ; and
there is no saying of our Divine Lord which is more
apt, or more fitted to raise the heart to Heaven, on
such a day than this, in which he foretells the labours
of His Apostles, and reveals to us that their success
is due to Him, and to Him alone.   For we are met
here to-day to praise and bless God for St. Augustine
and for the Christianity of England.

[1] Herbert Cardinal Vaughan, Archbishop of Westminster.

Between the day when the missionaries of St. Gregory stood here around the image of Jesus Christ, and this, on which, in sight of that same figure of our Lord and Saviour, a band of bishops, clergy, and faithful laity are gathered in thanksgiving and devotion, a long stretch of centuries has intervened—long enough to have seen generation after generation falling like the leaves of the autumn, to have seen the growing up and the decay one after another of a hundred works and institutions which have cost much labour and filled a great space in the world. In spite of the mists of time, which deepen as we gaze down the lengthening vista of the past, it is not difficult—it requires but little effort—to place ourselves in the company of those dark-robed men from Italy and France just landed on this shore. We may not be able to picture the scene—but that is no matter. It was this earth that they stood upon ; it was this sky which was over their heads ; it was these neighbouring cliffs which stood silently as now ; it was this curve of the sea's restless margin between the Forelands, into which their little ships ran with anxious hearts on board. But this shore, these waters, and these fields of Thanet, are very different now, when mysterious laws that never sleep, but always creep on resistless, have forced back the sea, emptied water-courses, and brought the habitations of man to desolation, silence, and ruin. Once the fleets that carried the legionaries, and the vessels of the traders of Gaul and Spain, lowered their sails as they drew near to the quays of the Roman city still majestic in ruin not far from where we stand. Now, populous towns of this nineteenth century have taken possession of the region, whilst great steamers hurry past, this way and that—a sign how near is what was once remote, and how changed is England from the day when St. Gregory called her " a little corner of the world."

Yet, in spite of every change—changes in the face of the land, in men, and in their works—there is no heart of a Christian and a Catholic which cannot pass over the great gulf of thirteen centuries, and feel that St. Augustine and his companions are known to him as he knows his friends. " Who are these that fly as clouds and as doves to their windows? For the islands wait for me, and the ships of the sea in the beginning; that I may bring thy sons from afar; their silver and their gold with them, to the name of the Lord thy God, and to the Holy One of Israel, because He hath glorified thee. And the children of strangers shall build up thy walls, and their kings shall minister to thee."[1]

Who are these? That is precisely what we know. That is what we can so well enter into and estimate. The islands were waiting for Jesus Christ. This land of Britain, separated from the world by its narrow sea, had not indeed been left without the mercies of God. But a new race had come to occupy a large part of it, and it was to be no longer Britain, but England. Thus it "waited" for the Gospel of grace and salvation. These men, therefore, of whom we

[1] Isaias lx. 8, 9, 10.

are to-day thinking, are servants of the loving Heart
of Jesus, whom He has sent to the land and the
race, which were waiting for Him. As to other
lands, over all the earth, so the earth's Redeemer has
sent these hither in His own good time. Like a
flight of doves they have come from afar, over seas,
over a continent, out of the unknown, to alight on
the shores where noble hearts are ready to hear and
respond to them. On their lips is the name of Jesus ;
in their hands is the banner of redemption. They
are Apostles. They are "sent" by Him Who alone
can send. They come to "make disciples" of the
heathen English. They come with the light of the
Gospel and carrying the very word of Christ—a word
which, although uttered by human lips, is yet stamped
with the inerrancy and the fruitfulness which make
it to be His, and His alone. They come with the
silver and gold of Calvary—the treasures of the Precious Blood. They come to set up the Christian
altar, and to dispense of the fountains of Christ—
those Christian Sacraments which will make this
heathen wilderness to blossom as the rose. They
come with a code, and a counsel, and a power, which
will bend the necks of kings, create a social order,
and cover the land with the temples and the trophies
of the reign of Christ.

These things speak to us—to us, who have so few
things in common with either Italians or Englishmen
of the sixth century ; to us, who know something of
the history of thirteen hundred years—of the vicissitudes of St. Augustine's work—of the sins, the wars,

the revolutions, that have followed each on the other's heels in this land of ours ; because Jesus Christ is yesterday, and is to-day, and is the same for ever. Souls are to be sought out and saved ; nations are to be converted and made to serve the living God ; the shadow of death is to be beaten further and further back ; the banner of Jesus Christ is to be carried further and further afield ; and the men who did this for our country all those centuries ago, need no laboured description to be recognised as kin, and to be loved in Christ Jesus, by every true friend and follower of His kingdom, not only now, but even if the world lasted ten times thirteen hundred years.

Yet it cannot but be that it is sweet and profitable in this year, on this day, to look more closely at this English Apostle, whose words were once heard with such power in this Kent, this Thanet, where we are gathered, and first of all upon this very spot. We have no biography of him. He has left no letters, no sayings, no record of mind, or heart, or life. Yet I for one seem to be able to gather his spirit and character from these few pages of Venerable Bede, which discover him to us starting for England at the age of thirty, and leave him, with his simple epitaph, honourably entombed seven years afterwards in the northern porch of the monastery at Canterbury which was soon to take his name. The broad and simple view of him is—that he is the Apostle of the English nation. What was said of him one hundred and forty years after his death by the Council of Cloveshoe was this : that he " was the first to bring to the nation of the

English the Faith, the Sacrament of Baptism, and the knowledge of our heavenly country." It may be laid down as a certain truth that no man is ever a successful Apostle unless he is a great Saint. Almighty God sometimes may use instruments that are unworthy and vile ; but not for the great operations of the Precious Blood. For there the effect or result is measured by the interior condition of the spiritual soul : by the intensity of love, prayer, and suffering. For in these more august and striking ministries which approach nearer to the triumphant and all-powerful work of the love and suffering of the Sacred Heart itself, it would be against all spiritual feeling and the traditions of the Saints to suppose that a great work is ever done for God unless the instrument is fashioned to the likeness of the Sacred Heart. Therefore it does not need St. Augustine's miracles to prove to a Catholic that he was, in a most excellent sense, a friend of God. We know it because he was a great Apostle. The few scanty gleanings which we have about his spiritual history confirm what on these irresistible grounds we cannot help believing. On St. Gregory's authority we know that he was deeply read in Holy Scripture, a devout and practical monk, and a man whose virtue had been proved beyond dispute. And there is one thing also that we know from St. Gregory—that he was especially beloved and esteemed by that illuminated man, led by the Holy Spirit, Gregory himself. Then, we can gather the hardships and the strenuousness of his apostleship : that long, interrupted, thankless, painful journey ; the anxieties

of leadership ; the heroic venturesome landing in
England.   After that, there were the seven years of
his labours in England itself ; the strict asceticism of
the life at Canterbury, which is described by the
Venerable Bede as " an imitation of the apostolic
life of the primitive Church," and a life of " continual
prayer, watching, and fasting "; a life in which they
would touch nothing but what was necessary for liveli-
hood ; a life in which there must at first have been
great probability of suffering and even of martyrdom,
for Venerable Bede says that they were prepared to
face all adversity and even death itself, for the sake
of the truth which they had come to preach.   Add to
this his preaching—a preaching to uncivilised fighting men, in a language that was strange to him ; his
journeys, not only all over Kent, but also to the Continent ; to the Severn, on that unsuccessful mission
to the British bishops ; very likely also to the North,
as some chroniclers have set down.   The ancient
Prophet said, " Whomsoever the Lord shall choose,
he shall be holy."[1]   And when the Lord chose Aaron
for his High Priest, straightway his rod burst into
blossom and fruit.[2]   And Isaias, prophesying of our
Lord and Saviour Jesus, and of His preaching, prophesied also of all those whom Jesus should choose
and send : " Behold My servant . . .   My elect,
My soul delighteth in him ; I have given My Spirit
upon him, and he shall bring forth judgment to
the nations."[3]   Great Saint, living now in the light of
God's face, in thee we honour the overflowing love of

----

[1] Numbers xvi. 7.   [2] *Ib.* xvii. 5.   [3] Isaias xlii. 1.

Jesus, Who first transformed thy soul to His own likeness and then sent thee forth to gather our forefathers to His fold !

I cannot pretend, on an occasion like this, to detain you long enough to review and estimate that great fact—the Christianity of the English nation—which in so true a sense took its rise on this spot. But in order to stir up the devout thanksgiving which should be the note and character of this celebration, I would ask you to observe that the Christianity which Augustine brought was the full and complete Christianity of the Catholic religion, which reigned and flourished in this country of England from the time of his landing for a thousand years.

There is only one Christianity—using the word in its adequate sense. It is the Christianity of the true doctrine of the Incarnation, of the sacramental system, of the Real Presence, of the Mass, of the Blessed Virgin's office, and of that which guards and secures the whole—the interpretation of the mind of God by the Church's pastorate, and primarily by the Sovereign Pontiff. We need not refuse the name of Christian to any one who claims that august name. But we know well what Christianity is—the complete faith and hope, and the supernatural love of God and of men, kept up by the peculiar grace-giving institutions of the New Law. These things St. Augustine brought. These things were realised in England. The change came with these forty men, and it spread as the clouds spread over the hot and dry desert, till all

the land was green and fertile. First, the idols
of the heathen were destroyed, and the name
of the Living God set up where they had been.
You read in Venerable Bede how gently this was
done, and how the ancient temples were not pulled
down, but purified, and how the old Teutonic open-
air superstitions and feastings were gradually transformed and moderated. Thus the English race
became a race of God-fearing men, all their native
seriousness and their awe of unseen powers sanctified
to the remembrance and worship of Him Who made
both Heaven and earth, and their love of homely
merry-making helping to accentuate the festivals of
Our Lord, and of that Blessed Mother of God and
those Saints who explain and illustrate Jesus Christ.
For the missionaries of England brought not only
God, but Jesus Christ. They brought Bethlehem,
Nazareth, and Calvary. They preached Him Who
has brought God near to all the powers of the soul
and all the emotions of the heart. They taught all
whom they baptised how each day and hour, and all
the work of the hands, must be sanctified by intercourse with the God made Man ; and there was
carried through England, and impressed upon the
English people, the spirit of prayer—of that Christian prayer which springs from the feeling of the
Incarnation ; that prayer which gave the vision of
Jesus Christ to St. Edward the Confessor—which
gave St. Edmund to see the Child Jesus in the Oxford
meadows—and which (as we read in the vernacular
prayer-books of the ages of Faith) taught gentle and

simple alike to end their prayers with "Good Jesu, grant it me," "Jesu, grant it may be thus," or "Sweet Jesu, Amen." They brought to the English people the persuasion of the sanctity of the moral law, the appreciation of the unseen and the spiritual, and of the value of the immortal soul. This noble spirit by degrees inspired the laws of England. It kept within bounds the powerful and violent men of the race, and moderated their wars. It abolished slavery. It protected the female sex, and covered England with their monasteries. It raised up some of the noblest prelates and pastors which Christian annals have known, to fight the battle of the kingdom of God against the world. It led Englishmen to the practice of the evangelical counsels, and often to the heights of sanctity, so that our history is full of the influence of Saints.

Moreover, as the Council of Cloveshoe emphatically says, St. Augustine and his companions brought to the nation the Sacrament of Baptism. By baptism the nation of the English became one in the faith of Christ. In the power of this unity, it was almost a necessity that the landmarks of tribes and petty kingdoms should disappear. How England became politically one, it is not my office to say. But it is certain that unity of faith and of Church government made it easy and natural. By baptism, moreover, the nation began to belong to that world-wide brotherhood of nations which is formed by the great Catholic Church. By her baptism, the great races and nations of the world

became her sisters in Christ ; and the varied life, the
literature, and the holiest glories of Christendom
began to be part of England's enjoyment and possession. Once mofe, by her baptism she entered
upon what the Apostle calls the " riches of the glory
of the inheritance of Christ."[1]   She began to use the
Sacraments—she began to cherish the Blessed Eucharist.   Is there any feature in any Christian
country so striking as the number and the excellence of the cathedrals and the parish churches of
this land ?   These were the symbols of her faith, the
homes of her piety, where the kingdom of God was
more sensible than elsewhere, and where her Saviour's
fountains more abundantly flowed.   These were the
dwelling-places of the Lord of Hosts, where her
children found that Presence which has dimmed the
glory of the Temple of Sion, and left us little to
envy even in Bethlehem or Nazareth.   And, therefore, the history of England is a history of the
building of churches great and small ; a history of
adding and enriching ; a history of never ceasing to
express her faith by nave and aisle, chancel and tower ;
of providing more and more lavishly for piety by
altar and chapel, by the tombs of the Saints, by
precious metals, by painted glass, by the warmth
of colour, by the beauty of her sanctuaries and the
solemn richness of her days of festival.   All these
things St. Augustine began ; of all this harvest of a
thousand years he sowed the seeds.   It would be
too long to enumerate everything that sprung up

[1] Eph. i. 18.

and flourished in the age which he inaugurated ; or
we might dwell on that deep appreciation of the Incarnation which made this country so devoted to the
Mother of God ; which led bishops, priests, and
people to look for her in every mystery of Redemption, to multiply her venerable name and her image,
and to lay at her feet all the Church and nation that
she might guard and cherish it for ever. Or we
might recall her schools, her doctors, and her monasteries ; her great primates, her many religious kings,
her canonised Saints. But above all details there
arises before us this day the thought of a great
noble, and powerful nation, for a thousand years
united in the full and adequate Christian faith,
honouring Christ, and believing in Christ's kingdom.
Throughout its broad shires and in its busy towns it
was Catholic. The sovereign, the peer, the knight,
the artisan, the tiller of the soil, in its castles and
hamlets, wherever its downs and plains spread out,
wherever its rivers ran, or its seas encompassed it,
wherever the winds of its seas blew over it from
shore to shore—all were Catholic. Be the drawbacks
or the blots what they may—and there is no need to
reckon them up to-day—this thought embodies a
real, solid, and inspiring truth—and for this we praise
our Lord and Saviour Jesus Christ.

Was this, then, the work of St. Augustine ? I
think that no one can mistake the sense in which it
was his work. He was the founder. His love, zeal,
holiness, labour, and suffering laid the foundation—a
deep foundation, a strong foundation, an enduring

foundation. We need not inquire, and we cannot know, how much we owe to the intense upliftings of the heart with which St. Gregory planned and followed the great work; we need not calculate the share of Columba, of Aidan, of Paulinus, of Chad, of Theodore, of Wilfrid. By priority, by leadership, by large and lasting success, by all that he did through other men, Augustine is our Apostle; and the mighty hidden forces which alone convert hearts to God are expressed in that antiphon which we sing to-day, which Augustine used, it may be on this spot: "We beseech Thee, O Lord, in Thy mercy to take away Thy wrath and Thine indignation from this city and from Thy holy house, for we have sinned."

It is strange that there can be any man so blind as not to see what it was, under God, wherein the strength and blessing lay of the Apostolate of St. Augustine. Christianity which is not complete and adequate, is not only not Christ's Christianity, but it is as sure before long to be disintegrated as a building is when the roof lets in the storms. The suggestion has been made, by those who must find theoretical support for a false position, that St. Augustine intended to found an independent Church. It is difficult to conceive that even the idea of an independent Church can ever have presented itself to him. Like every mind reared in Catholic tradition, he must have had the universal Catholic instinct, that independence in Christianity meant the falling to pieces of Christianity. It would not have mattered whence he came or who sent him. But it was from Rome he came, and to Rome he belonged. In St. Peter's strength he founded the English Church. That successor of St. Peter who sent him was a Pope who has left behind him in explicit terms his conviction that "every bishop is subject to the Holy See."[1] That Pope gave him the Pallium, defined the limits of his archiepiscopal jurisdiction, and made the priests of the British Church subject to him. It has been stated that St. Gregory expressly rejected the title of "Universal Bishop," and that therefore he could never have claimed authority over a national Church. But we have it in his own words that he only disclaimed that title in the sense in which he disclaimed for St. Peter the name of "Universal Apostle"; and in the very same passage he vindicates St. Peter's "princedom" over the whole Catholic Church.[2] Can there be a doubt as to the mind of St. Augustine? Not any more than there can be a doubt as to the mind of St. Gregory—or as to the mind of that English Church which owed him its beginnings. It was the union with Rome which alone, under God, kept away heresy, prevented schism and dissension, and saved the spiritual jurisdiction from the strangling and paralysing hand of the State, over and over again during these thousand years. And if we doubted what St. Peter has done for this nation when he was obeyed, we have only to glance at the last three hundred and fifty years, since dogmatic teaching has ceased, and at the present moment, when

[1] Ep. ix. 59.   [2] Ep. v. 20.

the body which calls itself the English Church is indefinitely at variance within its own bosom on every
point of Christ's religion—on the Eucharist, the reconciliation of sinners, the Sacrament of Baptism, the
world to come, and on the Bible itself.

And this leads to that inevitable note of mourning
which cannot be kept out of a celebration like the
present. Had God so willed, what a festival this
nation and race might have kept this year ! What a
gathering might have attended this Pontifical Mass
and *Te Deum* at Ebbsfleet ! We have to lament
that we are only a fragment ; that our countrymen,
in the mass, are cold to our devotion and strangers
to our enthusiasm. To have seen the English people,
represented by their highest and best, this day
honouring St. Augustine by joining in the great
sacrifice he himself was wont to offer, I know not
which of us here present would not have been
content to occupy the humblest place, and to have
wept whilst worthier voices spoke his panegyric !

Yet we have the right to hope. The Father
worketh until now—and Christ worketh—and St.
Augustine continues his work, for he is our Apostle
to the end. " You are they," said Our Lord to His
first Apostles, " who have continued with Me in My
temptations ; and I dispose to you . . . a kingdom, that you may eat and drink at My table."[1]
Being in the presence of the face of God, he can
help England better now than by his words on this
shore, by his journeyings, by his share in the Cross

[1] Luke xxii. 28.

—more than by all his going to and fro in Kent
and Britain—more than by the austere asceticism
and continual prayer of his monastic life at
Canterbury. It is our right, and it is also our
duty, to hope. There are those who would say
that to bring back England to Catholicism would
be harder than to bring back the salt sea waters
which thirteen hundred years ago ran up almost
to the spot whereon we stand to-day. But moral
laws are not as physical — immortal souls are
always dear to Christ—and God's mercy and compassion are infinite. And perhaps something is wanting on our own part. It is true, there is no one here
present, or indeed throughout the whole of the
Catholic body in this country, who does not pray for
England's conversion. And most warmly and plead-
ingly to-day does that prayer ascend, in the company
of the lifting up of Christ's heart in the sacrifice,
from every one here present : from the laity, who have
come here in all their faith and loyalty ; the clergy of
all ranks, in great measure representing flocks of a
race that is still united in honouring its Apostle ; the
monks, whose name is so bound up with England's
history ; the bishops, who are anointed with the same
unction that was laid on St. Augustine ; the Cardinal
Metropolitan, who chiefly represents St. Augustine
to-day by word and action as by position ; and, not
least, those brethren from the churches of France—
that most eminent prelate who brings back the
memory of the love and affectionate service of the
Church of Autun to our English Apostle.[1] The

[1] Cardinal Perraud.

memory of this day will swell and strengthen this choir of united prayer. But the office of the apostolate is an office of labour and of endurance. It is for these things that St. Augustine calls on the Catholic clergy of this country and their flocks for good and patient speech in due season, for the manning of forlorn hopes, the laying down even of life in work that brings no fame, for years and years of persevering intercession, for true and active zeal for souls. O country of our birth—England that we love—generous land that drawest thy sons together by cords and sympathies so many and so strong—would that Christ might give thee back that which Augustine brought! By all thy Saints, by all thy martyrs, by that fragrant incense of the Mass that has hallowed Thee through the centuries, by Mary, Mother of God, by St. Peter, by thy first Apostle, may God pardon our sins, answer our prayers, and lead thee back by gentle might to perfect faith and Catholic unity!

ST. JOHN THE EVANGELIST.

Preached in his church at Bath, December 26th,
1897.

"This is eternal life : to know Thee, the only true God, and
Jesus Christ, Whom Thou hast sent" (John xvii. 3).

THESE are the words of Jesus, as set down by St. John
the Evangelist. They are not a truism or a commonplace ; but a light that must never grow dim, a warning which must never be lost sight of. Eternal life
is the knowledge of God and of Jesus Christ. It
may be said that no one in these Christian days disputes it. Not to know God is to be a heathen ; not
to know the Incarnation is to miss redemption—to
find no way to the Heaven that awaits the saved.
Yet, if we do not deny it, we are far from seeing the
depth of its meaning. What do Our Lord and His
great Evangelist mean by "knowing" God ? Can
God be known ? Can the mind of the finite creature
ever attain to know the Infinite Creator ? And, on
the other hand, is the soul, which has God's image
impressed upon it, to be content with knowing Him
afar off, as one knows a planet, or the frozen Northern
seas, or the great deserts where lions roam and man's
foot has hardly trod ? What means the Prophet of
Patmos by "knowing" Jesus Christ ? Must a man
have lived with Him, heard His voice in the flesh,
grown familiar with His tone ? Or, again, is it

enough if we only set Him up in a niche among the
heroes of the centuries, and pay Him the respect of
a silent recognition, reserving the warmth of affection
for personalities whom we know more closely and
more intimately?

There are two great containing maxims which
bound and define the Christian and the Catholic
doctrine of the knowledge of God; first, that God
is incomprehensible even to the seraph most remote
from material condition; and, secondly, that every
heart is bound to study Him, for in that study there
is unfathomable light and salvation. The wide
extent, the surprises, the fertility of the study of
God and of the Incarnation, are only faintly known
by large numbers of these who shelter themselves
under the name of believer and of Christian. It was
to bring home to men what I may reverently call the
character of the God Who made us, that John the
Evangelist was commissioned to write three Epistles,
one great Prophecy called the Apocalypse or Revelation, and the Gospel which we call the Fourth, or
the Gospel of St. John.

I am not, on the present occasion, to address
myself to the infidel, or to any class of non-Catholics.
I am to speak to Catholic believers; even to those
who, may I not trust, are devout in their faith, and
are attached with some degree of warmth to the
illustrious Saint—Apostle, Evangelist, Prophet, and
Martyr—who is the venerated patron of this church,
and whose festival comes to us to-morrow, whilst yet
Jesus Christ is newly born in Bethlehem. But we all

have this disadvantage, Catholics as we are, that we live, few in numbers, in the midst of a nation which is not blessed with the full Catholic faith. This must be a misfortune. The men and women who sur- round us may have a hundred good qualities ; but if our ideal is a true one—that Jesus Christ has left a dispensation of infallible teaching, of sacramental ministration, of a real Eucharistic Presence and a true Eucharistic Sacrifice—then we must suffer from our environment, as a tree suffers which you trans- plant from a sunny slope on the Mediterranean to our own bleak Eastern sea-board. Coldness kills as well as contradiction. A faith that meets with no welcome, no encouragement—that sees no reflection of itself in other faces—that hears no echo of its utterances in the world in which it lives—a faith which is some- times stolidly ignored, sometimes lighty ridiculed, sometimes bitterly reviled—a faith which must exist under such conditions may well pine, dwindle, and even die. That it lives, and lives a life as hardy as it does, is to the praise of God and the glory of Divine grace.

In speaking, then, of the part which St. John the Evangelist has had assigned to him, in the impress- ing upon the world what kind of knowledge of God and of Christ a Christian man may have, and ought to have, it is always needful to take into account what is being said by non-Catholics. For if we have, in our own body, any errors, any shortcomings, they are —under the special circumstances—sure to be errors and shortcomings such as float upon the literature of

the day and are current among the men who preach,
who write, and who read, in the country we live in.

The Gospel of St. John, and his other writings so
far as they are on the lines of his Gospel, are neither
a treatise on God, nor an exposition of the human
nature of Christ. St. John's theme is the God-man ;
the Person Who existed, thought, spoke, in two
natures—the Divine nature and the human nature.
For of Jesus Christ we say, and say truly, " He is
God, He is Man."   We also say with complete truth,
when we are describing His thoughts, words, deeds,
or sufferings, " He is the Creator, He is the Judge,
He is the Last End "; and " He was born, His
Sacred Heart loved men, He sought sinners, He
was crowned with thorns, He died upon the Cross."
It is the same Person, in all these instances, Who is
designated by the word " He " or " His."   It is clear
that in this august mystery—this Incarnation of the
Word—it is not the mere human attributes of Jesus
that are so interesting to us whom He came to save ;
that is, not the human attributes apart from the
Divine personality.   Let us admit that our Blessed
Lord's human nature was the most perfect ever
formed ; that every organ and tissue of His sacred
Body was purer than gold, nobler than the diamond ;
that His human intelligence and all His spiritual
powers were, even naturally, comparable to those of
the angels ; that His aspirations and sympathies were
deep as the ocean, strong as fire, holy as those of the
seraphim.   Had He been only man and nothing
more, He would have been the first of the world's

heroes, the greatest of the world's Saints. But it is obvious that all this nobility must recede far into the background—must almost fade into space—in comparison with the master-thought of the Incarnation—that it was my God Who thought, spoke, acted, suffered when Jesus did these things : that this human nature was not only the Deity's tabernacle or dwelling, not only the Deity's instrument, not only the Deity's manifestation, but also the Deity's assumed nature.

In truth, we may look upon the Incarnation as a grand commentary on the character of God. Man, without the Incarnation, had never known what God truly is. I do not say that some knowledge, and even an extensive and a consoling knowledge, of the Infinite Creator would not in such circumstances have been capable of being acquired. But such knowledge, when compared with the clearness, the force, and the certainty of the knowledge we have now, would have been of very small value to draw human hearts, and to save wayward human souls.

The great danger to human nature, as we find it, is the danger of mistaking Almighty God, and so of forgetting Him. There have been instances in which God has been forgotten without being mistaken or misconceived ; and also instances in which He has been misconceived without being forgotten. We find an example of the former in those who have learnt their faith and yet turn their backs on their Creator ; of the latter in those who impute to God erroneous attributes in matters of predestination, vengeance, feeling, or universal toleration, and yet, in their way, continue to serve the God Whom they thus fashion to themselves like an idol. But generally forgetfulness follows misconception. Men easily come to think that they need not remember Him Whom they seem to find a difficulty in imagining.

Human nature, urged on by the activity of the enemy of mankind, has had three periods, or phases, of misconception or mistake about God. There is, first, the error which we may call essentially heathen —that God is too remote from men, and too high above them, to care for them or their concerns. The heathen ideal of God was, speaking generally, more or less idolatrous and irrational. But when, as happened sometimes, they formed to themselves some approach to the conception of a pure God, a holy God, a just God, an almighty and eternal God, it may be truly said that, invariably, they turned away from that vision in despair, as from one who could not possibly have any sympathy with the frailties, the limitations, and the sinfulness of men and women. Their gods, as Moses saw, were always "distant" from them, in the same proportion as those gods were godlike and not human ; it was Israel alone that believed in a true and living God Who was "near at hand "[1]— a God Who was "present to all their petitions "; a God Who, as the Psalmist said in His time, allowed His people to " draw nigh " to Him.[2]

The second error is that which we may call the heretical error ; the error of those who have accepted

<hr/>

[1] Deut. iv. 7.   [2] Ps. cxlviii. 14.

the Christian covenant, and yet distorted its most glorious feature. Christianity is reconciliation, salvation. It has always been a distinctive mark of heresy, and it is especially distinctive of the great Lutheran and Calvinistic heresy, to assert that salvation meant, not a regeneration of human nature, but a mere imputation or transaction on the part of God. The Church of Christ, firm in her grasp of God's word, and unfaltering in her exposition thereof, has uniformly proclaimed that we are saved by being moved, illuminated, cleansed, and glorified by grace even in this world. She has taught that the Holy Spirit comes to dwell within the human temple ; that supernatural influences surround, penetrate, and permeate the natural being and the natural powers, and that there is an august system of visible arrangements which are the occasions, and even the means, of a Divine communion, which the God of Heaven could—as He often does—bring about without any visible interposition at all. But the heretical spirit is to keep up a barrier, impenetrable as adamant, between human nature and its Redeemer. It asserts, indeed, that souls are saved ; easily, too easily, saved ; but it is only as the bodies of those who have been drowned in the wreck of a great ship are rescued after death from the hungry sea, and laid in stark and ghastly rows on the shore. The souls of the saved are saved in all their sin, in all their state of spiritual death. There is for them no mystery of regeneration, no elevation to a supernatural life. A visible Church is superfluous, a sacramental ministry is a mockery, good works are only a sham, even prayer itself—for certainly fiduciary assurance cannot be called prayer—is an empty breath. Such views, I will admit, are seldom found in any human breast in all their crudeness and unreasonableness ; unbelief is as inconsistent as it is perverse. But the poison pervades the religious systems of a Protestant country, as the pestilent breath of a land of marsh and jungle never ceases, even when the season is at its healthiest. And it is by no means certain that it does not affect even Catholics, and make them undervalue, or lose sight of, the work of Divine grace in the soul of a man who is travelling to his goal in the world to come.

But in these non-Catholic countries there is another false view of God, which is beginning to kill genuine Protestantism. It may be called the scientific error —or, more correctly, the error of the scientists. It is the error of those who assert that there may be, and probably there is, a God Who is in some sense the Creator and the Judge ; but that, even if there be, His attributes and character are so unknown to us as to make it practically impossible to assert anything about Him ; nay, that even as regards His being a person at all, whilst we cannot disprove it, neither can we form any consistent notion as to what it means. Some people call this attitude of mind agnosticism. Its evil effects are found in all the literature and all the talk of the present day. It is gradually extinguishing all belief in revelation. It is making people regard Christianity as a mere transitory phase of human development, which will itself be superseded as time goes on. It is blurring and confusing all the lines and shadows of right and wrong. It is leading to an entire scepticism as to the awful judgment after death ; and it is turning Heaven and hell into the terms of an antiquated myth which satisfied men when the world was younger. For if God is unknowable, then we cannot know what He would have us do and what avoid, whether we are to live or to die, whether He loves His creatures or whether His love is as remote and insignificant as the nucleus of some far-off comet, and His power as unsubstantial as the vapours that stream behind it in the skies.

What sort of a Gospel—what sort of a message from the Heavens—was needed to neutralise the deadly poison of such views as these ? What kind of a revelation was to be given, and to burn through the ages—as the warning fires burn through the night on the cruel headlands of the restless sea—in order to keep men, even in a Christian dispensation, from relapsing into heathenism, taking up with heresy, or losing themselves in the chill fog of agnosticism ?

That Gospel was to be the Incarnation. For the Incarnation, even as a mere naked fact, is an answer to all these errors ; and an answer which makes them impossible. But the Incarnation was not to be an isolated and unclothed fact. It was to be surrounded with every circumstance which could impress the intelligence and the heart. There were to be his-tories of birth and of childhood ; a birth-place, a mother, a holy home; words, acts innumerable and precious; and the record of human suffering and death. The men who were to hand down these things to all generations were to be called Evangelists. Of these, the Holy Spirit has vouchsafed four. Each of them wrote a history of the Incarnation, and of the God Who was Incarnate; and each from a different point of view. St. Matthew, St. Mark, and St. Luke agree in this—that they appear to have written what was the actual oral teaching about Jesus Christ which was made use of by the Apostles in their first preaching. Hence they relate, to a great extent, the same facts, the same utterances, the same miracles; and they differ from one another chiefly because these primitive instructions would, in a certain degree, differ, according as they were addressed to the Jews, to the heathen, or to a mixed community. These three voices of the Eternal Spirit preach Jesus, as a man might have pointed Him out upon the earth, or realised Him as he sat at His feet and heard His voice. What the world wanted first and foremost were the facts—the birth, life, passion, and death of the Son of God. These the Apostles preached assiduously, as men who had to deal with rude and unprepared intelligences—giving them milk instead of strong meat. But there was to be a fourth voice of the Spirit. There was to be a fourth Gospel—or rather, a final chapter in the one Gospel. I need not dwell upon its external features; they are known wherever the New Testament is known.

But let us see what is really done for the world in this Gospel of St. John. We call it the Gospel of the divinity of Jesus Christ. But let us be sure we understand what that means. It is not an exposition of the Godhead ; not an abstract treatise on the Divine nature. Nay, we find that it is wholly taken up with the Man, Jesus Christ. It gives us His picture, as a living and breathing man, far more forcibly and thoroughly than all the other three Gospels put together. Yet it is not a Gospel of His humanity, either. No! it is the grand Gospel of the Word made flesh ; not of the Word, not of the flesh, but of the divinity as Incarnate. The Man is before us ; but it is the Divine Person that we are bidden to observe. The Man speaks, acts, suffers ; but it is chiefly the way in which that speech, that action, that suffering reveal to the considering intelligence the qualities and attributes of God, that makes the fourth Gospel such a precious inheritance to Christian hearts. From the beginning the Word had been manifested ; but the darkness had largely overpowered its light. In the flesh, that Word, heralded by the Baptist, had come among its own—but its own had received it not. The fourth Gospel was meant to show to those who had goodwill that truth, that grace, that glory, which the Incarnation really meant ; that personal love of God for man, that longing for communion and intercourse, and that never to be quenched solicitude, which are God's essential attributes in relation to the human beings whom He has created.

It may seem that, in order to prove all these things,

it would have been enough to have left to the world no further record—no longer commentary—than we have in that single statement, " The Word was made flesh." For what other impulse could have urged the Lord of Eternity to break through the laws of His own creation, and set His foot on the gross and solid earth? What could have made Him take a Body to be subjected to physical vicissitudes, a Heart to feel, nerves to thrill, a voice to speak, and a soul to gather merit with it all—except that He would show what kind of a Father and Friend He was? What could have moved Him to throw across the widest chasm of universal being—the gulf which separates the finite from the Infinite—this rainbow bridge of Incarnation, but the wish to take hold of the creature, and draw us nearer and nearer to Himself? So that St. John's grand formulary was enough. He learnt it of the Holy Ghost, and he spoke it to men. As St. Augustine says : " Speaking with a voice of thunder, he lifted himself above the earth, above the skies, yea, above the hierarchies of Heaven, above all the spirit and powers in the heavenly places, and attaining Him by Whom all things were made, he said, ' The Word was made flesh.' "[1]

But this was not enough for John, because it was not enough for Jesus. The Gospel of the beloved disciple is the enforcement in detail of the reality of God in Jesus. St. Augustine says he learnt the things he said, or the significance of them, from the breast of Jesus, whereon his head was laid before

[1] *In Joan*, Tr. xxxvi. 1.

Calvary. For his picture of Jesus is, first of all, of One Who desires, and takes the means, to be a familiar friend of men. The first picture of Jesus in the fourth Gospel is this: One day—it was on the banks of the Jordan—the great Baptist saw Jesus coming to him, and he said, " Behold the Lamb of God."[1] The Baptist points Him out to Andrew and another—no other than John the Evangelist. The day after that, the Baptist sees Jesus walking, and again says, " Behold the Lamb of God."[2] As Jesus walks He stops and turns round, sees the two disciples, and asks them what they seek.[3] They wish to know where His abode is. He says, " Come and see." They go with Him ; it is the evening hour, and they stay and converse with Him until night— perhaps far into the night. A day or so later, St. Andrew brings St. Peter to Jesus. Jesus looks upon Peter, and says, " Thou art Simon ; thou shalt be called Cephas, the Rock." The day after that, when Jesus was preparing to go into Galilee—to go back to Nazareth—He finds Philip, and bids him follow Him. They depart—four in number with Jesus the fifth—and on the way from the Jordan to Galilee, perhaps as they are crossing near Bethel, the scene of Jacob's vision, Jesus sees afar off a Jew seated under a fig-tree ; it is Nathanael —the fifth to be called. Nathanael hesitates when Philip would bring him to Jesus ; but Philip says, " Come and see," repeating the words of the Master, with a thrilling sense of what happened to himself on

[1] John i. 29.   [2] *Ib.* 36.   [3] *Ib.* 38.

that first evening. And when Jesus has amazed Nathanael by reading his heart, He says, "Amen, amen, I say to you, you shall see the Heaven opened, and the angels of God ascending and descending upon the Son of Man."[1] To me, my brethren, that little party are the first-fruits of the universe, the nucleus of the saved, the representatives of the human race. I see One Who walks the soil of Palestine, Who abides in a hut of branches and leaves—a rude shelter, by the river, Who shows that he has come for men; Who seeks men, Who turns to men, Who invites men to His abode, Who keeps them conversing with Him for hours, Who draws men to follow Him over the mountains to His distant home, Who with a steady look of Divine inspiration gives a stranger a new and significant name, as God gave in the Old Testament, and who claims the heavens as His witness and the angels of Heaven as His ministers. And if I go on through the chapters traced by the hand of him who was one of that first little company, I see the Lord of Heaven and earth for three years seeking, calling, finding men out, looking into their face, moving them to surprise or to joy by His presence. I read of four never to be forgotten interviews; interviews in which Jesus is alone with one person; but each of which, with its words and circumstances, is adapted to make all generations feel what the great and Eternal God would do, longs to do, for the whole human race. First, the interview with Nicodemus by night. To a weak and timid man,

[1] John i. 51.

the Lord and Saviour reveals the law of the "new birth." Thus would He, in all times to come, raise infirm hearts to believe in the supernatural life. Next, the interview with the Samaritan woman at the well. To a sinner, Jesus preaches in earnest words, the "living water"—the redeeming grace which can both purify and give strength to live purely. Not on her alone, but on you and on me, would the God Who loves us press these words of salvation—individually, personally, as He did with that woman; scorning fatigue, despising food and rest, trampling on human respect; making a conquest of her soul, but showing in the same hour what God would do for every soul. Thirdly, the interview with the man whom He healed at the Pool of Probatica. That man, as you know, after He had healed Him, He sought; He sought Him, and found him in the Temple. "Sin no more," He said, "lest some worse thing befall thee."[1] Have we not here an illustration of the mercy and charity of that Heavenly Father Who uses every outward incident of human life to reach the inward souls of His creatures? Our God is not a God Who can be content without our immortal souls. His universe will go on, His laws will act, His seasons will follow each other, the day and the night without cessation will testify to His glory; but that is not enough. In the temple, in secret places, in sacred moments, our God will always seek us out, and in the ways that He knows will make the heart feel that all is vain and empty unless it leads to

[1] John v. 14.

repentance and to love. And, finally, the interview with that blind man to whom He gave sight. Him again He seeks. It is after the Jews have cast him out that Jesus seeks him. " Dost thou believe in the Son of God ? " " Who is He, Lord, that I may believe in Him ? " " It is He Who talketh with thee ! "[1] Is it not a lifting of the veil from the holy of holies?—a revelation of the very heart of God ? For it proves that God would seek out individual men and women, to make them feel that He is their only Father and Friend. It proves that He feels—to use a human phrase—that a man must have a friend, even when the hour comes in which earthly friends avail him not ; that He offers Himself ; that He presses Himself; that He can always find a way to make Himself present, and that he will always do so ; and that He is not satisfied with the creation of the universe, and the awful power of the Infinite, but rests not till He makes the individual atom, the frail human unit, of all the millions that are and shall be, fall down before His all-sufficing Pre-sence, and give Him the worship which alone is pledge of life and bliss.

It is here, as it seems to me, that we have the grand characteristics of the Gospel of St. John—that it shows men their God as One Who burns to deal personally with every human heart. This conviction is the all-necessary conviction that every man must have. If I have not this conviction—if my God to me is only afar off, or too mighty, or only a force, or

[1] John ix. 36, 37.

only a name—then my being will never blossom into what it is made for. But when I rise from reading the Gospel of John, I must either feel that conviction in every fibre of my essence, or I must fling the book away and disbelieve.

We might dwell on many more details which illustrate this. Observe, for example, how, in St. John, the Word made flesh not only seeks out men and deals with them personally, but seems to interest Himself in all the concerns that can be called human. He turns the water into wine to befriend a poor bridegroom. He cannot think of the men and women around Him without seeing them as a harvest, white for the sickle of His apostolate. He loves Lazarus, John, Mary, Martha ; He weeps at the grave of His friend, He is troubled at the treachery of Judas ; He prays for His Apostles, and for the flock of every age and country ; He will not allow them to disturb Magdalen. He prophecies, with the vision of Calvary before His eyes, that He will draw all things to Himself. Let us notice, again, how He rejoices at the good things which His holy coming, His Precious Blood, are to bring to His people. He announces that He is to give them life, light, holiness, and the Holy Spirit. His words are burning ; His zeal is infectious ; those who come near Him feel that a new era, a new dispensation, is about to dawn. The Gospel of St. John is full of this stir and motion of the New Covenant. You have seen, on a calm and cloudy day, a lake lying grey and still ; and you have seen the wind rise suddenly and the sun come out,

and then the waters began to stir and move, to ripple
and to sparkle as if some spirit, as in the beginning,
had moved over them. It was thus that, in the
Christian inheritance, a new life—the life of grace—
was to be breathed over the spiritual universe of the
souls of men. And it is in the Gospel of St. John
that we can watch the God of souls, with human
speech and teaching, revealing the new dispensation,
inventing the terms by which men were to know it,
insinuating its laws and conditions, and causing the
awe-struck generation to feel the coming on of that
Pentecostal storm and fire which was to be the
official beginning of the new time. It is in St. John
that we hear chiefly of the "life" that the Son of God
is to bring ; that we read of the new baptism ; the
new birth ; the taking away of sin ; the banishing of
the darkness ; the Eucharistic gift, life and antidote
of the spirit. It is in St. John's revelation that we
read of God's servants overcoming spiritual fear,
wearing white robes on earth, becoming as refined gold,
living on a hidden manna of Paradise, holding white
counters on which are written new names that no
man knew. And these things appear in the writings
of this beloved disciple, not as lessons or homilies,
not as the proverbs of a sage or the didactics of a
Solomon ; but as the record of the earthly career of
the God-Man. He has taken upon Him human
nature ; and His human nature is not dead and
silent, like a painted face upon the canvas ; it
lives, moves, acts with a warm and abundant life,
in a long and varied career, from the manger to the

Cross, and even to the Ascension. And every one of
its recorded manifestations is a manifestation of the
inmost mind and heart—let the expression be pardoned—of the everlasting and eternal God. And to
John the Evangelist it has been given above all other
men to write these things down, and to leave them
for you and for me. The Gospel of John, then, is
beyond others that utterance of the one great Gospel
of the Incarnation which is best fitted to keep out
heathenism, to neutralise heresy, and to make agnosticism impossible.

The best panegyric of St. John is that he was the
instrument of the Holy Spirit in thus enforcing on
the Christian generations this true knowledge of
God and of Jesus Christ, Whom He had sent.
That which he heard, that which he saw with
his eyes, that which he looked upon and touched
—that he has declared to the Church.[1] No—not
only that; but also that He whom his senses
thus took note of was the "Word of Life";[2] the
Word which was to reveal to men Who and what
their God was. You remember what happened after
the resurrection, on the shores of the Sea of Galilee.
Jesus came to the spot where the Apostles laboured
at their fishing, and stood, in the early morning light,
as they drew to land. He asked them for food; they
had none; he bade them cast the net again; they
did so, and drew a miraculous draught of fishes.
How really and truly on that morning Our Lord
must have shown Himself a man! Not one of the

[1] 1 John i. 1.　　[2] *Ib.*

disciples recognised Him—neither Peter, nor Thomas, nor Nathanael, nor James, nor the two others. Even John did not see at first who it was; but at the miraculous draught he looked more intently, and then he said to Peter, "It is the Lord!" His was the truest sight, his was the deepest perception. A pure and innocent youth had prepared him to follow the Lamb with all the promptness of love; a high and enthusiastic spirit had been disciplined by his Divine Master into the spirit of the Apostle, the shepherd of souls, the martyr; the Supper and his place there, Gethsemani and his watch there, Calvary and his station beneath the Cross, had given to him visions more piercing and transforming than when afterwards he saw the opened heavens; the company of Most Holy Mary had helped him as the years went on to absorb more and more the meaning of the Word made flesh; and at last, in his old age, at the inspiration of the Holy Ghost, he had taken his pen and begun, "In the beginning was the Word"—these words to begin with; and, for the end, the charge of Jesus to Peter, "Feed My lambs, feed My sheep." My brethren, you are truly His sheep; you belong to Him; He will not, He cannot be, anything but your Friend and Father. St. John would have you never forget these things. Have a little courage to walk forward where the light seems to cease and the shadows to thicken; have a little courage, with such a Gospel as John has left you, to follow your faith. Peace, comfort, repose, happiness—they are all not far off. Only yield to this leading, believe this voice; take St. John's view of the world, and his view of your spiritual enemies ; and then, learning from him lessons that will sink deeper with every hour of prayer and every day of Christian life, you will at length come to know something of the riches, of the mercy, of the solicitude, and of the everlasting love, of the God Who made us all for Himself.

Selection

FROM

Burns & Oates'

Catalogue of Publications.

Latest Publications.

A Form of Prayers following the Church Office. For the use of Catholics unable to hear Mass upon Sundays and Holidays. By the MARQUESS OF BUTE. Limp cloth, 1/- net (postage 2d.); or bound in leather, with gilt edges, 2/6 net (postage 3d.).

Life of St. Gerlach. By F. A. HOUCK. Crown 8vo, cloth. 2/-.

A Martyr of Old York. Being a Narrative of the Life and Sufferings of the Venerable Margaret Clitheroe. By J. B. MILBURN. With 13 Illustrations. 1/- net (postage 2d.).

Hymns for Congregations, Convents, and Missions. By the the Very Rev. L. C. Canon COELENBIER. Wrapper, 3d. net; limp cloth, 4d. net (postage 1d.).

Consolations of the Sick Room; and the Christian Nurse's Guide. Compiled, with the help of kind friends, by the Rev. JOSEPH EGGER, S.J., author of "Meditation Leaflets." Cloth. 1/-.

The Soldier of Christ; or, Talks before Confirmation. By MOTHER MARY LOYOLA, author of "First Communion," &c. Edited by Rev. H. THURSTON, S.J. Crown 8vo, cloth, gilt, Illustrated. 5/-.

The Passion Play of Oberammergau. The Complete Text, with the addition of the Choruses in Rhyme and Rhythm. Translated from the German by MARY FRANCES DREW. Crown 8vo, cloth. 1/6 net (postage 2d.).

A Month's Meditations. By CARDINAL WISEMAN. From MS. left by his Eminence, and now first published. Crown 8vo, handsomely bound in quarter leather. 4/-.

Our Mother. A Story by FRANCES I. KERSHAW, author of "Mrs. Markham's Nieces," &c. Crown 8vo, cloth, extra gilt, gilt top. 5/-.

Honour Without Renown. A Novel by Mrs. INNES BROWNE, author of "Three Daughters of the United Kingdom." Crown 8vo, cloth, gilt. 5/-.

BURNS & OATES, LIMITED,
Granville Mansions, 28, Orchard Street, London, W.

ALLIES, T. W. (K.C.S.G.).

A Life's Decision. Second and Cheaper Edition. Crown 8vo, cloth. 5/-.

THE FORMATION OF CHRISTENDOM SERIES.

Vol. I. The Christian Faith and the Individual. Popular Edition. Crown 8vo, cloth. 5/-.

Vol. II. The Christian Faith and Society. Popular Edition. Crown 8vo, cloth. 5/-.

Vol. III. The Christian Faith and Philosophy. Popular Edition. Crown 8vo, cloth. 5/-.

Vol. IV. Church and State. Popular Edition. Crown 8vo, cloth. 5/-.

H. E. CARDINAL VAUGHAN says :—" It is one of the noblest historical works I have ever read. Now that its price has placed it within the reach of all, I earnestly pray that it may become widely known and appreciatively studied. We have nothing like it in the English language."

The Throne of the Fisherman, built by the Carpenter's Son. The Root, the Bond, and the Crown of Christendom. Demy 8vo, cloth. 10/6.

The Holy See and the Wandering of the Nations. Demy 8vo, cloth. 10/6.

Peter's Rock in Mohammed's Flood. Being the Seventh Volume of Mr. Allies' great work on the " Formation of Christendom." Demy 8vo, cloth. 10/6.

ALLIES, MARY.

Pius the Seventh, 1800-1823. Crown 8vo, cloth gilt. 5/-.

" Miss Allies has narrated the history of the long and memorable Pontificate of the first Pope of this century with a thoroughness of research and a dignity of style worthy of her illustrious father."—*Irish Monthly.*

Leaves from St. John Chrysostom. With Introduction by T. W. Allies, K.C.S.G. Crown 8vo, cloth. 6/-.

History of the Church in England, from the Beginning of the Christian Era to the Death of Queen Elizabeth. In Two Vols. Crown 8vo, cloth. Vol. I. From the Beginning of the Christian Era to the Accession of Henry VIII. 6/-. Vol. II. From the Accession of Henry VIII. to the Death of Queen Elizabeth. 3/6.

BAKER, VEN. FATHER AUGUSTIN (O.S.B.).

Holy Wisdom (*Sancta Sophia*). Directions for the Prayer of Contemplation, &c. Edited by Abbot Sweeney, D.D. New and Cheaper Edition. Crown 8vo. Handsomely bound in half leather, xx.-667 pp. 6/-.

BEST, REV. KENELM DIGBY (of the Oratory).

The Blood of the Lamb. Crown 8vo, cloth. 2/6 net (postage 3d.).

" These essays should serve as a revelation to those outside the Church in search of the truth, and could not fail to awaken an echo in the mind of even the most prejudiced. Short enough to avoid all chance of exciting a sense of weariness, each chapter will be found to contain ample food for meditation and reflection."—*Tablet.*

BIBLES, &c.

N.B.—*For full particulars of Bindings, &c., see Illustrated Prayer Book Catalogue, sent post free on application.*

Holy Bible. POCKET EDITION (size, 5¼ by 3¼ inches). Embossed cloth, red edges, 2/6; and in leather bindings, from 4/6 to 7/6. MEDIUM EDITION (size, 7¼ by 4¾ inches). Cloth, 3/6 ; and in leather bindings, from 6/- net to 10/6 net (postage 6d.). OCTAVO EDITION (size, 9 by 6 inches). Cloth, 5/- ; and in a great variety of leather bindings, from 8/- to 35/- net. Family Editions in quarto and folio. Prices upon application.

New Testament, The. POCKET EDITION. Limp cloth, 6d. (postage 2d.). Cloth, red edges, 1/-. Roan, 1/6. Paste grain, round corners, 3/-. Best calf or morocco, 4/6 each. ROYAL 8vo EDITION (size, 9 by 6 inches). Cloth, 1/- net (postage 3d.). NEW MEDIUM EDITION. LARGE TYPE. Crown 8vo (size, 7½ by 5 inches). 500 pp. Cloth, boards, gilt lettered, 2/-. Paste grain, limp, round corners, red or gold edges, 4/6. German calf, limp, round corners, red under gold edges, 8/6. Morocco, limp, round corners, red under gold edges, 8/6. Also in better bindings for presentation.

Novum D.N. Jesu Christi Testamentum. 48mo. 4¾ by 3 inches. Printed within red line border. Cloth, gilt edges. 2/10. Ditto. 32mo. 5 by 3¼ inches. Cloth, red edges. 2/. Ditto. 32mo. 5 by 3¼ inches. With red line border and marginal notes, cloth. 4/5.

Biblia Sacra Vulgata. Paris Edition. 12mo, half bound morocco, 6/8. Ditto. Large Type. Paris Edition. 2 vols., 8vo, half bound morocco. 14/-. Ditto. Fillion's elegant Edition. Printed on tinted paper, within red line border, with marginal notes and analyses of chapters. 8vo, half bound. 11/-.

BOWDEN, REV. H. S. (of the Oratory), Edited by.

The Religion of Shakespeare. Chiefly from the writings of the late Mr. Richard Simpson. Crown 8vo, cloth. 7/6.

Dante's Divina Commedia: Its scope and value. From the German of Francis Hettinger, D.D. With an engraving of Dante. Second Edition. 10/6.

Natural Religion. Being Vol. I. of Dr. Hettinger's "Evidences of Christianity." With an Introduction on "Certainty." Third Edition. Crown 8vo, cloth. 7/6.

Revealed Religion. Vol. II. of Dr. Hettinger's "Evidences of Christianity." With an Introduction on the "Assent of Faith." Crown 8vo, cloth. 5/-.

BRIDGETT, REV. T. E. (C.SS.R.).

Sonnets and Epigrams on Sacred Subjects. Crown 8vo, cloth, extra gilt, bevelled boards. 3/6.

"An exquisite little volume, filled with uplifting and higher thoughts that cannot help but be beneficial to any who read it."—*Monitor.*

BRIDGETT, REV. T. E. (C.SS.R.)—*(continued)*.

Lyra Hieratica : Poems on the Priesthood. Collected from many sources by the Rev. T. E. Bridgett, C.SS.R. Fcap. 8vo, cloth. 2/6 net (postage 3d.).

"The idea of gathering an anthology of Poems on the Priesthood was a happy one, and has been happily carried out. Priests and laity alike owe a debt of gratitude to Father Bridgett for the many beautiful things he has brought together."—*Tablet*.

The True Story of the Catholic Hierarchy deposed by Queen Elizabeth, with fuller Memoirs of its last Two Survivors. By the Rev. T. E. Bridgett, C.SS.R., and the Rev. T. F. Knox, D.D. Crown 8vo, cloth. 7/6.

Wisdom and Wit of Sir Thomas More, The. Crown 8vo, cloth. 6/-.

"Every page in this delightful volume bespeaks the master hand, the clear head, the deep and tender heart. It is lively, eloquent, impressive, genial ; without stiffness of parade of learning, but as full as good things as it can hold."—*Catholic Times*.

BROWNLOW, BISHOP.

Memoir of Mother Rose Columba Adams, O.P., first Prioress of St. Dominic's Convent, and Foundress of the Perpetual Adoration at North Adelaide. With Portrait and Plates. Crown 8vo, cloth. 384 pp. 6/6.

BUCKLER, REV. REGINALD (O.P.).

A Few Aids to Faith. Wrapper. 6d.

A Good Practical Catholic. A Spiritual Instruction to Working Men and Women. With a Prefatory Letter by H. E. Cardinal Vaughan. Neat wrapper. 6d.

The Perfection of Man by Charity. A Spiritual Treatise. Second Edition. Crown 8vo, cloth. 5/-.

BUTE, MARQUESS OF, K.T.,

A Form of Prayers following the Church Office. For the use of Catholics unable to hear Mass upon Sundays and Holidays. Limp cloth, 1/- net (postage 2d.) ; or bound in leather, with gold edges, 2 6 net (postage 3d.).

BUTLER, REV. ALBAN.

People's Edition of the Lives of the Saints. Twelve Pocket Volumes, each Volume containing the Saints of the Month. Superfine paper, neat cloth binding, gilt lettered. 1/6 each ; or the complete set (comprising over 6,000 pp.), in handsome cloth case to match, 18 -.

CATHOLIC DIRECTORY, THE. Ecclesiastical Register, and

Almanac for 1900. Prices : Directory, 1/6 net ; Directory and Ordo, 2/- net (postage on either, Inland 4d., Foreign 7d.)

"The mass of information contained in this useful work is wonderful, and no household should be without it. '—*Pall Mall Gazette*.

DALE, REV. J. D. HILARIUS.

Ceremonial according to the Roman Rite. Translated from the Italian of Joseph Baldeschi. New and Revised Edition. Crown 8vo, cloth. 6/6.

"This work is our standard English directory on the subject. Few functions of any importance are carried on without a glance at it. It is a familiar guide and friend—in short, a classic."—*Catholic Times*.

The Sacristan's Manual ; or, Handbook of Church Furniture, Ornament, &c. Fourth and Enlarged Edition. Crown 8vo, cloth. 2/6.

DE ESTELLA, DIEGO.

Meditations on the Love of God. Translated from the Spanish of Fray Diego de Estella by Henry W. Pereira, M.A. Crown 8vo, cloth. 3/6.

" Twenty-six in number, and leaving little to be desired as to form and length, breathing love and faith, these Meditations will have a welcome not given by some to more set and scientifically arranged aids to mental devotion."—*Weekly Register.*

DE PARAVICINI, BARONESS.

The Life of St. Edmund of Abingdon, Archbishop of Canterbury. Crown 8vo, cloth, gilt. 6/-.

" This account of St. Edmund's life is probably the fullest that has yet been given to English readers. It is a readable, and, to all appearance, a faithful rendering down of the mediæval authorities for the Saint's biography, which will prove useful to students of ecclesiastical history, as well as edifying to the Faithful."—*Scotsman.*

DOMVILE, LADY MARGARET.

The King's Mother. Memoir of Margaret Beaufort, Countess of Richmond and Derby. Crown 8vo, cloth, gilt top, with Portrait. 3/6.

" In this book we are made to realize something of the intimate and domestic life of that age when mediævalism was drawing to its close, amid scenes of violence and the clash of arms. All the charm and nothing of the hatefulness of that wonderful age appears in the Lady Margaret, who, while ruling great fiefs with a steady hand, and holding the threads of the conspiracy which put her son (Henry VII.) on the throne, maintained an inner life of devotion, and made herself a steward of God's bounties, justly deserving to be inscribed, as Newman has inscribed her, in the list of uncanonised saints."—*Daily Chronicle.*

DREW, MARY FRANCES.

The Passion Play of Oberammergau. The Complete Text, with the addition of the Choruses in Rhyme and Rhythm. Translated from the German. Crown 8vo, cloth. 1/6 net (postage 2d.).

EGGER, REV. JOSEPH, S.J.

Consolations of the Sick Room ; and the Christian Nurse's Guide. Cloth. 1/-.

" A very delightful little book, full of sound common sense and real Christianity. It is crammed with good advice to nurses."—*Church Gazette.*

EMMERICH, SISTER ANNE CATHERINE.

The Nativity of Our Lord Jesus Christ. Translated by GEORGE RICHARDSON. Cloth, gilt. 2/6.

" A striking characteristic of this book is the sweet simplicity with which the holy nun deals with the subject, and the intensely practical character of her remarks. There is, nevertheless, a peculiarly winning power in her words, and an unction which is redolent of the Divine source from which they came. The book will be found a most useful and suggestive one for spiritual reading."—*Child of Mary's Journal.*

The Flight into Egypt. Translated by GEORGE RICHARDSON. New and Cheaper Edition. Wrapper. 1/- net (postage 1½d.).

FABER, FATHER.

All for Jesus; or, The Easy Ways of Divine Love. 5/-.

Bethlehem. Crown 8vo, cloth, 500 pp. 7/-.

Ethel's Book; or, Tales of the Angels. A New and Cheaper Edition. Beautifully bound in cloth, extra gilt, gilt edges. 2/6.

FABER, FATHER—(continued).

Growth in Holiness; or, The Progress of the Spiritual Life. 6/-.

Hymns. Complete Edition. Crown 8vo, cloth, 427 pp. 6/-.

Notes on Doctrinal and Spiritual Subjects. Two Vols. 10/-.

Poems. Complete Edition. Crown 8vo, cloth, 582 pp. 5/-.

Spiritual Conferences. 6/-.

The Blessed Sacrament; or, The Works and Ways of God. Crown 8vo, cloth, 548 pp. 7/6.

The Creator and the Creature; or, The Wonders of Divine Love. Crown 8vo, cloth, 416 pp. 6/-.

The Easiness of Salvation. Cloth gilt. 1/-.

The Foot of the Cross; or, The Sorrows of Mary. 6/-.

The Precious Blood; or, The Price of our Salvation. 5/-.

The Life and Letters of Frederick William Faber, D.D. By Rev. John E. Bowden, of the Oratory. 6/-.

Father Faber's May Book. 18mo, cloth, gilt edges, with Steel Frontispiece. 2/-.

A Brief Sketch of the Early Life of Frederick William Faber, D.D. By his Brother. Limp cloth. 1/-.

FITZGERALD, PERCY.

Jewels of Prayer and Meditation from Unfamiliar Sources. Fancy cloth, gilt. 2/6.

Jewels of the Imitation. A Selection of Passages with a Little Commentary. Cloth, extra gilt. 2/-.

Eucharistic Jewels. Second Edition. Fancy cloth, gilt. 2/6.

Jewels of the Mass. A Short Account of the Rites and Prayers used in the Holy Sacrifice. Sixth Edition. Fancy cloth gilt. 2/-.

The Layman's Day; or, Jewels of Practical Piety. Second Edition. Cloth, extra gilt. 2/-.

GAY, MONSEIGNEUR CHARLES.

The Religious Life and the Vows. Translated from the French by O.S.B. With an Introduction by the Rev. William T. Gordon, of the Oratory. Crown 8vo, cloth. 5/-.

This is a translation of three admirable chapters in Monseigneur Gay's work on "The Christian Life and Virtues," which has been so greatly appreciated in France. Though primarily addressed to Religious, the book is written with a largeness of view and a poetic enthusiasm which will make it attractive to all classes of Christians.

GIBSON, REV. HENRY.

Catechism made Easy: being a Familiar Explanation of the Catechism of Christian Doctrine. Eleventh Edition. Two Vols. Fcap. 8vo, cloth, 800 pp. 7/6.

"Contains a course of fifty-eight instructions on Catholic doctrines, each accompanied by from one to eleven stories, legends, anecdotes, &c., expressly designed to illustrate their meanings and to fix them in the minds of children."—*Irish Monthly.*

GILLOW, JOSEPH.
Biographical History, and Bibliographical Dictionary of
the English Catholics. From the Breach with Rome in 1534 to the Present Time. Vol. I., A-C, 612 pp. Vol. II., D-Grad, 557 pp. Vol. III., Grah-Kem, 688 pp. Vol. IV., Kem-Met, 572 pp. Demy 8vo, cloth. 15/- each.

HAMMERSTEIN, REV. L. VON (S.J.).
Foundations of Faith: The Existence of God Demonstrated.
From the German of Fr. Ludwig von Hammerstein, S.J. With an Introduction by the Very Rev. W. I. Canon Gildea, D.D. Crown 8vo, cloth. 6/-.

"Popular, interesting, forcible, and sound. It is well to have a book like Father von Hammerstein's to put into the hands of serious inquirers; it forms a valuable addition to our apologetic literature."—*Tablet.*

HEDLEY, BISHOP.
The Light of Life. Crown 8vo, cloth, gilt, gilt top. 6/-.

"The Bishop of Newport is invariably thoughtful, eloquent, and incisive; he speaks the language of the age: he has a wide, strong grasp of subject, and he answers modern questionings about religion with very unusual expository power. His sermons are finished productions, excellent models for young priests, instructive and edifying for all Catholics, and persuasive and illuminating for educated non-Catholics."—*Ave Maria.*

The Christian Inheritance. Second Edition. Crown 8vo, cloth gilt, 430 pp. 6 -.

Our Divine Saviour, and other Discourses. Third Edition. Crown 8vo, cloth gilt. 6/-.

A Retreat : Consisting of Thirty-three Discourses, with Meditations: for the use of the Clergy, Religious, and Others. Fourth Edition. In handsome half-leather binding. Crown 8vo, 428 pp. 6/-.

LIGUORI, ST. ALPHONSUS.
A Translation of the Works of St. Alphonsus, edited by the late Bishop Coffin :—

Christian Virtues, and the Means for obtaining them,
The. Cloth gilt. 3/-. Or separately, cloth flush—1. The Love of Our Lord Jesus Christ. 1/-. 2. Treatise on Prayer (in many Editions a great part of this work is omitted). 1/-. 3. A Christian's Rule of Life. 1/-.

Eternal Truths. Preparation for Death. 2/6.

The Redemption. Meditations on the Passion. 2/6.

Glories of Mary. New Edition. 3/6.

LIVIUS, REV. T. (M.A., C.SS.R.).
St. Peter, Bishop of Rome ; or, the Roman Episcopate of the Prince of the Apostles. Demy 8vo, cloth. 12/-.

Explanation of the Psalms and Canticles in the Divine
Office. By St. Alphonsus Liguori. Translated from the Italian by Thomas Livius, C.SS.R. With a Preface by his Eminence Cardinal Manning. Crown 8vo, cloth, xxx.-512 pp. 7/6.

LIVIUS, REV. T. (M.A., C.SS.R.)—*(continued)*.

Mary in the Epistles; or, The Implicit Teaching of the Apostles concerning the Blessed Virgin. Crown 8vo, cloth. 5/-.

The Blessed Virgin in the Fathers of the First Six Centuries. Demy 8vo, cloth. 12/-.

LOYOLA, MOTHER MARY.   Edited by Rev. H. Thurston, S.J.

First Communion. A Book of Preparation for First Communion. Fourth and also a Better Edition. With nineteen Illustrations. 3/6.

The Child of God; or, What comes of our Baptism. With five Full-page Illustrations. Boards, 2,6. Cloth, gilt, 3/6.

The Soldier of Christ; or, Talks before Confirmation. Illustrated. 5/-.

Confession and Communion. Intended for the use of Religious and those who communicate frequently. 18mo, cloth. 1,6.

MACDONALD, HON. LADY.

Christian Rome. A Historical View of its Memories and Monuments, 41—1867. Translated from the French of E. de la Gournerie, K.S.G., by the Hon. Lady Macdonald. With a Preface by His Eminence Cardinal Vaughan. Two Vols., crown 8vo, cloth. 15/-.

MANNING, CARDINAL.

Confidence in God. 32mo, neat cloth gilt. 1/-.

Lost Sheep Found. A Sermon. Wrapper. 6d.

Miscellanies. First Series. Crown 8vo, cloth, 387 pp. 6/-.

Miscellanies. Second Series. Crown 8vo, cloth, 391 pp. 6/-.

Pastime Papers. With Portrait. 2/6.

Sermons on Ecclesiastical Subjects. 6/-.

Sin and its Consequences. Crown 8vo, cloth. 4/-.

The Blessed Sacrament the Centre of Immutable Truth. 32mo, neat cloth gilt. 1/-.

The Eternal Priesthood. Crown 8vo, cloth. 2/6.

The Four Great Evils of the Day. Crown 8vo, cloth. 2/6.

The Fourfold Sovereignty of God. Crown 8vo, cloth. 2/6.

The Glories of the Sacred Heart. Crown 8vo, cloth. 4/-.

The Grounds of Faith. Crown 8vo, cloth. 1/6.

The Holy Ghost the Sanctifier. 32mo, neat cloth gilt. 2/-.

The Independence of the Holy See. Crown 8vo, cloth. 2/6.

The Internal Mission of the Holy Ghost. 5/-.

The Love of Jesus to Penitents. 32mo, neat cloth gilt. 1/-.

The Office of the Church in Higher Catholic Education. 6d.

MANNING, CARDINAL—*(continued)*.

The Temporal Mission of the Holy Ghost; or, Reason and Revelation. Crown 8vo, cloth. 5/-.

The True Story of the Vatican Council. 2/6.

The Workings of the Holy Spirit in the Church of England. New Edition. Crown 8vo, cloth. 1/6.

Why I became a Catholic. Crown 8vo, cloth. 1/-.

MARTIN, LADY.

A Daughter of France. 1464–1505. Being Records of Blessed Jane, Foundress of the Order of the Annunciation. Curtailed from the French of the Countess de Flavigny. 1 6 (postage 3d.).

Life of Don Bosco, Founder of the Salesian Society. Translated from the French of J. M. Villefranche. New Popular Edition. Crown 8vo, 302 pp. Wrapper. 1/- net (postage 3d.).

Life of Princess Borghese (*née* Gwendalin Talbot). Translated from the French. Crown 8vo, tastefully bound in cloth gilt. 4/-.

MEMORIES OF THE CRIMEA. By Sister Mary Aloysius. With Preface by the Very Rev. J. Fahey, D.D., V.G. Crown 8vo, cloth gilt. 2/6.

MORRIS, REV. W. B. (of the Oratory).

The Divinity of Our Lord Jesus Christ. From Pascal. Crown 8vo, cloth. 3/-.

The Life of St. Patrick, Apostle of Ireland. Fifth Edition. Crown 8vo, cloth. 5/-.

Ireland and St. Patrick. A Study of the Saint's Character and of the Results of his Apostolate. Second Edition. Crown 8vo, cloth. 5 -.

NEWMAN, CARDINAL.

The Church of the Fathers. Fcap. 8vo, cloth, 361 pp. 4/-.

An attempt to illustrate the tone and modes of thought, the habits and manners, of the early times of the Church.

Detailed List of Cardinal Newman's Works on application.

PERRY, REV. JOHN.

Practical Sermons, for all the Sundays of the Year. First and Second Series. Sixth Edition. Fcap. 8vo, cloth. 3/6 each.

POPE, REV. T. A. (of the Oratory).

Life of St. Philip Neri. Translated from the Italian of Cardinal Capecelatro. Second and Revised Edition. Two Volumes. Crown 8vo, cloth. 12/6.

PORTER, ARCHBISHOP (S.J.).

The Banquet of the Angels: Preparation and Thanksgiving for Holy Communion. New Edition. 18mo, blue cloth, gilt. 2/-. Also bound in a variety of handsome leather bindings suitable for First Communion memorial gifts. From 6/6 to 12/6 net.

PRACTICAL MEDITATIONS FOR EVERY DAY IN THE
Year, on the Life of our Lord Jesus Christ. Chiefly for the use of
Religious. By a Father of the Society of Jesus. With Imprimatur
of Cardinal Manning. New Edition, Revised. In two Volumes.
Cloth, red edges. 9/-.

PRAYER BOOKS, &c.

N.B.—For full particulars of Prayer Books, see *Illustrated
Prayer Book Catalogue*, sent post free on application.

Catholic's Daily Companion. With Epistles and Gospels. Roan,
1/-; and in various leather bindings, 1/6 to 5/-.

Catholic Piety. Containing a Selection of Prayers, Reflections,
Meditations, and Instructions adapted to every state in life. By the late
Rev. Wm. Gahan, O.S.A. 32mo Edition, with Ordinary of the Mass.
Cloth, 6d. ; post free, 8d. ; roan, 1/-. With Epistles and Gospels,
1/6, 2/-, 2/6, 4/6, &c. Messrs. BURNS & OATES also publish two
other Editions of this book.

Catholic's Vade Mecum. A Select Manual of Prayers for Daily
Use. Compiled from approved sources. 36th Thousand. With Epistles
and Gospels. Calf, 5/6, and also in better bindings.

Children's Pictorial Mass Book. (Abridged.) New Edition.
Forty-three Illustrations. 2d. ; cloth, 6d.

Daily Exercise. Cloth limp. 6d.

Flowers of Devotion. Being a Collection of Favourite Devotions,
for Public and Private use. Compiled from approved sources, and
with the Imprimatur of His Eminence Cardinal Vaughan. New
Edition. Leather bindings. 1/6 to 6/-.

Spirit of the Sacred Heart, The. A new large-type Prayer
Book. Cloth, 3/6 ; leather, 5/6 ; German calf or morocco, 8/6.

Garden of the Soul. 715th Thousand. Approved by the Cardinal
Archbishop of Westminster, and revised by a Priest of the Archdiocese.
New Edition. In which many devotions will be found which now form
a necessary part of every Catholic Prayer Book. Cloth, 6d. ; post
free, 8d. ; roan, 1/-. With Epistles and Gospels, cloth, 1/-; and in
leather bindings, at 1/6, 2/-, 2/6, 3/-, 3/6, 4/-, 5/-, and upwards.
    Messrs. BURNS & OATES have just issued a new Pocket Edition of
the " Garden of the Soul," size 3¾ by 2½ inches, with red line borders,
and Devotions for Mass in large type. This Edition can now be had
in various bindings, from 1/- to 5/-. Also three other Editions.

Golden Manual. A Guide to Catholic Devotion, Public and Private,
Compiled from approved sources. Fine Paper. Leather, 6/-. With
Epistles and Gospels, 7/- and upwards.

Imitation of Christ, Of the. By Thomas à Kempis. NEW
POPULAR EDITION FOR DISTRIBUTION. Cloth, red edges, 6d.
(postage, 2d.). Leather, red edges, 1/-. SUPERFINE POCKET EDITION.
Fancy cloth extra, with red borders, 1/6. And in leather bindings,
from 2/6 to 10/-. PRESENTATION EDITION (size, 6¼ by 4½ inches).
With red border on each page. Cloth extra, 3/6. And in leather
bindings, from 7/- to 15/-.

PRAYER BOOKS, &c.—*(continued).*

Key of Heaven. A Manual of Devout Prayers. 32mo Edition. Cloth, 6d. ; post free, 8d. ; roan, 1/-. With Epistles and Gospels, 1/6, 2/-, 2/6, 3/-, 4/6, &c. Also two Smaller Editions.

Manual of Prayers for Congregational Use. As authorized by the Bishops of England and Wales. With an Appendix containing Prayers for Mass, Confession, and Communion. Cloth, 1/- ; leather, 2/6, 5/-, and upwards.

Manual of the Sacred Heart. Compiled and Translated from approved sources. New Edition. Cloth. 2/- upwards.

Missal. New and Complete Pocket Missal, with the Imprimatur of H. E. Cardinal Vaughan, in Latin and English, with all the New Offices, and the Propers for Ireland, Scotland, and the Jesuits. (Size, 5¼ by 3¾ inches). Roan or French morocco, 5/- ; Rutland roan, limp, 7/- ; best calf or morocco, four styles, 8/6 each. Also in better bindings, from 11/- to 30/- net.

Missal for the Laity. Cheap Edition. 6d. ; post free, 8d. ; and in leather bindings, at 1/6, 2/6, 4/6, and 5/-.

Path to Heaven. Containing Epistles, Gospels, and Hymns, &c. Cloth, 2/- and 2/6 ; leather, 3/-, 4/-, 4/6, 6/-, and upwards.

Prayers for the People. By the Rev. F. D. Byrne. Imperial 32mo, cloth, extra gilt. 2/-.

PYE, H. J.

The Course of Conscience. Being a Short Inquiry as to the Transmission of Revelation. Crown 8vo, cloth. 2/6.

" A better or more useful book of its kind there could not be. Mr. Pye comes with a most helpful hand to clear away the obstacles felt by some searchers to lie in the path of Catholic unity. The objections of the man in the street, the well-meaning and intelligent man, are met fairly and fully, with no excitement, no rhetoric, no quibbling. We predict for the little volume a long career of value as a *vade mecum* for thoughtful pilgrims from Canterbury to Rome."—*Weekly Register.*

QUARTERLY SERIES. Edited by the Jesuit Fathers. **99** Volumes published to date.

SELECTION.

The Life and Letters of St. Francis Xavier. By the Rev. H. J. Coleridge, S.J. Second Edition. Two Volumes. 10/6.

The Life and Letters of St. Teresa. By the Rev. H. J. Coleridge, S.J. Three Volumes. 7/6 each.

The Life and Teaching of Jesus Christ in Meditations for every Day in the Year. By Fr. Nicholas Avancino, S.J. Two Volumes. 10/6.

The Life of St. Alonso Rodriguez. By Francis Goldie, of the Society of Jesus. 7/6.

Letters of St. Augustine. Selected and Arranged by Mary H. Allies. 6/6.

QUARTERLY SERIES—(continued).

Acts of the English Martyrs, hitherto unpublished. By the Rev. John H. Pollen, S.J. 7/6.

The Life of St. Francis di Geronimo, S.J. By A. M. Clarke. 7/6.

Aquinas Ethicus; or, The Moral Teaching of St. Thomas. By the Rev. Joseph Rickaby, S.J. Second Edition. Two Volumes. 12/-.

The Spirit of St. Ignatius. From the French of the Rev. Fr. Xavier de Franciosi, S.J. 6/-.

Jesus, the All - Beautiful. A Devotional Treatise on the Character and Actions of our Lord. Edited by the Rev. J. G. Macleod, S.J. Second Edition. 6/6.

The Manna of the Soul. By Fr. Paul Segneri. New Edition. In Two Volumes. 12/-.

Life of Ven. Joseph Benedict Cottolengo. From the Italian of Don P. Gastaldi. 4 6.

Life of St. Francis Borgia. By A. M. Clarke. 6/6.

Life of Blessed Antony Baldinucci. By the Rev. F. Goldie, S.J. 6/-.

Distinguished Irishmen of the Sixteenth Century. By Rev. E. Hogan, S.J. 6/-.

Journals kept during Times of Retreat. By the late Fr. John Morris, S.J. Edited by Rev. J. Pollen, S.J. 6/-.

Life of the Rev. Mother Mary of St. Euphrasia Pelletier. By A. M. Clarke. 6/-.

Jesus: His Life, in the very Words of the Four Gospels. A Diatessaron by Henry Beauclerk, S.J. Cloth. 5/-.

The Life and Letters of Fr. John Morris, S.J. By Fr. J. H. Pollen, S.J. Cloth. 6/-.

The Story of Mary Aikenhead, Foundress of the Irish Sisters of Charity. By Maria Nethercott. Crown 8vo, cloth. 3/-.

Life of the Blessed Master John of Avila. Secular Priest, called the Apostle of Andalusia. By Father Longaro Degli Oddi, S.J. Edited by J. G. Macleod, S.J. Cloth. 4/-.

Notes on St. Paul; Corinthians, Galatians, Romans. By Joseph Rickaby, S.J. 7/6.

The Life of St. Hugh of Lincoln. Translated from the French Carthusian Life, and Edited with large additions by the Rev. Herbert Thurston, S.J. 10/6.

RENDU, A. (LL.D.).

The Jewish Race in Ancient and Roman History. Translated from the Eleventh Corrected Edition by S. T. Crook. Crown 8vo, 440 pp. 6/-.

RICKABY, REV. JOSEPH (S.J.).

Oxford Conferences. Lent and Summer Terms, 1897. Second Edition. Crown 8vo, wrapper. 1/- net (postage 2d.). SECOND SERIES. Lent Term, 1898. 1/-.

Cambridge Conferences. Michaelmas Term, 1898. Crown 8vo, wrapper. 1/-. SECOND SERIES. Lent Term, 1899. 1/-. THIRD SERIES. Easter Term, 1899. 1/-.

Oxford and Cambridge Conferences. Complete Edition. Containing the above five volumes. Crown 8vo, cloth. 5/-.

Commentary on the Gospel of St. Matthew. Crown 8vo, boards, with Map, 2/6.

Commentary on the Gospel of St. John. Crown 8vo, boards, with Map. 2/-.

(See also Quarterly Series.)

RIVINGTON, REV. LUKE (D.D.).

Rome and England ; or, Ecclesiastical Continuity. Crown 8vo, cloth. 3/6.

" Fr. Rivington's method of exposition is admirable—brief and lucid without meagreness, pointed and telling without harshness. . . . . A book to be grateful for ; useful alike to the controversialist, the historical student, and the general reader."—*Tablet.*

RUSHE, VERY REV. JAMES P. (O.D.C.) (Father Patrick of St. Joseph).

Carmel in Ireland. A Narrative of the Irish Province of Teresian or Discalced Carmelites. A.D. 1625-1896. Crown 8vo, cloth. 3/6 net (postage 4d.).

" . . . . Written in an easy, historical style. The history of the Carmelite Abbeys in Ireland is here told with much graphic power in a series of interesting chapters, which will be valued by very many readers. . . . . The author is most painstaking, and has consulted all available books of reference to make his record complete."—*Irish Times.*

RUSSELL, REV. MATTHEW (S.J.).

Vespers and Compline. A Soggarth's Sacred Verses. Crown 8vo, cloth, gilt, gilt top. 3/6.

"All the poems are both scholarly and fervid, and enjoy the rare distinction among sacred verse of showing genuine poetical feeling. The book cannot but prove cordially welcome to those readers to whose sympathies it makes so tender and graceful an appeal."—*Scotsman.*

At Home near the Altar. Fifth Edition. Cloth, gilt. 1/- net (postage 1½d.).

ST. FRANCIS DE SALES, The Works of. Translated into the English Language by the Very Rev. Canon Mackey, O.S.B., under the Direction of the Right Rev. Bishop Hedley, O.S.B.

Vol. I. Letters to Persons in the World. Third Edition. Crown 8vo, cloth. 6/-.

Vol. II. The Treatise on the Love of God. Fr. Carr's Translation of 1630 has been taken as a basis, but it has been Modernised and thoroughly Revised and Corrected. Second Edition. 6/-.

ST. FRANCIS DE SALES —(continued).

Vol. III. The Catholic Controversy. New and Revised Edition. Crown 8vo, cloth, 6/-.

Vol. IV. Letters to Persons in Religion, with Introduction by Bishop Hedley on "St. Francis de Sales and the Religious State." Second Edition. Crown 8vo, cloth. 6/-.

" We earnestly commend these volumes to all readers, and we desire their widest diffusion, as we desire also that the doctrine and spirit of St. Francis may reign in all our hearts, both of pastors and of people."-- Cardinal Manning in the *Dublin Review.*

St. Francis de Sales as a Preacher. Wrapper. 1/-.

SALVATORI'S PRACTICAL INSTRUCTIONS FOR NEW

Confessors. Edited by Fr. Anthony Ballerini, S.J., and Translated by Very Rev. William Hutch, D.D. Third Edition. 18mo, cloth gilt, 314 pp. 4/-.

SCHOUPPE, REV. F. X. (S.J.).

Purgatory : Illustrated by the Lives and Legends of the Saints. Second Edition. Crown 8vo, cloth. 6/-.

SMYTH, JOHN.

Genesis and Science. Inspiration of the Mosaic Ideas of Creative Work. Crown 8vo, cloth, with Illustrations. 3/6.

SOULIER, REV. P. M., Edited by.

Life of St. Juliana Falconieri, Foundress of the Mantellate or Religious of the Third Order of Servites ; to which is added a short account of the Lives and Virtues of her Daughters in Religion. Crown 8vo, cloth, gilt, with Illustrations. 5/-.

" A valuable addition to English hagiology. St. Juliana's example cannot fail to influence for good. A womanly woman, a sympathetic personality, a practical, sensible Christian, the disciple of St. Philip Benizi has every characteristic which should call up the attention, love, and imitation of Catholic womanhood in the nineteenth century."—*Dublin Review.*

SWEENEY, RIGHT REV. ABBOT (O.S.B.).

Sermons for all Sundays and Festivals of the Year. New and Cheaper Edition. Crown 8vo, handsomely bound in quarter leather. 7/6.

THOMPSON, EDWARD HEALY (M.A.).

Letters and Writings of Marie Lataste, with Critical and Expository Notes. By two Fathers of the Society of Jesus. Translated from the French. Three Volumes. 8vo, cloth. 5/- each.

Life of Jean-Jacques Olier, Founder of the Seminary of St. Sulpice. New and Enlarged Edition. Post 8vo, xxxvi.-628 pp. 15/-.

The Hidden Life of Jesus. A Lesson and Model to Christians. By Henri-Marie Boudon. Translated from the French by E. Healy Thompson, M.A. Third Edition. Cloth gilt. 3/-.

The Life and Glories of St. Joseph. Grounded on the Dissertations of Canon Vitali, Fr. José Moreno, and other Writers. Second Edition. Crown 8vo, cloth. 6/-.

The Unity of the Episcopate. Crown 8vo, cloth. 4/6.

THOMPSON, EDWARD HEALY (M.A.), Edited by.

LIBRARY OF RELIGIOUS BIOGRAPHY.

Life of St. Aloysius Gonzaga (S.J.). Eleventh Edition. Globe 8vo, cloth, xxiv.-373 pp. 5/-.

Life of Marie Eustelle Harpain; or, The Angel of the Eucharist. Fifth Edition. Cloth, xxi.-388 pp. 5/-.

Life of St. Stanislaus Kostka. Sixth Edition. Cloth. 5/-.

Life of Marie Lataste, Lay Sister of the Congregation of the Sacred Heart. With a Brief Notice of her Sister Quitterie. Second Edition. Cloth. 5/-.

Life of Leon Papin-Dupont, The Holy Man of Tours. Fourth Edition. Cloth. 5/-.

Life of Jean Baptiste Muard, Founder of the Congregation of St. Edme and of the Monastery of La Pierre-qui-Vire. 8vo, cloth, xix.-540 pp. 6/-.

' **Life of St. Charles Borromeo,** Cardinal Archbishop of Milan. Second Edition. Cloth gilt. 3/-.

ULLATHORNE, ARCHBISHOP.

Christian Patience: The Strength and Discipline of the Soul. Sixth and Cheaper Edition. Demy 8vo, cloth, 256 pp. 7/-.

The Endowments of Man considered in their Relations with his Final End. Fifth and Cheaper Edition. Demy 8vo, cloth, 404 pp. 7/-.

The Groundwork of the Christian Virtues. Fifth and Cheaper Edition. Demy 8vo, cloth, 411 pp. 7/-.

Memoir of Bishop Willson, first Bishop of Hobart, Tasmania. With Portrait. Crown 8vo, cloth. 2/6.

The Autobiography of Archbishop Ullathorne. Edited by Augusta Theodosia Drane. Second Edition. Demy 8vo, cloth. 7/6.

The Letters of Archbishop Ullathorne. Arranged by A. T. Drane. (Sequel to the "Autobiography.") Demy 8vo, cloth, 550 pp. 9/-.

Characteristics from the Writings of Archbishop Ullathorne, together with a Bibliographical Account of the Archbishop's Works. By the Rev. M. F. Glancey, Crown 8vo, cloth. 6/-.

WALPOLE, F. GOULBURN.

A Short History of the Catholic Church. Crown 8vo, cloth. 3/-.

This work may be described as a Skeleton History of the Church. It is been compiled from notes made by the author for his own instruction, and he hopes that it may prove useful to those who may not have leisure or inclination to study the voluminous standard works upon which it is based.

WHITEHEAD, REV. H. (S.J.).

India: A Sketch of the Madura Mission. With Map and Illustrations. Cheaper Edition. Wrapper, 1/- net; cloth, 2/- net (postage 3d.).

"There are few books of missionary experiences which equal this in interest. This sketch will be deeply appreciated by all who read it."—*Catholic Times.*

WISEMAN, CARDINAL.

A Month's Meditations. From MSS. left by h's Eminence, and now first published. Crown 8vo, quarter leather. 4/-.

Meditations on the Incarnation and Life of Our Lord. With a Preface by H. E. Cardinal Vaughan. Crown 8vo, cloth. 4/-.

"In these Meditations we have Wiseman at his best. Though passionately devotional, they are distinguished by breadth of thought aud true Catholicity of tone, and are suitable for every variety of those who call themselves 'Christians.'"—*Church Gazette.*

Meditations on the Sacred Passion of our Lord. Crown 8vo, cloth. 4/-.

In the Preface H. E. Cardinal Vaughan says :—"The characteristic of these Meditations, as indeed of most of Cardinal Wiseman's writings, is that you will nearly always find in them a 'Hidden Gem.' The beauty and richness of his mind seemed to illustrate and justify every topic he treated by suddenly striking some vein of thought or some point of feeling which, if not new, is at least presented in a new light or reference."

Fabiola. A Tale of the Catacombs. New Cheap Edition. Crown 8vo, cloth, xii.-324 pp. 2/-. Also an Edition on better paper, bound in cloth, richly gilt, gilt edges. 3/6. And an *Edition de luxe* printed on large 4to paper, embellished with thirty-one Full-page Illustrations and a Coloured Portrait of St. Agnes. Handsomely bound. £1 1/-.

A Few Flowers from the Roman Campagna. Small 4to, cloth gilt, printed in red and black. 1/- net (postage 2d.).

New Visits to the Blessed Sacrament. Edited by Cardinal Wiseman. Containing Devotions to the Quarant' Ore and other Occasions of Exposition and Benediction. Cloth, red edges. 2/-.

Characteristics from the Writings of Cardinal Wiseman. Edited, and with a Preface by the Rev. T. E. Bridgett, C.SS.R. Crown 8vo, cloth. 6/-.

ZIMMERMAN, REV. BENEDICT (O.C.D.).

Carmel in England. A History of the English Mission of the Discalced Carmelites, 1615 to 1849. Drawn from documents preserved in the Archives of the Order. Crown 8vo, cloth. 6/-.

"Father Zimmerman has given to the world a book that, besides being accurate and exact in every historical detail, contains in addition many pages as thrilling and exciting as those of a romance."—*Tablet.*

New Classified Catalogue of Standard Books, comprising every class of book in demand among Catholic Readers, post free on application.

BURNS & OATES, LIMITED,
28, Orchard Street, London, W.